Becoming Intimately Mobile

WARSAW STUDIES IN CULTURE AND SOCIETY
Edited by Jacek Wasilewski

Vol. 2

PETER LANG

Frankfurt am Main · Berlin · Bern · Bruxelles · NewYork · Oxford · Warszawa · Wien

Paula Bialski

Becoming Intimately Mobile

PETER LANG
Internationaler Verlag der Wissenschaften

Bibliographic Information published by the Deutsche Nationalbibliothek
The Deutsche Nationalbibliothek lists this publication in the Deutsche Nationalbibliografie; detailed bibliographic data is available in the internet at http://dnb.d-nb.de.

Cover Design:
© Olaf Gloeckler, Atelier Platen, Friedberg

The publication was financially supported by
the Warsaw School of Social Sciences and Humanities

ISSN 2192-4961
ISBN 978-3-631-63070-9
© Peter Lang GmbH
Internationaler Verlag der Wissenschaften
Frankfurt am Main 2012
All rights reserved.

All parts of this publication are protected by copyright. Any utilisation outside the strict limits of the copyright law, without the permission of the publisher, is forbidden and liable to prosecution. This applies in particular to reproductions, translations, microfilming, and storage and processing in electronic retrieval systems.

www.peterlang.de

About this book

As more and more people become mobile to visit friends, family, and business colleagues using social networking websites, technologies in use today like Couchsurfing.com or online hitchhiking websites (OHWs) are allowing people to create new, planned encounters between other strangers. This book adds to the small body of work currently existing in the social sciences which describes ways in which the internet aids such face-to-face intimacy. Based on 5 years of ethnography of Couchsurfers and OHW users and insights from over 3500 open-ended survey responses, this text explains the way meetings are initiated, relationships are strengthened or avoided, and the way hospitality and homemaking are negotiated. Here, the concept of "intimate mobility" helps theorize the significance of sociality in tourist travel as well as more broadly – with a view to how friendship and people's relationships to strangers are being reshaped. These technologies like Couchsurfing and OHWs, and frequent close contact with strangers among the intimately mobile produce new rules of engagement, and new relationships that blur the boundaries between friend, acquaintance, stranger, and enemy. This work defines these relationships and their rules of engagement, while also explaining that closeness is not always producing friendship, trust and social capital. Such technologies also allow people to exert their status and power during interaction, creating moments of tension, awkwardness, or distrust, and also force people to strategically accept or reject others, commodifying their relationships. By explaining the process of 'becoming intimately mobile,' this work creates an in-depth account of the relationships being created today as well as the problems that arise when defining friendship and closeness in a mobile world.

Acknowledgements

My sincerest thanks go out to my supervisors Monika Büscher and John Urry who were always eager to provide help and direction, whether co-present or at-a-distance. John's years of incredible scholarship and professionalism and Monika's drive and creativity of ideas became my constant assurance that my work was in good hands.

Thank you to my community of friends at Lancaster for sharing their intimate insights on life and scholarship. I also would like to thank Casey Fenton and his friends for starting Couchsurfing and embracing me into their community. My gratitude also goes out to my mother, father and family for their financial, moral, and spiritual support as well as the Dolphinholme pub farers and village hall yoga-goers for helping me make ends meet and keeping me a participant observer in their curious, lively community.

My thanks also goes out to Karol for coaching me along in my double-life as both a doctoral student and musician.

And finally, I would like to thank all the intimately mobile people I met along my journey for opening up, giving, and sharing a piece of their life with me.

Table of Contents

Chapter 1
Systems of Intimate Mobility 13
    Formalizing mobile systems 16
    What is Couchsurfing.com? 19
    Online hitchhiking websites 26
    Searching out new patters of interaction 29

Chapter 2
(Intimately) Mobile Methods 31
    Where it began 34
    Couch and Car Participant Observer 35
    Interviews 36
    Open-Ended Survey Responses 38
    Desk Research 40
    Emerging Practices in a Global Culture 40

Chapter 3
Mobile Intimacy: Research Paths 43
    Mobility – Physical mobility 44
    New Modes of Communication 46
    Mobile Networks 49
    Social Networking: a union with others 54
    Mobile spaces 56
    The intimate people 57
    Mobile sociability 61
    Some Conclusions 63

Chapter 4
Technologies of Hospitality: issues of interaction in planned encounters between strangers 65
    Opening the doors of hospitality 67
    Technologies of power 68
    Guests and passengers: the guest 70
    The passenger 73
    Payment as reciprocity 74

Spaces of hospitality: the host and their home 75
In-car hospitality 78
A new familiarization process 80
Discussion 83
Conclusion 85

Chapter 5
Rituals in mobile homemaking: Food, dwelling, and talk 87

Global communities 89
Home Rituals: food 91
Dwelling, Locking, Grooming 94
The Good Conversation 95
Participatory culture 97
Native to somewhere 98
Familiarity, home, and community 100

Chapter 6
Technologies of Friendship 103

Fluid friendship 105
The excitement of chance 107
Missed opportunities 109
Choice encounters: online profiling 111
Homophily and compatibility 114
Homophily and friendship 115
Part-time friends 116
Conclusion 117

Chapter 7
The Avoidance of Intimacy: escaping interaction on-the-move 121

Sturating the self 123
Not my cup of tea: 'faulty' interactants 125
Ideal interactions 126
Goffman and forms of alienation 128
External preoccupation 130
Objects of preoccupation 131
Blame mobility 133
The offensiveness of preoccupation 134
Interaction-consiousness 135

    Self-consiousness 137
    Other-consciousness 138
    Conclusions 139

Chapter 8
Sentiments of Mobility 143
    The origins of the sociology of emotions 144
    Emotional space 146
    New emotions 147
    Emotional technologies 148
    Objects of emotion 149
    Co-presence and emotion 151
    A culture of of interacting 152
    Anticipation: the first date affect 153
    The meeting: clicking with someone 154
    Gaining and offering 155
    Emotional currency 157
    Emotional encounters 158
    Mobility, self-understanding and personhood 159
    Emotions: artefacts of mobility 160

Chapter 9
Intimate Mobilities: Cosequences and Conclusions 163

Ethnographic Appendix 173

Bibliography 175

Websites Used During Ethnography 190

Chapter 1
Systems of Intimate Mobility

It was late in October, 1978, and my mother was standing on the northbound side of the highway outside Warsaw, heading in the direction of Olsztyn, her hometown. Sticking out her thumb, her 6-foot-1 frame, and light blond hair meant that cars would just stop for her. Taking advantage of her privileged position, she waved off those who did not make the cut – those who looked dodgy or 'uninteresting.' After the sixth car, a man pulled up in a new Peugeot. He was dressed better than most people living in socialist Poland at the time – wearing a neat shirt and sharp-looking sunglasses which looked American or French or German. She decided to go with him, which was a pretty good choice as I see it, given the fact that this man would later turn out to be my father.

I tell this story not to indulge in my own biography, but rather as a precursor to the story-to-come – a story of meetings between individuals on-the-move. I realized long after beginning my work that this meeting between my mother and father had everything that this book aims to address – the way a mobile context of interaction changes the dynamic of interaction, the way intimacy and closeness is formed between two strangers on-the-move, and the ways in which people come to trust strangers in mobile contexts. Their meeting would take on a different quality if they had met at the supermarket, through the village matchmaker, or at their local park. It is the urgency, passion, and sense of intensity in these types of "crossroad meetings" that I wish to examine here.

My mother did not think twice about hitchhiking alone, mainly because the practice was institutionalized under socialist Poland and at the time, 95 per cent of drivers accepted hitchhiking as something positive (Czuprynski 2005). Older generations of Poles recall nostalgically the days of the centralized "Hitchhiker's Booklet" (Ksiazeczka Autostopowicza) which was practiced in Poland in their youth. I stumbled across the existence of this booklet quite recently, four years after I became interested in mobile interactions. The booklet was part of a plan to legalize hitchhiking, which began in 1957 in Poland – the only state under Soviet rule which promoted such mobility. It was known as the "Hitchhiker's Action" (Akcja Autostopowicza), and at the start of the summer season in May it issued small booklets to hitchhikers containing coupons with set kilometre increments printed on them. This booklet, which had a red stop sign printed on it, acted as a reward system for drivers picking up passengers. Instead of 'thumbing a ride,' hitchhikers would wave down drivers by waving the booklet, and after going a certain distance, would rip off a coupon and give it to the driver. After collecting a certain number of 'points,' drivers would send off these coupons to the Hitchhiker's Action in order to collect a valuable prize like a washing machine or refrigerator. Yet like any socialist-led system, the Hitchhiker's Booklet was full of rules and regulations (Czuprynski 2005). At the back of each booklet coupon was a set of information for the driver:

> Please ask for the booklet for the duration of your trip. Collect the coupons prior to departure. During the trip, the booklet will be held with the driver. The number on the coupon is the hitchhiker's 'calling card.' Send the coupons by registered mail by the 10th of October to the Hitchhike Office – Warsaw, Narbutta street 27a. Using one booklet for more than one person is an offence (enforced by the Ministry of Defence). Every hitchhiker has received, and must give each driver to look over, the 'Letter to the Drivers – Regulations;' this letter contains news regarding prizes and the driver's responsibilities when driving a hitchhiker. The hitchhiker thanks you for your goodwill and help" (Ksiazeczka Autostop, 1968 in Czuprynski 2005).

Possible roadside gestures as well as the way in which hitchhikers actually 'hitched' their ride was outlined, stating that "the hitchhiker must stand on the right side of the road, and upon seeing an oncoming car at the distance of 150-100m, lift up their booet [...]. Hitchhikers must never walk onto the middle of the road and force the driver to a sudden stop" (Hitchhiker's Action Booklet 1968).

In the 1960s and 1970s, hitchhikers numbered roughly 30,000 annually (Czuprynski 2005). Possession of a booklet would also provide the hitchhikers with insurance, and those wanting one had to sign up by providing the Hitchhiker's Action with their personal documents or parental consent. While my mother, and many others, did not own a hitchhiker's booklet, those using this system found a sense of support and institutional security by signing up with the Hitchhiker's Action.

The Hitchhiker's Action also formalized a hospitality system – which promoted farmers and villagers to open up their homes and barns out of goodwill. The system enabled people (mainly living in the countryside – free space was scarce in the cities with families packed into two-room apartments), to post information regarding the possibility of accommodation. More importantly, it promoted home owners to take in young travellers. The notice regarding this service was found in the Hitchhiker's booklet:

> "If there is no room in a hotel, hostel, at a camping cite – you may have to sleep in a barn. Farmers are hospitable, and keeping that in mind, please be gracious guests. Last year we awarded 50 prizes to those landlords whom you voted for – this year we are also hoping to hear your feedback. Information regarding the prizes for farmers and landlords is being disseminated widely throughout the country, providing you with many friends among the village citizens...
>
> We do not have any way of enforcing our requests, we only hope you practice this service wisely. Please act accordingly. Remember that village landlords are very fearful of fire – this is their number one enemy. Quite often, the fear of inviting fire into one's home prevents the landlord from providing you with a place to stay. Please hand over your matches to the landlord before entering the barn. Help in any work that needs to be done around the farm; you can bring in the water, cut down some wood, help fix the farm machinery, or you can fix their radio (if you know how). The possibilities are endless; you just have to have the desire to do them." (Hitchhiker's Action Booklet 1968)

After staying at a farm, the hitchhiker was requested to fill out a small carton slip titled "Kind Landlord," providing positive feedback for the farmer. This was then sent off to the Hitchhiker's Action, and each farmer was then placed into a draw to win a prize like a new refrigerator, or a smaller kitchen appliance.

This type of mobility that organized under the Hitchhiker's Action formalized an exchange between people which always existed among gypsies, vagabonds, or ancient sages. Yet as the Hitchhiker's Action became an institution, a technology which provided a gateway for people like my mother, father, as well as many other hitchhikers and landlords, to engage in something I call intimate mobility – where people travel in order to meet and interact in a close, personal, and trustworthy way, exchanging ideas, thoughts, and experiences. People could have always been intimately mobile in the past, yet now, intimate mobility was made more accessible for a wider public through its formal nature.

The Hitchhiker's Action fell away along with communism, and Poland's hitchhikers, as well as services providing hospitality to strangers became informal and decentralized. Today, Poland becomes part of a world which is digital, mobile, and capitalist. Entering this world which is complex and constantly in-flux, inhabited by people who are on-the-move and transnational, formalized state-run systems such as the Hitchhiker's Actions cannot function on a strictly national level. With the socialist ideal of creating a utopian culture of hospitality and citizen-wide sharing on a nation state level nonexistent, the internet is now emerging as a place where these utopian ideals are being formalized, from the ground-up. Online car-sharing as well as online hospitality networks are reviving, while quite indirectly, what the Hitchhiker's Action under Socialist Poland aimed to achieve on a nation state level.

Formalizing mobile systems

One such formalized system of intimate mobility which has emerged online is known as a hospitality network. These networks are internet-based social networks of hundreds of thousands of individuals who use an online space to search out accommodation in the home of another network-member. Instead of staying at a hotel or hostel, the members of this virtual community prefer to encounter individuals online who are willing to host them in their home, apartment, or sometimes like in the Hitchhiker's Action, a barn. Hospitality networkers must establish an online profile of themselves, and this profile communicates information about oneself which is crucial for those hoping to host or visit. Additionally, users may be motivated to engage in the hospitality network not to travel, but to host members from various parts of the world. Other users simply enjoy meeting other network members for a coffee or a tour of a new city. These are networks in which interaction between members originates online with the purpose of meeting offline. Today, there are over five such networks, and Couchsurfing.com is the largest community with over 3,000,000 (September 2011) members globally.

Other formalized systems of intimate mobility are online hitchhiking websites. Alternately to flagging down a ride while standing at the roadside, e-hitchhikers browse through various hitchhiking websites (Craigslist.com rideshare is popular in North America, the German mitfahrzentrale.de or mitfahrgelegenheit.de are most popular across Europe) in order to find someone driving to their given destination. Unlike on Couchsurfing.com where profiles are highly detailed, drivers who post room in their car on online hitchhiking websites only have to provide a contact number or email for any potential hitchhiker. And unlike traditional hitchhiking or even the hospitality network exchange, drivers on online hitchhiking websites most often expect payment from travellers to cover petrol and/or car costs.

As "people's spread-out lives are nevertheless relational, connected, and embedded" (Urry 2007, 228), I chose to investigate specific types of mobile systems which foster relations and connections not only between friends and family, but mainly between strangers. Only by identifying and describing these systems of 'intimate mobility' are we able to fully understand the way in which access to virtual and physical mobility is increasing the amount of interaction between people in the world's rich, northern societies. Such interactions between strangers are becoming increasingly widespread and need to be addressed in order to understand the nature of trust and people's sense of closeness between strangers. Today, people can learn, trust, or feel closeness and intimacy with other people both online and offline, close by or at-a-distance (Elliott and Urry 2010). Despite the fact that people are spending more time online than ever before, a large increase in the percentage of online community members take actions offline at least once a year that are related to their online community, such as attending a meeting. A growing majority of online community members meet their counterparts in person (World internet Report, 2008), adding to the number of people who are now travelling specifically to meet with friends and family (Larsen, et. al. 2006). Wang and Wellman recently termed this type of friendship which was initiated online and subsequently established offline as "migratory friendship" (Wang and Wellman 2010).

As research within the area of mobility suggests, analysis should focus on "those processes by which co-presence and intimacy are on occasions brought about, and the social ties involved when people are not involved in daily interactions with each other but with whom a sense of connection is sensed and sustained" (Larsen et al. 2006). Experiencing this 'sense of connection' between strangers when mobile is what I call Intimate Tourism, or Intimate Mobility – when people move with the desire to experience a new space and interact with the people inhabiting those spaces (Bialski 2008).

The book you are holding in your hand is entirely based on my doctoral thesis, which was completed at the Center for Mobilities Research in the wonderful sociology department at Lancaster University in Lancaster, England in the fall of 2011. It will outline the conditions fostering intimate mobility and the consequences of interaction between individuals in a state of intimate mobility. The fact that people are attracted to mobility is not new. Movement has always promised a shift in the pattern of whom people interact with on a regular basis, and the way in which they do so. The difference is that today, people are able to move and network on a much larger scale. This increasing practice of networking depends upon "an extensive and growing array of interdependent mobility systems" (Urry 2007, 89), which include social networking technologies like Couchsurfing.com or OHWs. According to Google, social networks comprised four out of the top 10 global fastest-rising queries[1]. Social networking technologies create new opportunities of interaction en mass. A fraction of those who network, are intimately mobile - people who interact face-to-face with strangers using online social networking sites. If someone wants to meet a stranger in Paris, new technologies such as online hitchhiking, Couchsurfing, and cheap

---

1   Www.google.com accessed December 2008

airline travel make such interaction readily available. What I wish to outline using the concept of intimate mobility is that mass networking has direct impact on the way in which people interact if they engage in intimate mobility. Among the intimately mobile are people who engage in mobility with the hope of intense interactions, spontaneous interactions, and interactions with an imagined 'other' which are not available when stationary.

In this work, I will describe how people are expanding their social networks because of the opportunities these interactions provide. It will also show that when intimately mobile, people must renegotiate their definition of the stranger, trust, intimacy, and utility in order to enter into interaction/exchange with another. This renegotiation creates a desire for trust and intimacy with strangers, and also creates a lasting impact on the way a person interacts once returning home. This shift in the process of interaction provides a lasting impact for society, and the consequences of these experiences will also be addressed.

As I stated earlier, we can understand the changing processes of interaction by focusing on formalized systems of intimate mobility. Here two systems will be taken into account as mentioned earlier - Couchsurfing.com as well as online hitchhiking websites (OHW). In order to explain this further, it would be useful to introduce the way in which such formalized systems function. Before doing so, I will explain key aspects of my methodology.

All Couchsurfer's experiences are derived from interviews and participant observations conducted throughout the course of my 5-year study. Since joining Couchsurfing in February, 2005, I hosted and visited over 35 people. I became accepted into the Couchsurfing community as their researcher, and spent two months in the summer of 2006 living with a group of volunteers at the "Couchsurfing Collective" in Montreal – a temporary commune-of-sorts established in order to remodel, debug, and improve the website. Most of my interviews (conducted nearly 20) took place in there in Montreal between July and August, 2006, among Couchsurfers who had been actively hosting or visiting other members of the community. Other insights are derived from informal conversations with Couchsurfers while hosting or surfing. Some community and website statistics, collected after November, 2008, which are constantly being updated and made available to the public through Couchsurfing.com are also used. Additionally, I draw certain information from my own online survey which was conducted between August, 2006 and March, 2007. This online survey was programmed into the website and was made available to users through their individual profiles, by adding an extra tab named "My Survey" onto their profile. Much of my analysis of Couchsurfing as it specifically relates to the tourism process and tourism industry was explored in <u>Intimate Tourism: Enquete dans</u>

un reseau d'hospitalite (see Bialski 2008), and some concepts and analysis from the book will also be developed further here to support my argument.

Research for the OHW was also supported by participant observation. I used four different forms of OHWs – Craigslist.com in Canada and the United States, Gumtree.co.uk in the United Kingdom, Mitfahrzentrale.de across Europe, Mitfahrzentrale.de in Austria, and Nastopa.pl in Poland. The observations and interviews were conducted in the car during the journey. Five interviews were conducted among frequent users of OHWs outside of the use of OHWs. In total, I have taken 15 journeys using OHWs. I focused on interviews and participant observations because they provided the in-depth insights needed to compare the two technologies of intimate mobility.

What is Couchsurfing.com?

The knowledge of an online community such as Couchsurfing often travels in two ways – one, through the media, and secondly, through one's personal network, often through weak-ties (Granovetter 1973) – acquaintances and people we meet through casual encounters, meetings-in-flux, in public spaces – in airports, hostels, bars, and sports clubs. Couchsurfing.com is a talking-piece. As I stated earlier, it is a community of individuals who use the online social networking website in order to find accommodation in the homes of other members of the network. It is quirky. It sounds risky. It seems like something your mother would disprove of. If you haven't heard of Couchsurfing, you'll certainly want to hear about it. It has slowly entered the small-talk of the rich north – an icebreaker, a piece of small-talk, a note for the back-page of a lifestyle magazine.

Nana is an IT consultant from Helsinki. She likes her job, she earns enough money to live comfortably, she is still in her late 20s. She likes meeting new people, but complains that she can't really find anyone to "connect with." "The Finnish are quite closed people," she explains. One day, after work, she goes to a pub with some of her colleagues. She knows three out of five of the other people. A friend-of-a-friend starts telling them a "funny story" about his last city break to Berlin, where he went "Couchsurfing." Some have vaguely heard of Couchsurfing, also through word-of-mouth, through friends-of-friends, through loose ties. The new acquaintance begins to explain the nature of the community. Instead of staying at a hotel or a hostel, he stayed on somebody's couch. The group gets excited. This idea seems too good to be true. Questions and skepticisms start flying. Did you know them? No. So they were complete strangers? Yes. Weren't you scared that they would hurt you? Not really. Why? Why aren't you afraid? Nana does not say anything and listens to the questions. She is not afraid of the idea. The concept intrigues her. A cheap place to stay. The feeling of home in a foreign place. And insider's view on a place. This is so simple, why hasn't anyone thought of this earlier, she asks herself.

Couchsurfers are often drawn to the idea out of either an understanding of the practice (i.e. they have created informal networks of hospitality, where they used to stay on the couches of friends-of-friends or hosted people they met in a pub or at a party), or a desire to engage in a practice that promises friendship and trust - an alternative to the risk society (Beck 1992) under an individualistic, consumer capitalism – it is a utopian altruism. Moreover, while one could possibly come to the conclusion that Nana wanted to become part of Couchsurfing because she has the time, financial resources, and accommodation to host another individual, this is often not the case. Couchsurfers have many faces. They can be families, single bachelors living in bachelor apartments, young mothers, students living in residence, or farmers. Calling "Couchsurfing" by its name is deceiving – visitors sleep in tents, on the floor, on blow-up mattresses, on children's beds (the children then sleep with their parents), in a barn, or sometimes share a bed with the host. Thus, the individual's lifestyle is irrelevant – if an individual is interested in the idea of Couchsurfing, they will arrange their lives around their practice. The main slogan which appears on the website is a call to "Participate In Creating A Better World – One Couch At a Time." So in order for Nana to become engaged in the website she must identify herself with the ideology behind the website. The barebones structure of this type of exchange promises new users a cheap way to travel – a free couch. Yet Couchsurfing aims to weed out this type of utilitarianism but providing an ideology with a free couch – "this is not just a free couch. This promises intense, frequent, diverse interactions," stated the founder of the website.

Couchsurfing is based on a common purpose and ideology, where members express that opening up one's home to strangers will provide them with various cultural, educational, and self-reflective benefits. What is also worth noting is that trustfulness becomes a mandatory practice in order to become part of this community. In other words, you can not be a Couchsurfer if you don't want to trust another person enough to let them into your own home, your own private space.

Those who gain the desire to join the website first have to understand what a virtual community is, how it functions, and, quite basically, be able to log onto a website. Those who desire to join Couchsurfing must understand and trust the system that is the internet. Without already holding a narrative of the internet, the belief in the functionality of this type of virtual community is impossible.

The process of self-presentation online is an important aspect in relational development offline. Couchsurfers must establish an online profile of themselves, and this profile communicates information about oneself which is crucial in creating a sense of knowledge about the other person, which influences familiarity. The profile also plays a crucial role in a user's social navigation through the website, when he/she chooses whom to initiate contact with. As the average age of Couchsurfers is 27, and 70 per cent of users are from Europe or North America, most new Couchsurfers are like Nana – have a high level of media literacy and are proficient in navigating through websites. It takes her a matter of minutes to register her profile. Nana fills in a variety of boxes that ask for her "personal interests" and "life approach." She types in that she likes Finnish literature. Her interests are "strange lands and languages." Couchsurfing asks her to fill in her "Current Mission." She writes: "To have brand new adventures." She is asked to explain the "types of people she enjoys." She writes: "Seekers. People who are curious, creative, laid-back, insightful without being pretentious and intelligent without being arrogant about it. Those who prefer shaking the world with their thoughts rather than just making noises."

According to website statistics, 60.1 per cent of the members present photos, and most active members have a number of photos attached to their profile. Profiles with text and no photos can be considered less trustworthy, and users are encouraged to post a photo online in order to get better feedback. One of the main aspects, which make Couchsurfing distinct from all other websites of its sort, is its high use of photo images. Unlike on other virtual communities like Facebook.com, the photos attached to the profile must be actual likenesses of the members themselves. And although this does not guarantee that a member will use somebody else's headshot, photos of celebrities, animals, or objects are never used and are deleted by the website administrators.

Couchsurfing also features a "buddy list" or a "friendship list." Every profile shows a list of other members that the given person knows. As an example of how the friend-list works, lets consider the profile of Andrew in Warsaw, Poland. He has over 180 friends linked to his profile, and most of them are people he has surfed or hosted, although they also include high school friends, university friends, and family members. Every time somebody clicks on Andrew's profile, they can look at all of Andrew's friends, and all their "testimonials" to Andrew as well as their "link strength" (which I will explain in detail below). By using simple common sense, a user will come to the conclusion that somebody with many friends is, in fact, more likely to be trustworthy. It is also worth mentioning here that the type of person one is friends with matters just as much as the number of friends one has. For example, a person who has all of the website administrators and a few ambassadors as their friends could also be considered more trustworthy.

Members who become very involved in the development of the Couchsurfing project, want to help promotion of Couchsurfing, or are simply highly active surfers and hosts, have the potential of becoming a Couchsurfing "Ambassador." The Ambassador's job comes in all sorts of shapes and sizes. Sometimes an ambassador can help translate the website into a new language, or send "greetings" to new members. The title of "Ambassador" is given to a surfer by members of the administrative team, which is a collective of individuals who helped found and develop the website. The fact that a person is an ambassador, or a founding member, has the potential to make him more trustworthy.

Each member has the opportunity to enter the process of vouching. One member can "vouch" for another member by clicking on an icon next to their profile. In doing this, one member makes a sort of promise to the rest of the Couchsurfing community that the member they are vouching for is, in fact, trustworthy. Often people could vouch for their good friends, or people they have hosted or surfed with. New users like Nana obviously cannot vouch for anyone if they do not have anybody linked to their profile. Vouching implies that you have been a member for some time.

Verification is something slightly different than vouching, and involves a 4-step process in which a member sends their credit card number to the members of the administrative team, the founder of the website. The members of the administrative team in charge of verification then take 25 US dollars from the member's account (there are discounts for those who cannot afford it). Upon payment, the user is sent a verification number to their home address. The member enters the number onto the website and receives the full level of verification. Verification guarantees others that this member lives at the address he or she indicated on the website, and that their identity is correct. The downside of this process is that it excludes those without a credit card and financial means to pay for it. Verification is not a requirement of the website, and many members visit or host other users without it.

Relationships on Couchsurfing are recorded with a set of variables and descriptions - meaning, when Nana adds a friend to her "friendship list," she must answer a set of questions about this friend. These questions are based on the origin and duration of the relationship. From a drop-down menu, the user chooses from a list of 13 answers as to the relationship origin. Nana would also have to explain how strongly she trusts the friend and would have a choice of six text-based answers which range from "I don't know this person well enough to decide" to "I would trust this person with my life" (other answers are "I don't trust this person," "I trust this person somewhat," "I generally trust this person," and "I highly trust this person"). This friendship list is an indicator of both how popular one individual is, and through the 'trust strength' they gain information on how reputable (and hence, trustworthy), they are.

The final, and one of the most important features on Couchsurfing explicitly relating to trust is the reference system – similar to online auction websites like Ebay.com, in which a user is given a positive/negative rating from people who have interacted with them either through hosting or visiting, or elsewhere. This feature functions in addition to the friendship list – and under any Couchsurfer's profile there can appear a list of references from old school friends, family members, or former hosts and guests. Note that a reference is usually left by someone whom we have met and interacted with face-to-face, over a period of time. One of Nana's references written by her former host was:

> Another CS enthu(siastic) person. [Nana] is one of the first people I hosted through CS... hosted her in Bombay with her friends from England, then met up with her in Goa and traveled a bit together and again hosted her at my place... It would be funny if [Nana] wrote a mail asking me whether she can surf my couch.. she has become family now... the wanderer spirit in her and in me will ensure that we meet some day in some corner of this not so lonely planet and I am really looking forward to it

None of the received references can be deleted by the user – and some profiles include negative references. According to website statistics, 99.8 per cent of experiences are positive, but the negative experiences are also posted on a user's profile. These references are textual and depend on the detail - a lot of information is contained on the descriptive opinion of each user. The level of enthusiasm can differ from user to user. The meaning these references cannot be understood by reading just the "positive" or "negative" rating, yet rather by reading the detailed description of the author. Knowledge of this reference feature may also implicitly encourage community members to be good hosts or guests during the offline interaction so that they may gain a positive reference, and hence, a positive reputation, online. In general, the profile serves as an introduction – and Couchsurfing acts as the mediator in this introduction, helping acquaint one person with another, offering various affordances within the profile in which a member could communicate who they are.

After Nana builds her profile, she then searches couches to stay on. If she types "Stockholm" into the search engine, 13 pages showing 25 users per page appear. These profiles are smaller versions of the larger profiles and include information such as the user's photo, their age, gender, location, date of last login, languages spoken, hobbies and 'philosophy' – which is a short sentence describing the user's approach to life. The number of photos, friends, and email response rate is also shown.

Despite Nana's sense of trust in the ideology of Couchsurfing, some first time users want to understand how to communicate trust online. A section of the website is devoted to answering questions regarding first time interaction between potential host and guest. The following is an extract from a page found on the website, outlining the precautions new Couchsurfers should take when hosting or surfing.

> A profile can give you valuable information about a person, so first find out what kind of people will surf your couch! Read the profile carefully Is their profile filled out? Do they have photographs? Who left them references? How much CouchSurfing experience do they have? Did that glowing reference come from someone who hosted or surfed with this person?[2]

The fields which are filled in by each user not only allow Nana to familiarize herself with another user, but also allow her to discern whether or not the other user would be a person she wishes to interact with. This decision is quite subjective, and often based on homophily – or an attraction to those who are similar to Nana. Among all the users in Stockholm, Nana found a woman her age who, like her, is interested in creative, adventurous, and open-minded people. Similarity instantly connects Nana to this stranger – and in this case, this sense of connection is based on the stranger's perceived worldview. This user in Stockholm has now shifted from being a stranger, to being a familiar, likeminded individual – all before any verbal dialogue was exchanged. The design of Couchsurfing enabled this connection to take place.

Once Nana has found someone she would like to visit, she sends them an email through the messaging system which is built into the website. This message is forwarded to the user's regular email provider – yet the actual email address of any user is not shown on the website. It is not guaranteed that the first person Nana chooses will accept her as a visitor. Those who receive email requests to Couchsurf may not respond to the request for a variety of reasons – sometimes, the user may not have any free time to host a visitor that specific weekend. They may already have other Couchsurfing guests, or any other guests, staying with them on the weekend Nana requested. Another reason is that they may not have the energy, the will to host – as hosting can sometimes be quite time consuming and can also take the host away from their daily routine. Other reasons which have more to do with the user requesting to visit rather than with the individual hosting, is that the potential host may not want to host the person sending the request. This may be for a variety of reasons, but they come to reject a request after socially navigating through the user's profile, and after reading their request email.

Emails requesting a couch are often sent out to a number of people in a given city. Many respondents and friends have expressed the difficulty finding

---

[2] Profile on homepage of www.Couchsurfing.com accessed October 2008

accommodation in certain cities – among all the reasons provided above, this also has to do with the time of travel as well as the number of Couchsurfers in a given city. Yet Couchsurfers have expressed the sense that Couchsurfing is about choice – the profile offers them the ability to choose one member over the other – and the host chooses the visitor (and vice versa) based on the perceived ease of interaction. Specifically, Couchsurfers aim to minimize the high risk of social awkwardness when the two go from interacting online to meeting offline. Thus, the profile helps a) a guest or host to express who they are, and b) allows the host or guest to discern if the given person will be someone they want to interact with.

As soon as the host accepts the guest, only a few emails are exchanged between the two – mainly emails providing directions and sometimes include a short informal description of the host or guest's expectations. The administrators of the website created a field on the user profile titled "Couch Information" in which "will give surfers information on what they can expect and also might be expected upon their arrival." Dana, a 50-year-old American, is an experienced community member – hosting over 50 Couchsurfers on separate occasions. Under her "couch information" she outlines a set of expectations.

> I have a guest bedroom with bath available for one or two people, 2 couches, one quite small, and a little travel trailer. I have plenty of bedding. I live alone with my dog Luna about One and a half miles from town. the park is about half a mile so you can walk or ride bikes (I have 4 extras) to town or through the beautiful park. Smoking is allowed outside. I work from home so most the time I will have plenty of time to show you around. If you stay more than two days it would be great if you chip in for food and drinks if you want to have dinners here. I love to cook and you won't regret it! Please let me know at least a week in advance so I can Plan for your stay3

Note that this feature in the user profile provides Dana with space to express her expectations, and allows the potential guest to understand what Dana's expectations are of them.

Couchsurfers often meet in public places for the first time. The daytime or evening activities are dependent on the host's lifestyle, and it is also frequent that the two individuals stay in the vicinity of their host's home, immersed in dialogue. The fact that the design of the website structures a response of relative self-disclosure online, the users involved in this interaction (looking at each other's profiles, gathering information about each other, interacting through email) become part of a dialogue which continues offline with an openness to self-disclosure and candid intimacy. Nana explained that "When I talk to people I do not wish to discuss the superficial things like 'what went on in the football

---

3 Profile quote from www.Couchsurfing.com accessed October 2008

game' or 'which model has the biggest boobs,' so with Couchsurfer there's an excuse to avoid all that stuff because they're only there for a short time. So you get closer faster." But this feeling of 'getting closer faster' is still instigated by the candidness found through the profile. Nana may approach her host in Stockholm by stating, "So you mentioned on your profile that you've been to Nepal. Tell me about that" or perhaps "I saw on your profile that you lived in South Africa and Italy. What were you doing there?" Reading another person's online profile provides an illusion that Couchsurfers in fact know their host or guest. A Couchsurfer like Nana may stay with a host usually between two days and a week, and upon returning home, only around half (couchsurfing survey 2006) the time keeps in contact with their host.

Online hitchhiking websites

OHWs are more explicitly utilitarian compared to Couchsurfing.com. The purpose is simply to find a ride to wherever one needs to get to. Whereas Couchsurfing.com has an explicit utopian ideology of "connecting the world, one couch at a time," Mitfahrgelegenheit's slogan is "Klicken. Fahren. Sparen", which can directly be translated as "Click. Ride. Save." Other OHWs such as Mitfahrzentrale, Craigslist, as well as the Polish Nastopa.pl are also quite straightforward, lacking an ideology. The websites look functional and impersonal.

Despite the fact that within Europe, there are over a dozen websites organizing this type of travel, I chose to look at Mitfahrgelegenheit (directly translated to "Rideshare Opportunity") because, through word of mouth, it has become the most popular out of the OHWs I mentioned above. It is also the least commercial, meaning that it does not ask for membership fees from new users, and also unlike some sites, charges nothing for contact between passenger and driver.

Mitfahrgelegenheit provides any user with the option of placing an advertisement either searching for a ride, or offering a ride to any given destination on any given date. Unlike on Couchsurfing, creating a profile is not mandatory and users can search for a driver or passenger without having "logged in." The only benefit to logging into the website and creating a profile is that doing so allows users to send internal emails to drivers or passengers. Most often doing so is not necessary since drivers and passengers provide their mobile phone numbers when advertising a journey – this phone number is visible to anyone who clicks on the given advertisement, users and non users alike.

Antonio was born in Vienna to a Serbian mother and a Hungarian father. Now in his late 30s, he works in as an economist in a large Balkan business development company. His new wife lives in Bolzano, north of Trento, in the upper Italian Alps.

Because of her job as a psychologist, and her lack of German, she decided to stay in the Alps for one year before learning enough language to move to Vienna. Antonio accepted the distance, and the difficult commute. Each weekend or fortnight, he drives 590km (around 6 hours driving) one way in order to spend three days with his wife, and returns on Monday morning to work. Despite the fact that the drive takes him through the Alps, Antonio can't help find the drive to be quite monotonous. To liven his journey and help him with petrol costs he uses Mitfahrgelegenheit. Each weekend, he places his advertisement on the website, stating that he is driving from Vienna to Bolzano. Sometimes he departs at noon on Friday. Some weeks he has to leave in the late afternoon.

I want to get from Vienna to Vocklabruck, which is halfway between Linz and Salzburg. I click on Mitfahrgelegenheit.de and search click under "suche" (search), and click in all rides being offered from Vienna to Vocklabruck. Because Vocklabruck is such an obscure town, I find no offers. I then look at all the departures leaving Vienna on the day I want to go. This is the second main difference between OHWs and hospitality networks – because of the lower numbers of people using this website, drivers and passengers often have to compromise their route in order to accommodate the wishes of either the passenger or driver. When searching a given destination, they often have to be flexible and change either their departure town (they must first get to a larger city or place themselves near a major roadway), or they have to change their destination town (get to a larger city or major roadway near their destination-of-choice).

On my search I notice Antonio is driving to Bolzano, and will be driving along the A1 highway passed Linz and near Vocklabruck. I alternate my route, and realize that I will have to be flexible and take a bus from the trans-national highway near Vocklabruck to the town center. Each advertisement shows the journey's origin as well as the destination, the exact date and time of departure. It also lists the number of available places in the car (sometimes only 1, sometimes the entire car except for the driver is free). There is also a space for the driver's contact numbers, email and name. Next to the name there is a small icon which links up with their personal profile (if they decided to establish one). There is also a space for the driver to place additional details and comments regarding the rideshare. Some details include the cost of the journey (at times it is not specified, at times there is a price per km) and drivers also wish to add if they allow smoking, or the types of music they enjoy listening to. Antonio's additional comments explain that he is driving to Bolzano but is willing to drop off passengers who need to get to destinations along his route like Linz, Salzburg or Innsbruck.

As in most cases, I first send Antonio a text message asking if there is still space available in his car. Contact is usually initiated by mobile phone, and by text message. Text messaging is more direct than emails and offer a quicker response rate for those who need to organize their journey last-minute. Passengers and drivers often first communicate via text messaging in order to save on costs linked with phoning one another. After Antonio writes back, I phone him telling him I would be happy to go with him, and explain that I want to go to Vocklabruck, which is along the A1. Our initial contact over the phone is a lot lets detailed and personal than the contact initiated over Couchsurfing. At this point, I know nothing about Antonio, nor do I care to know anything about him. Antonio is also not expecting any details about who I am or why I am going to Vocklabruck. He tells me that he will meet me, as well as another passenger who showed interest in coming with us, at a bus stop in an Eastern district of Vienna on Friday at 1pm. It is unusual for drivers to pick up passengers at their homes – a neutral departure point usually near a major highway is often preferred.

It takes me 5 minutes to find Antonio on Friday. He calls me a few minutes before noon to make sure I am there waiting for him. Mobiles phones are crucial accessories to OHWs, and most contact offline is kept up via mobiles, especially around the time of departure, in order to locate a passenger or driver. We greet each other with a handshake and Antonio takes my backpack and loads it into his Volvo. He explains that we have to wait another 10 minutes for Julia, the other passenger who is going to Innsbruck. She had just phoned Antonio to tell him she would be late. Note that without a mobile phone to express her delay, Antonio would likely drive off without her, thinking she was not coming. The fact that Antonio has to compromise his departure time is also something each driver has to take into account when using an OHW. This is not a regular roadside hitchhike, where a driver picks someone up and within a matter of seconds, drives off. Usually a drop off or pick up puts another 30 minutes on top of the journey time for each driver.

Julia finally arrives and I sit in the front seat and she sits in the backseat behind me. My German is poor, so we speak English to one another, and I initiate the conversation. We talk about our background and what are doing in Vienna, and why we are going to Innsbruck, Vocklabruck, and Bolzano. This type of interaction can happen, but some frequent users of OHWs expressed that this is not necessary. Because a passenger is paying for the trip, they "have the right to do what they want," meaning, they can sleep, look out the window, or listen to their iPod. In the case of more than one passenger, the front seat next to the driver is known as the "less-privileged" seat. Being more proximate to the driver, the front seat driver is expected to speak to entertain the driver, which can, or cannot be a nuisance.

Antonio drives the 10km out off the highway into Vocklabruck town in order to make my journey easier, and I pay him 20 Euros – more than he was expecting – in order to thank him for the favour. I keep his number in my phone in case I want to return with him on his journey back on Sunday. Quite often, if passengers and drivers are going the same route for the same period of time, a driver will take the passenger back on their return journey.

Searching out new patters of interaction

Using the cases of Couchsurfing.com and Mitfahrgelegenheit.de as my empirical examples throughout my work, I argue that certain technologies in use today are enabling closeness, intimacy and trust between strangers. Those living in a rich, northern society, using modern technologies, can and do expand their network of friends. This book will focus on the way networks of intimacy and closeness are created or avoided. While friends can be made virtually or at-a-distance, face-to-face interaction still remains the most detailed method of interaction (Boden and Molotch 1994), and as such, I will also show the way in which proximity still provides the depth and detail and value in a relationship, mobilizing people to move and meet others in distant places. While on one hand, this increase in choice can be termed a "supermarketization of friendship," (which shall be discussed in the fourth chapter), I argue that among the intimately mobile, interaction is not disposable. The subsequent chapters will heavily draw from my respondent's experiences of meeting when on-the-move, and the personal value it has for them. Interaction, as I will explain, is not simply about empty fun. Just as travel can be about self-discovery, certain people desire to meet and interact because of the 'psychological' or 'spiritual' value it provides them with.

The following section will explain the way interactions, within a mobile dimension, differ from people's everyday, localized contexts. New places are not safe places. Familiarity creates safety. Unfamiliarity creates unease. When people are in a place they do not know (a place full of new sights, sounds, objects, etc.), and are faced with people they have never met before (people with certain customs, desires, expectations, obligations, etc.) they must adapt to this new context. In the chapter on the sentiments of mobility as well as the rituals of homemaking, I will look at the way people adapt to a new space, (re)negotiating their way of interacting with another person in order to create a sense of familiarity in the unfamiliar context. This section relies on my ethnography of Couchsurfing and Online Hitchhiking Networks in order to outline the ways mobile interaction is (re)negotiated.

These new patterns of interaction among people who are intimately mobile create certain consequences for the way in which people define friendship. I argue that an increase in mobility shifts the way people interact with one another. People who use these technologies frequently develop a sensitivity of intimate mobility – and upon returning 'home,' the stranger is redefined, becoming somebody closer and accessible. With more interactions with strangers we are creating intimacy with individuals we would never have created before. The idea of the "faceless mob" of urban life is rejected. Here, responses from interviews will be utilized to understand the way in which closeness can and is achieved through contact with another person on-the-move. One chapter in this work will address the precise ways in which individual's understanding of interaction shifts when intimately mobile. Another theme I wish to address is that while the individual engages in interaction, he/she feels autonomous, and thus an encounter becomes an interaction between two separate individuals. Yet a popular theme among my respondents is that they return home understanding the world as a commons – with a sense of grasping the complexity of the world through their interactions.

Chapter 2
(Intimately) Mobile Methods

Because methodology is closely connected to theory and the kinds of empirical worlds a researcher creates, it may seem strange to separate the methodology chapter from the theoretical chapter that will follow. The theory used in this work is much more entangled in the actual research process, but I separate the two in order to outline the scope and detail of my research methods.

The research in this dissertation is a much more theoretical, in-depth development of the work which began, and was only partially documented, in my masters thesis (a monograph on tourism and Couchsurfing, published as a book, titled <u>Intimate Tourism: Enquete dans un reseau d'hospitalite</u>, 2009). My work here draws on some material which was given preliminary analysis in my MA dissertation.

As my introductory chapter suggested, I became fascinated with online/offline communities as well as the users of such websites by first becoming part of these communities, and observing the emergent social relations between myself and others around me. As a result of this fascination, my research throughout the past years employed a variety of methodological approaches and research phases that started in the spring of 2005 and lasted until the completion on my final chapters. As I mentioned in my introduction, this dissertation is based on mainly qualitative methods derived from online social networks being used in a variety of locations around the world – specifically, Couchsurfing.com (global), as well as a collection of online hitchhiking websites (OHWs): carpooling.pl and nastopa.pl (Poland), mitfahrgelegenheit.de (Germany), mitfahrzentrale.de (Germany and Austria) and classified advertisement websites which offer online hitchhiking/ridesharing options including gumtree.co.uk (England), craigslist.com (Canada and the USA). The following short chapter will introduce the research approach used to investigate the emergent mobile practices of the intimately mobile.

My methodology was inspired by the research being conducted at The Centre of Mobilities Research (CeMore) at Lancaster, namely Urry and Sheller (2006), as well as other works by Cresswell (1997, 2004, 2006), Castells (1996), Adey (2006), the methodological approach to the mobilities paradigm presented by Büscher and Urry in <u>Mobile Methods and the Empirical</u> (2008), and more recently, their edited book <u>Mobile Methods</u> (Büscher et al. 2011). The mobilities paradigm, they explain, "enables the 'social world' to be theorised as a wide array of economic, social and political practices, infrastructures and ideologies that all involve, entail or curtail various kinds of movement of people, or ideas, or information or objects. And in so doing this paradigm brings to the fore theories, methods and exemplars of research that so far have been mostly out of sight" (Büscher et al. 2011, 4). This research hopes to answer the call for "mobility-oriented social science" which "highlights the importance of investigating how worlds (and sense) are made in and through movement" (Büscher et al. 2011, 13).

While I will further explain and position this paradigm in existing influential and explorative social theory pertinent to this work, when it came to developing my research methodology, I searched for an approach that would help me understand how strangers are creating worlds that are both intimate and mobile, fleeting yet also somehow deep and lasting. Law and Urry (2004) explained that the main problem with existing methodological approaches in the social sciences is that they fail to address those social occurrences which are "fleeting," or "that which is here today and gone tomorrow, only to reappear again the day after tomorrow":

> They deal poorly with the distributed – that is to be found here and there but not in between – or that which slips and slides between one place and another. They deal poorly with the multiple – that which takes different shapes in different places. They deal poorly with the non-causal, the chaotic, the complex. And such methods have difficulty dealing with the sensory – that which is subject to vision, sound, taste, smell; with the emotional – time-space compressed outbursts of anger, pain, rage, pleasure, desire, or the spiritual; and the kinaesthetic – the pleasures and pains which follow the movement and displacement of people, objects, information and ideas (Law and Urry 2004, 403).

The intimately mobile, and the interactions and relationships that are negotiated online and then offline when being intimately mobile, including people's experiences of intimacy, trust, love, awkwardness, avoidance, isolation, hospitality, and gift giving are part of this "fleeting" complex social movement of people online and offline. I did find that my research subjects went through sensory interactions, relationships, and experiences that took shape in different places. These interactions were also not always anchored geographically and often did "slip and slide between one place and another." In order to deal with the difficulties of studying these fleeting and mobile interactions, Büscher and Urry suggest that it is "necessary to develop research methods that are 'on the move' (Büscher and Urry 2008, Büscher et al. 2011). To employ this approach, I focused on:

a. Various forms of tracking – including physically travelling with my research subjects in order to understand the many and interdependent forms of intermittent movement of people, images, and objects (Sheller and Urry 2006).
b. Investigations of how people, objects, information and ideas move and are mobilized in interaction with others in order to understand the way 'grammars' or orders of social, economic and political relations are being shaped (Garfinkel 1967, Büscher and Urry, 2008).

In my work on the technologies of friendship and hospitality (Chapter 4 and 6), as well as my chapter on alienation and emotion (Chapter 7 and 8) I describe the way the intimately mobile experience face-to-face conversation, non-verbal interaction, virtual communication, and the way space influences these interactions, accepting that "bodies are not empirically fixed and given but involve performances to fold notions of movement, nature, taste and desire, into and through the body. Bodies sense and make sense of the world as they move bodily in and through it, creating discursively mediated sensescapes that signify social taste and distinction, ideology and meaning" (Büscher and Urry 2009, 102). My observation of the way in which my hosts, visitors, and drivers sensed and made sense of their mobile interactions became a key component in creating my own sense of their practices.

As I described in my introduction, I began as a member of Couchsurfing.com rather than a researcher. After comparing the website to other online hospitality networks, I decided on researching it specifically because its design features were much more developed than any other website of its kind, enabling also a unique quantitative approach. Additionally, my participation in the online and offline community, including my introduction to the founders of the website, gave me access to the inner community of Couchsurfing.com.

With these qualitative and quantitative approaches with the Couchsurfing community (which I will explain in detail below) that I began when writing my masters thesis, I found it crucial to add a third dimension of my research – a comparative example using another online social network that enables people to meet offline, in a mobile setting. In the first year of my doctoral studies (early in 2008) I became a member of a variety of online hitchhiking networks – in the UK, Canada, Germany, Austria and Poland. The way I conducted and recorded my interviews within this community will also be explained below.

Where it began

I became a member of Couchsurfing.com at the beginning of February, 2005 and began my study as participant observer after first hosting an American named Ben in Warsaw in February, 2006. For the following five years, I was engaged in Couchsurfing as both a host and visitor. My main endeavour from the start was to use this case study in order to illustrate and develop a theoretical framework for understanding and posing questions about the process of mobile intimacy.

All Couchsurfer's experiences are derived from formal and informal interviews conducted throughout the course of my 5-year study of the website. Since joining Couchsurfing in February, 2005, I hosted, visited and met over 50 people (listed at the end of this book) in Canada, the United States, England, France, Germany, Austria, the Czech republic, Spain, Holland, Sweden, and Poland. I spent between one and five days with these hosts and guests, and would be constantly observing rituals, eliciting stories regarding their own experiences, tracing trust and property lines, and keeping a journal.

The year I joined Couchsurfing, the website was just 4 months old, and when starting to host in Warsaw, Poland, the website had under 30,000 registered members worldwide. The founder of the website, Casey Fenton, came to visit Warsaw in April, 2006 and, along with two other website programmers, stayed on my couch. This immediate access to the "core" members of this website – those creating and maintaining the concept and content allowed me to gain insight into the creation of the website and the ways in which these people designed and structured its content.

Geertz explains that "doing ethnography" is like trying to read (in the sense of "construct a reading of") a manuscript-foreign, faded, full of ellipses, incoherencies, suspicious emendations, and tendentious commentaries, but written not in conventionalized graphs of sound but in transient examples of shaped behavior" (Geertz 1973, 10). Throughout my chapters, various new ways of becoming intimately mobile are illustrated as "examples of shaped behaviour" (Geertz 1973, 10) when on-the-move.

In ethnography, Geertz used the term "thick description," which was a notion borrowed from the British metaphysical philosopher Gilbert Ryle (1971). in order to define a form of ethnography where the researcher's aim "is to draw large conclusions from small, but very densely textured facts; to support broad assertions about the role of culture in the construction of collective life by engaging them exactly with complex specifics" (Geertz 1973, 10). Throughout my chapters, I explored various concepts and "systems of concepts" (Geertz 1973, 10) such as "emotion," "ideology," "hospitality," "reciprocity," and the "stranger" into a "body of thick-description ethnography in the hope of rendering mere occurrences scientifically eloquent" (Geertz 1973, 10).

In order to engage in this thick description suggested by Geertz, I used a variety of research episodes to engage in tracking the relationships between mobile strangers using OHWs and Couchsurfing.com. I will explain each research phase in detail in order to explain the scope and depth of the empirical work that has been done and the methodological approaches that were used in this research.

Couch and Car Participant Observer

My first approach to research included note taking and photography as participant observer in both the Couchsurfing and online hitchhiking website. My mobile methods were similar to the approach of Bærenholdt et al. (2004), who used "participation-while-interviewing" in their research on mobile tourists in Denmark: "Here the researcher first participates in patterns of movement, and then interviews people, individually or in focus groups, as to how their diverse mobilities constitute their patterning of everyday life" (Büscher and Urry 2008, 105). I also identified with the work of Burawoy, who became a participant observer for 10 months as a factory worker in order to describe the labour process under "monopoly capitalism" (Burawoy 1979). Burawoy "took the job with the explicit consent and knowledge of management as to why [he] was there" (Burawoy 1979, 34), and much like in Burawoy's case, the Couchsurfing founding team "agreed to provide me with records and data" (Burawoy 1979, 34).

While hosting or visiting when Couchsurfing, or being the driver or passenger, I would often, but not always, keep my identity as sociologist hidden (only when someone asked me what I was studying or what my research was about would I reveal my subject of inquiry). This corresponded with the methodology of Goffman (1963) who employed total participation in which the role and the activities of observation themselves were totally hidden. Later, joining the team of Couchsurfers at the "Couchsurfing Collective" in Montreal – a volunteer-run house established for three months to run and further develop the website – I became an overt participant observer. My research activities (such as asking questions, taking notes) became a taken-for-granted part of my participation.

I kept Goffman's research in <u>Interaction Ritual</u> (1967) as a model of ethnography throughout my work. In this work, as well as in <u>Behaviour in Public Places</u> (1963) Goffman systematically describes the way in which strangers come into contact with one another, in what he termed focused and unfocused interactions. The detailed way in which sociality occurs between Couchsurfers and OHW users will be described in this work with heavy reference to Goffman's methods and terminology, especially using the above mentioned texts, as well as <u>On face-work: An analysis of ritual elements in social interaction</u> (1955). As this work shall show, understanding certain rituals that arise from being mobile and meeting new people become key in understanding the general process of mobile intimacy. For example, the processes of microcoordination (Ling and Yttri 2002) – the way in which objects like keys, maps, mobile phones, ipods, or laptops aid in creating or avoiding ties among the intimately mobile, or the way in which strangers navigate through private and public spaces are explored in terms of rituals and detailed exchanges. In doing so, it was my aim to update Goffman's efforts of showing how forms of interactions are done in cities, and how new mobile social configurations are created.

I would like to underline that much of this work is based on my own interaction with the mobile world of friendship-making. I would take notes, photographs, and reflect on my own interaction, becoming fully involved and committed as a host or guest, driver or passenger. This auto-ethnography (Ellis and Bochner 2003) of my own involvement and interaction while Couchsurfing or using OHWs became especially useful in this entire work, and my descriptions of the practices in interaction, the use of these various online social networks, the avoidance of intimacy, the performance of hospitality, and the way in which friendship is negotiated resulted from my five year history as somebody intimately mobile. This created compromises, negotiations, and tensions that fostered further insight into mobile interactions.

Research for the OHWs was also supported by participant observations. I traveled using six different forms of OHWs – Craigslist.com in Canada and the United States, Gumtree.co.uk in the United Kingdom, Mitfahrzentrale.de across Europe, Mitfahrzentrale.de in Austria, and Nastopa.pl and carpooling.pl in Poland, and travelled across distances in cars to track the changes and practices of OHW users.

Interviews

Research that is conducted under the mobilities perspective is oftentimes ethnographic and thereby intrinsically connected into practice – as Büscher and Urry explain, "many are part of collaborative innovation projects, art and design interventions, or form part of policy advisory panels, programmes and literatures" (Büscher and Urry 2008, 111). Being the first academic to study this community, after meeting with the founder of the website in Warsaw, I became accepted into the Couchsurfing community as a collaborative researcher and began my ethnography as both an ethnographer and collaborator in their creative team. This approach was used here in order to create an interdisciplinary, academic and practitioner/community collaboration – which is an integral part of mobilities research and mobile methods.

In the summer of 2006, Casey invited me to spend two months living with a group of volunteers at the "Couchsurfing Collective" in Montreal – a temporary commune-of-sorts established in order to remodel, debug, and improve the website. Based on a co-working environment model they exported from their days in the silicon valley dot-com boom many of them were once a part of, the "Collective" worked out of the first floor of a row house in Montreal's mile-end district – with computers and programmers packed into a room, intensively tapping away on their keyboards. By June of 2006, the news had spread throughout the 40,000-strong Couchsurfing global community that a Collective was established to help improve the website, and throughout the summer, volunteers and eager Couchsurfers would come through the house for a day, or a few weeks at a time, lending help in the form of baking or programming skills. This was an ideal period for me as a researcher – to gain insight into the motivations that drive Couchsurfers to become part of the community, and the experiences and practices that shaped their view of the community. Couchsurfers coming through this house were eager to help and eager to express their thoughts. Thus, most of my 20 interviews took place in Montreal between July and August, 2006, among Couchsurfers who had been actively hosting or visiting other members of the community.

The methodological benefits of interviewing Couchsurfers at the Collective were numerous. Specifically, neither I nor the person I interviewed was at the time a host or a guest, nor were we inhabiting a space that was either mine or theirs. This absolved us of any norms or responsibilities as host or guest to maintain a face of hospitality, politeness, or honesty (as my chapter on hospitality explains), and created a very informal interview setting where we both felt comfortable.

Additionally, the people I interviewed mostly volunteered their time to talk to me. As I explain in chapter 6, the process of discussion and intimate, candid dialogue is part of being a Couchsurfer – and it was common practice for two Couchsurfers who met at the "Collective" to set up a time to meet – often the apartment was filled with two people talking on the back porch, or in the kitchen, discussing topics that covered motivations to become a Couchsurfer, or their background and travel history. These topics were similar to the ones I covered in my interviews, and because of this common practice of face-to-face dialogue, interviewees did not fear me, but rather became eager to meet with me – and treated our interview as "Paula time." At the end of my research stay at the collective, a few people became disappointed that they did not get a chance to be interviewed.

Over the five years of hosting and visiting others, I also led informal interviews and discussions which were less formalized, yet often took notes in order to create a detailed description of the hospitality process.

My interviews with OHW members were also less formalized. Only on two occasions did I record my interviews with my OHW drivers – and the reason that I avoided recording these interviews is linked to the notion of hospitality mentioned above. As a passenger, I felt the recorder and my presence as a researcher could be intrusive. The car is also a confined space, a space that is in motion, and the act of driving often involves a person's immediate attention. As a passenger I did not want to put my host – the driver – in any discomfort. I asked him/her questions, and at times jotted down notes during or after my drive. On a few other occasions as the passenger in the back seat, I recorded an interview with another passenger – here, again, we were both passengers, and being of equal status, I felt no obligation to cater to them. I did gain a great deal of important insight from my drivers, and despite not having recorded these interviews, they were much longer in duration than my interviews at the Couchsurfing collective, because they lasted for the duration of my car trip. Some journeys lasted for 4 hours, and sometime for nearly 12 hours. Three interviews were conducted among frequent users of OHWs whom I met in a non-OWH context. In total, I took 12 journeys using OHWs. As I will explain, OHWs are quite simplistic. Most do not ask users to provide any profile information or personal details, making finding any sorts of online statistics about users impossible. This is the main reason I only relied on research done during participatory observation.

Open-Ended Survey Responses

Couchsurfing was a unique social network, in the sense that relationships between users were registered with variables such as the origin and the duration of acquaintanceship, as well as how strongly the individuals trust one another on a scale of 1-6. Together with one of my lecturers at the sociology department – a Polish expert in social network analysis, in February, 2006, we wrote to Casey requesting a "network dump" of the data set on Couchsurfing. He agreed, and sent us a large anonymized whole network data – meaning a data set with all the connections between users. At that point, CS had almost 45,000 active users, and this included 221,180 friendship dyads. This friendship data set was used to write a chapter on trust in <u>Social Computing and Virtual Communities</u> (edited by Ang and Zaphiris 2009), and published prior to the completion of the book you are holding in your hands. This quantitative research was revealed the factors fostering trustworthiness between members of an online community. While the ways in which gender, age, and the origins of relations factors into creating trustworthiness is an important topic in studies on online-offline relationships, my data does not provide insight into the motivations, experiences and practices of intimate mobility. This is best investigated with qualitative methods, which is the focus of this book – which ethnographically describes the rituals, and acts, and skills of becoming intimately mobile. Further quantitative analysis here was not necessary to create this description.

Another dimension of the qualitative research included my online survey. While at the Couchsurfing "Collective" in Montreal, I created an online survey which was conducted between August, 2006 and March, 2007. This online survey was programmed into the website and was made available to users through their individual profiles, by adding an extra tab named "My Survey" on to their profile. In those months, a little over 3609 Couchsurfers responded to my survey – answering 24 questions about their motivations to travel using Couchsurfing, the duration of their host-guest interaction, why/why they don't stay in touch with their host and guests, and other questions relating to the nature of their interaction on the website.

The open-ended questions derived from over 3609 responses in this survey became the main body of responses that helped verify and further support my autoethnography and interviews. These open-ended answers included description of the Couchsurfers' primary motivations to travel, what they hoped to gain from new friendships, what they learned from their hosts/guests, words which would describe their relationships made via couchsurfing, as well as their reasons for not keeping in touch with their previous hosts/guests after their visit. Analyzing and interpreting thousands of responses helped me create a rich, highly specific, detailed description of the host-guest relationship – creating an unprecedented thick description of relationships initiated online via hospitality networks. In this book, all responses and quotes derived from this survey will be identified using the respondent's age, their country of origin, as well as their gender. In all instances where I refer to "survey respondent" I am referring to the survey which was conducted between August, 2006 and March, 2007. In the instances where I identify a response using "respondent" without using the terms "survey respondent," or in the instance where I use first names (pseudonyms), I will be referring to my in-person interviews.

Desk Research

Some community and website statistics, collected after November, 2008, which are constantly being updated and made available to the public through Couchsurfing.com, shall also be used throughout this work. These statistics are collected and analysed by a research team at Couchsurfing hired specifically for this task. As was already mentioned, much of my analysis of Couchsurfing was used to write <u>Intimate Tourism: Enquete dans un reseau d'hospitalite</u> (Bialski 2008), and some concepts and analysis from the book will also be used to support my argument here. I also browsed through user profiles both on OHWs and Couchsurfing in order to understand the online space of both the websites (Markham 1998).

The combination of ethnography, survey, social network data analysis, and desk research in a variety of online/offline social networks has created a multidimensional approach to this analysis. The methodology became a "mobile methodology" when tracking the intimately mobile in their various practices (traveling, interacting in cars and in foreign homes of strangers).

Emerging Practices in a Global Culture

What is also worth noting is the way in which I omit a cross-cultural analysis in my thesis. This is directly linked to my definition of culture, which is understood in this work as a set of practices and norms that are created and negotiated when mobile, on a transnational setting between transnational people. This culture of the intimately mobile is part of a rising transnational culture (Featherstone 1990). I did not take into account the customs and mores of gift giving, trust, hosting, visiting, intimacy, and interaction between strangers that were specific to the host or traveler's country-of-origin. The choice to omit such descriptions and comparisons was strategic – this work is the study of a culture of the intimately mobile, and as such, it describes the rituals of their behaviour and the ways in which intimacy and closeness are achieved offline. My online survey was taken by over 3000 members in a variety of countries, but in no way does this study unveil the cultural (local) conditions that may foster someone to become intimately mobile, nor do I compare the different practices of travelling, mobility, and hospitality in a variety of local cultures. The cultural differences that help determine the way in which people become close and intimate are not critical in explaining the emerging practices of a *global culture*. I found characteristics of the intimately mobile through a cross section of Spanish, Canadian, Cuban, Colombian, Japanese, and a multitude of other nationals that I hosted and visited. Yet all shared common practices that will be described in this book, making up an emerging culture on a global field (Robertson 1992).

Also, my approach in this study at times leans towards social psychology – especially my online survey, which specifically dealt with the motivations to travel and create relationships with other Couchsurfers. Yet to fill an ethnographic gap in mobilities studies – I steered away from ideas like motivation and agency in my thick description of the intimately mobile and as you shall read in my chapters, focused on the way new technologies create new social situations between people, and the way people have to renegotiate their ideas of friendship, intimacy, and strangerhood. This work aims to add to the growing literature on mobilities studies and new forms of computer mediated communication, I focused on this idea of re-negotiation and re-mediation – asking how exactly OHWs or websites like Couchsurfing help create new social situations between people and how people deal with these new situations. Now that I have clarified how I went about researching the intimately mobile, the following chapter will explain the theoretical choices I made in this work. The appendix attached will provide a more precise timeline of respondents I came into contact while completing my ethnography and the length of time I spent interacting with each of them. Their pseudonyms are used to help narrate my description.

Chapter 3
Mobile Intimacy: Research Paths

Conceptualizing the forces mobilizing, driving, and energizing individuals to act, interact, and organize remains a controversial problem in the area of psychology, social psychology, and sociology. Applying the existent approaches to study interaction to the current trends found in mobile social networking becomes even more problematic when taking into account that many social theories were conceived before the virtual, before people engaged in mass mobility and mass sociality using computer-based technologies (Larsen et al. 2007, 2008, Wittel 2001).

When people like Couchsurfers or Hitchhikers engage in mobile encounters they are creating a hybrid of meeting contexts – meeting strangers both online and offline, fluctuating their interaction from co-presence to interaction at-a-distance. By doing so, norms and meanings inherent in co-presence, trust, and intimacy become reconfigured. Thus, if the characteristics of interaction change along with the flows of such societal trends and norms, and theories in the social sciences which once were applicable when discussing interaction must be re-evaluated. How can existing theories account for the temporal, fluid, mobile nature of our interactions today? Is research today on computer-mediated-communication taking into account these migratory relationships that form online in order to meet offline? Does mobilities theory take into account the way in which co-presence, self-disclosure, and relationship development unfolds among mobile people?

This chapter reviews the current research on computer mediated communication, social networking, as well as mobilities theory in order to bring to light issues regarding stragerhood, the development of social networks, and the way intimacy is mediated and negotiated when on-the-move. This chapter will also link these new developments with certain theories of interaction, friendship, strangerhood, and networking that arose at a time before the virtual, but which will be helpful in developing an in-depth understanding of the intimately mobile. As a paradigm which will be presented in this chapter,

> social science has...been static in its theory and research. It has not sufficiently examined how, enhanced by various objects and technologies, people move. But also it has not seen how images and communications are also intermittently on the move and those actual and potential movements organize and structure social life" (Sheller and Urry 2006, 212).

New research developments in the area of social interaction that coincided with the developments of new technologies and new mobilities will be taken into account here.

Mobility – Physical mobility

It goes without saying that due to the discovery of oil, the developments in transportation infrastructure, and a variety of technologies from the bicycle and car, to the fast train and the internet, the mobility of people has been increasing. In the 20th century, with the development of technologies that help people move physically to visit a friend or meet somebody new, or virtually, new social issues arise that relate to space, place, trust, co-presence, identity, or isolation.

The new mobilities paradigm which arose out of the notion that current debates in the social sciences "do not deal with the complex consequences of diverse mobilities; the intersecting sensuous relations of humans with diverse objects; the timed and spaced quality of relations stretching across societal borders; and the complex and unpredictable intersections of many 'regions, networks and flows'" (Urry 2000). Urry outlined five interdependent types of mobilities:

- The *corporeal travel* of people for work, leisure, family life, pleasure, migration and escape, organised in terms of contrasting time-space modalities (from daily commuting to once-in-a-lifetime exile).
- The *physical movement* of objects to producers, consumers and retailers, the sending and receiving of presents and souvenirs, as well as the assembly and (re) configuration of people, objects, and spaces as part of dwelling and place-making.
- The *imaginative travel* effected through talk, but also the images of places and peoples appearing on and moving across multiple print and visual media.
- *Virtual travel* often in real time that enables presence and action at a distance, transcending geographical and social distance (e.g. internet bank transfer, or attending conferences 'in' Second Life').

- *Communicative travel* through person-to-person contact via embodied conduct, messages, texts, letters, telegraph, telephone, fax and mobile (Urry 2007).

An increase in various types of movement had many consequences for different peoples and places located in "the fast and slow lanes of social life," meaning that mobility inevitably led to the "proliferation of places, technologies, and `gates' that enhance the mobilities of some while reinforcing the immobilities of others" (Hammam et al. 2005). As migration became a larger issue, studies of migrant's assimilation patters and their maintenance of ties with their home country became a research agenda (Burrell 2008). As did various consumer studies on the consumption of "mobile" technologies like those surrounding the car (Sheller 2004, Bijsterveld 2010), the ipod (Bull 2004), as well as the entire socio-economic and socio-cultural process of tourism (MacCannell 1976, Urry 2002).

What is worth underlining in the context of the intimately mobile, is that as people began to migrate, move, and transport themselves from one place to another, they became "involved in occasioned, intermittent face-to-face conversations and meetings within certain places at certain moments that seem obligatory for the sustaining of families, friendship, workgroups, businesses and leisure organizations" (Hammam et al, 2005; Larsen et al. 2005; Amin and Thrift 2002). Hammam et al. outlined the necessity to draw upon interactional, conversational and biological analyses of how people read and interpret the face and the body, taking cues from Simmel and Goffman (which will be outlined in later paragraphs), as well as conducting new forms of 'mobile ethnography' (Büscher and Urry 2009). In order to study these new mobilities, Büscher and Urry also proposed the "researchable modes" that the mobilities paradigm wished to tackle. The mobilities paradigm created a research agenda that related to:

- moves and ethnomethods of creating and seeing scenic intelligibility',
- the importance and effervescence of co-presence,
- the relation of (imagined) presences, absences, deferrals
- practically achieved phenomena of trust, emotion, appreciation
- the emplacement of professional judgement, affect, and sense making
- boundaries between multiple presents and futures, users and designers, critique and engagement
- patterns of movement recalled or automatically recorded
- sensory experiences
- practices of seeing, imagining, remembering, formulating places
- the cultural biographies of objects
- interactional adaptations and adoptions of new mobile technologies
- interspaces, places on the move (Büscher and Urry 2009, 110).

This paradigm filled the gap previously left in social sciences discourse which attempted to understand the ways in which people adapt and reconfigure their social norms when mobile. While the mobilities paradigm proposes these areas of research, there has been little done thus far to investigate the "importance of co-presence" (Büscher and Urry 2009, 110), and the ways in which trust, emotion, and appreciation are achieved. Much travel today thus "involves making new connections and extending one's network or sustaining one's existing networks" (Elliott and Urry 2010, 45).

New Modes of Communication

While networks will be discussed in the following section, the process of "making new connections" were also computer-mediated connections, fostered by the proliferation of the internet in the early 90s. Computers, laptops, and all other mobile technologies also introduced "opportunities for new continuities across space and time, previously disjoined through centralization" (Green 2002, 290).

With the growth of new communications media also came a whole field of internet research in the mid-1990s, where researchers began to explore the impact of computer-mediated-communication (termed CMC).

The way in which people made choices, or discerned who to interact with offline, and who to trust offline, became a very pertinent issue in internet research. Research focusing on the effects of telephones versus CMC in the persistence or dissipation of pre-interaction expectancies (Walther et al. 2010), suggested that CMC was at times superior in transmitting positive impressions to other interactants (Walther 1995).

Not only was online interaction, romance, flirting, friendship, and acquaintanceship becoming a topic of interest – certain research was also looking into the impact of internet-initiated relationships. For example, Parks and Roberts in their survey of relationships created, via real-time, text-based virtual environments known as MOOs (Multi-User Dimensions, Object Oriented), showed that a third of all relationships resulted in face-to face meetings (Parks and Roberts 1998). Other early internet research found similar insights, stating that "relationships that started online rarely stayed there" (Parks and Floyd 1996, 92), where "about a third had used the telephone, the postal service, or face-to-face communication to contact their on-line friends" (Parks and Floyd 1996, 92). Early on, those researching CMC friendships termed online relationships which continued offline as "migratory."

Researchers studying the internet from a computer science or communications orientation were "guided by the engineering concept of 'communication bandwidth'" and "assumed at a metatheoretical level that the reduction in social cues during internet communication compared to the presumably richer face-to-face situation (with all of its attendant nonverbal, expressive cues) must necessarily have negative effects on social interaction (Bargh 2002, 2).

The "reduced cues" or " diminished bandwidth" of internet communication compared to face-to-face settings created, as Bargh termed it, "an atmosphere of ambiguity" (Bargh 2002, 3).

Only ten years later, as CMC became socially adopted at home, for work, and leisure, strictly face-to-face communication became less possible as the only method of communication with another person. Due to the prominence of CMC technology in people's lives, Turkle recently explained that humans developed new skills of interaction. Turkle suggested that the values of human sociality shifts as "technology offers us substitutes for connecting with each other face-to-face" (Turkle 2001, 11). She wrote: "We don't ask the open ended 'How are you?' Instead, we ask the more limited 'where are you?' and 'What's up?' These are good questions for getting someone's location and making a simple plan. They are not so good for opening a dialogue about complexity of feeling. We are increasingly connected to each other but oddly more alone: in intimacy, new solitudes" (Turkle 2011, 19).

In the beginning of internet research, internet pessimists and journalists also warned that isolation, not connectivity, will be the result of CMC:

> "while all this razzle-dazzle connects us electronically, it disconnects us from each other, having us 'interfacing' more with computers and TV screens than looking in the face of our fellow human beings. (Jim Hightower 1994[4]).

Noll (1995) also warned that "the information superhighway has not been as super as many have promised. The many potholes and washed out bridges have jolted our sense of reality" (191). In the mid-1990s, Kraut et al. (1998) reported negative effects of using the internet on social involvement and psychological well-being among new internet users. This was a big issue among researchers at the time – linking internet use to social and psychological problems like addiction (Kandell 1998) and depression (Young and Roberts 1998).

Other research explained the opposite, that CMC in fact helps enrich lives and bring people closer together. There was "less evidence that the internet is pushing people away from traditional social ties or making them less trusting" (Uslaner 2000, 22). In a follow-up study, Kraut et al. found that negative effects of internet use dissipated, showing that the internet can lead to positive effects on communication, social involvement, and well-being (Kraut et al. 2002). According to several large-scale American and international surveys of internet users, the great majority of respondents consider internet use to have improved their lives (McKenna and Bargh 2000), that a substantial proportion (over 50%)

---

4   See: http://www.jimhightower.com/node/2134 (accessed July 2011)

of over 600 internet users surveyed had brought an internet relationship into their real life (i.e., met in person), and that over 20% of those respondents had formed a romantic relationship and were now living with or engaged to someone they met on the internet (McKenna 1998).

Thus, the internet proved even helpful in offline relationships. Bargh et. al. found that in first-time encounters an individual will be liked better if the encounter takes place in an internet chat room than if the two strangers were to meet face to face. In their study, those who first met on the internet and then talked face to face liked one another more than did those who met face to face in both encounters" (Bargh et al. 2002, 65).

As these two research camps were developing in the discussion of the impacts of CMC penetration, others had a different, less radical perspective. Some researchers explained that the internet is not in fact revolutionary, nor is it a transformative technology that has fundamentally changed patterns of either interpersonal or group processes. "The internet seems more like a new way to manage long-standing social problems and meet long-time social needs... internet may be a new way for people to do old things" (Tyler 2002, 195).

Barry Wellman's work, including his article 'Net Surfers Don't Ride Alone' (with Milena Gulia, 1999) arose in counter-argument to the research being done at the time, warning both against claims that CMC creates isolation and pathology, or that it has the ability to revolutionize interaction. Wellman explained that the internet was simply "a new technology following the path of other promoters of transportation and communication connectivity, such as the telegraph, railroad, telephone, automobile, and airplane... community dynamics continued to operate on the internet – this was not a totally new world – and how intertwined offline relationships were with online relationships" (Wellman 2004, 127).

Along with his research team at NetLab in Toronto, Wellman proposed that "the evolving personalization, portability, ubiquitous connectivity, and wireless mobility of the internet is facilitating a move away from interactions in groups and households, and towards individualized networks. The internet is helping each person to become a communication and information switchboard, between persons, networks, and institutions" (Wellman 2004, 127).

Sociality was becoming less based upon a shared common history and narrative (Elliott and Urry 2010, 57). Rather, the new institutional process includes the unfolding of a new type and form of "life politic", involving personal autonommy and self-actualization (Elliott and Urry 2010, 88) – would also support the development of more individualized, globally-dispersed networks that CMC and other forms of mobile sociality (technologies of hospitality and friendship) foster.

While research focusing on CMC was developing, little was understood regarding internet initiated relationships, or in other words, CMC that migrates offline. Studies relating offline with the online thus far focused less on aspects of social practices of internet-initiated-relationships and relationship development, and more on the way in which CMC supports the development of social capital or social connectedness in physically-based communities. Wellman and Gulia (1999) argued that close proximity and continued face-to-face (FtF) interaction increases frequency of online contact. Studies on migration, for example, showed that migrants go online in order to establish new ties, maintain old ties and find lost ties (Hiller and Franz 2004, 743).

Yet intimately mobile interactions which will be discussed in this work, are those which involve the latter – CMC research related to issues of online trust, social presence (Short et al. 1976), online interactional cues, identity creation, and other linguistic issues involved in interaction in a person-computer-person configuration. The anonymity of CMC "is a special and important difference between it and other forms of social interaction" (McKenna and Bargh 2008, 64). While these issues of anonymity and online trust undoubtedly created new issues in interaction, these issues that internet-intiated-relationships faced were quite different, due mainly to the fact that interaction was merely initiated online and unfolded face-to-face. The intimately mobile are never anonymous, and the face-to-face is the main method of interaction and relationship development. In order to provide more research in this area, this work will show the ways in which technologies of friendship and hospitality that the intimately mobile use to interact with one another are only initiated online, yet quickly migrate offline.

Mobile Networks

The increased ability to manoeuvre through one's network: to date, couchsurf, host, link, friend, de-friend, hitchhike, meet-up, tweet, text message, skype, or IM somebody means an increase in the acts of mobile sociality today. In order to analyze these new forms of sociality, new modes of analysis were taken into account in order to show how and why people manoeuvre through their network, the nature of these interactions that take place when people meet-while-mobile, and the relevance these meetings have for people.

Additionally, the process of "social networking" was present prior to social networking technologies and geographical mobility, and as the study of sociology began to take form at the end of the 19th century, questions regarding 'why' people interact with one another and how sociality impacts a person's sense of 'self' became one of the central modes of analysis.

As CMC became prevalent, and people were meeting in new virtual settings, some theorists began contemplating a new order of community – a networked society. Due to in-depth transformations within the systems of economic production and individualisation (Castells 1996), some believed a new mechanism of sociality began creeping its way into society, thus reshaping relational discourse. At the turn of the 21st century, Andreas Wittel observed a phenomenon he termed "Networked Sociality" – a process of relationship-making in which contacts were based on the information they shared rather than their shared narrative involving emotion and obligation. Networked sociality, according to Wittel, became "a sociality based on individualization and deeply embedded in technology…informational, ephemeral but intense, and it is characterized by an assimilation of work and play." In his article, Wittel proposed the question: 'how do people build, maintain and alter these social ties? (Wittel 2001).

For Wittel, "network sociality will become the paradigmatic social form of late capitalism and the new cultural economy" (Wittel 2001, 72). People started to engage in networked sociality not strictly in order to gain their own forms of capital (economic, social, cultural, and symbolic), but for the experience which those "fleeting and transient, yet iterative social relations of ephemeral but intense encounters" (Wittel 2001, 72) provide.

Seven years after it was written, Wittel's definition of Networked Sociality has changed as the platforms and technologies for networking expanded. Networked sociality according to Wittel, supposes that creating new ties is about cold, hard, *networking* – meaning acquiring new ties in order to acquire a bigger network capital. And as we shall see, networking is also about the moments of co-presence rather than the resulting structure of one's social network.

Yet years before Wittel, certain social psychologists were inspired to map out the relationships between people in a process known as sociometry. In the 1930s, Jacob Moreno started to question exactly how interaction structures and ties the individual to others and vice versa. In his view, "if God would come into the world again, he would not come into it as an individual, but as a group, as a collective" (Moreno 1934, xxi). It was his network models that were first used to study interpersonal communities (White 1992), and his sociometric graphs were the precursors to Social Network Analysis (SNA) (Scott 2000).

While the exact beginnings of studying networks seem to stem from a variety of theorists in a variety of disciplines during the mid-20th century, the common thread which brought SNA to a consistent whole was the search for structural determinants of individual behaviour. Just as Moreno's sociometry focused on the scientific study of patterns of social behaviour (Moreno, 1953), SNA also aimed to "describe networks of relations as fully as possible, tease out the prominent patterns in such networks, trace the flow of resources through them, and discover what effects they have on individuals who are or are not connected into them in specific ways." (Wellman and Berkowitz, 1988). SNA became predominantly used for:

a. Mapping the social configuration that comprises a community, as well as the relationships between the subgroups within the community;
b. Sociometric relational networks (Moreno 1953), popularity, homophily, etc.;
c. Small group research - triads, loyalty, peer pressure, (Scott2000)

As an example of this theory-in-development, in the 1950s, the (then) prominent sociologist, Paul F. Lazarsfeld, used the sociometric technique in order to study people's job-hunting experiences, with special groups as well as in the setting of a whole community. In a similar vein to Wittel's networked sociality theory which was conceived almost 40 years later, Lazarsfeld discovered that "in a community there are real networks along which news about available jobs is passed on. Anyone who is outside such a network has a much smaller chance to get a job" (Moreno 1953). Twenty years later, Mark Granovetter would follow this with his now highly influential article, The Strength of Weak Ties. Granovetter's text (1973) was one of the seminal works of social network analysis' early years – merging rational choice theory with new, networked methods. In his analysis, he showed that effective social coordination does not arise from densely interlocking "strong" ties. Rather it derives from the presence of occasional weak ties between individuals who frequently did not know each other that well or have much in common (Granovetter 1973). The actor benefits from maintaining 'weak' ties with a number of acquaintances, rather than keeping a close-knit, traditional, tribal-like network of strong ties. Maximizing the number of people an individual knows would in-turn increase the flows of information, and therefore increase the actor's access to such information. Action would therefore be easier, the more 'weak' ties one acquired, due mainly to the fact that opportunity to act would be made more accessible. As Abell (1991) outlined, in Granovetter's text all individuals were expected to act in such a way which would optimize his/her immediate situation. SNA explained that the actor was a person holding the power to reason over his given situation. Within structural analysis there was an understanding that all action was caused by structural norms to which a person adhered to. The theory implicitly proposed that the actor had a sense of agency and influence upon his/her own decision and the decision of others as they manoeuvred through their own, (sometimes chosen) structural network of acquaintances, institutions, etc.

The questions of structure, as well as the idea of rational choice, created branches of social theory known as mathematical sociology, and then finally SNA. Within mathematical sociology, developed by Harrison White at Harvard in the 1950s, choice within interaction became an underlying theme, and creating models for the prediction of the probabilities of these choices called for a mathematical/statistical foundation. The research group around White at Harvard in the 1960s and 1970s played an especially important role in the efforts to study more members of social systems and a large number of ties. White stated that "network concepts may provide the only way to construct a theory of social structure." (Wellman 1988). Applying quantitative methods to interaction moved the study away from interpretive behavioural sociologists such as Georg Simmel and Erving Goffman, and into a sphere of mathematical sociology, economic sociology, and game theory.

In the 1960s and 70s, SNA was identified with the specific ideas of the Manchester anthropologists, mainly concerned with informal, interpersonal relations of a 'communal' type, and the method was seen as specifically concerned with the investigation of ego-centric networks (Scott 2000). New research coming out of the Harvard school and beyond moved SNA away from the pure study of interpersonal relations and into other phenomena such as corporate interlocks and institutional structures and relations.

In the 1950s, Moreno hoped that sociology, with its dependent social sciences, and revolutionary socialism, will converge and meet on a new level of social insight -- the sociometric. In the subsequent years, the sphere of social sciences witnessed a development of network theory due to, as I mentioned in a previous paragraph, its stress on structuralism. As relations were viewed as the basic units of social structure, the groupings of similarly situated actors were the result of this type of structuring (Wellman and Berkowitz 1988). This who's-who approach helped locate actors in occupational, educational, and friendship networks. Sociologists began to understand that if one could locate people in such networks, researchers could then make some useful estimates as to who and what they know, the resources to which they have access, the social constraints on their behaviour, and how they are likely to think and act (Wellman and Berkowitz 1988).

SNA was thus helpful in understanding *connections* between individuals. Yet in the attempt to understand the details of a meeting, or the way in which a connection is formed, the way trust, intimacy, conversation, proximity, closeness, or solitude is negotiated, SNA had few answers. SNA dealt with data, and as such, could not provide researchers with answers regarding the individual value attached to each interaction. For example, social network analysts, when faced with a data set, do not (and must not) treat data generically. Scott outlines three categorizations of data, which take into consideration the notion that all interaction is not similar. He proposes the following:

Attribute data: relates to the attitudes, opinions and behaviour of agents in so far as these are regarded as the properties, qualities or characteristics that belong to them as individuals or groups.
- Relational data: are the contacts, ties, and connections, the group attachments and meetings, which relate one agent to another and so cannot be reduced to the properties of the individual agents themselves. Relations are not the properties of agents, but of systems of agents; these relations connect pairs of agents not larger relational systems. The methods appropriate to relational data are those of express analysis, whereby the relations are treated as expressing the linkages which run between agents.
- Ideational data: describe the meanings, motives, definitions, and typifications themselves. According to Scott, techniques for the analysis of ideational data are less well developed than those for attribute and relational data, despite their centrality to the social sciences (Scott 2000, 3).

Structural analysis aimed to point out that social structural features greatly determine the milieu in which dyadic ties operate. For example, social structures created the foci of activity in which dyads are created - kinship groups, cafes, etc. (Feld 1981). Wellman's approach was that many personal community ties persisted because the participants were embedded in social structures - kinship, work groups, friend circles, etc -- that constrained them to continue, and not because either dyad member enjoys being with the other.

While SNA developed to explore the structure of human connection, human behaviour was not (and is not) determined by the structural constraints on such behaviour. People creating new ties, migrating to create new communities, and initiating interaction online with strangers were impeded yet not limited by their own structural constraints. Taking this into account, network theorists could not predict the way in which an interaction will unfold, or new norms of intimacy or connection will develop and transcend their previous limitations. This will is multi-causal, both based on inner inertia which stemmed from one's own self-reflexivity, as well as the socialization which aided in the individual's levels of self-reflexivity.

What seemed problematic within SNA was that if network analysts attempted, as they so hoped, to "describe networks of relations as fully as possible, tease out the prominent patterns in such networks," (Garton et al. 2006, online), they had to account for the more personal, micro-details found in interactions. Terminologies like "nodes" and "dyads" dehumanized the act of interaction, the processes before and after a personal reflection on the act, or the feelings of significance a person experiences while creating their network. These terms also did not help define the social organisation of relationships.

Social Networking: a union with others

For others, another completely different potential of networking, CMC and the internet, was the way in which people were creating a sense of connection to the global community of strangers, or "a grand intellectual and social commune in the spirit of the collective nature present at the origins of human society" (Hauben and Hauben 1997, 5). Some explained that media, even before the internet, was a way people could achieve "the communitas of good neighbourliness and shared spirituality" (Dayan and Katz 2004, 132). In his book *Community*, Bauman took another stance, and saw the mobile, connected, mediated as not in search of union, but rather a class of globals he termed the "succession of the successful – escapees who are keen to join company with other escapees just like them" (Bauman 2001, 52). These individuals lived by an 'I need more space' slogan, where the flight from the 'messiness of real intimacy,' became more akin to a herd-like stampede than to an individually conceived and undertaken journey of self-exploration.

As Georg Simmel explained, the intention while interacting was to experience another person's features. Both the intentions and purpose within a relationship may shift within a relationship. Someone may need to borrow a cup of sugar from their neighbour. Sharing resources is the purpose behind their sociality. Yet over time, the purpose of their interaction changes – shifting into an ends relationship, where the experience of their own co-presence, becomes the intention.

Couchsurfers began to notice that certain sentiments also arose from certain interactions both online and offline – a sense of comfort, coziness, intimacy, and love – and provided the 'individual' with a sense of returning to a holistic oneness – a part of the entire network whole. Simmel explained this feeling of a social commune as an inherent part of interaction by stating that, "... all the associations are accompanied by a feeling for, by a satisfaction in, the very fact that one is associated with others and that the solitariness of the individuals is resolved into togetherness, a union with others" (Simmel and Hughes 1945, 255). This sentiment may help drive the individual to interact with others, and to search out connections that may help them feel more part of the whole.

> "Of course this feeling can, in individual cases, be nullified by contrary psychological factors; association can be felt as a mere burden, endured for the sake of our objective aims. But typically there is involved in all effective motives for association a feeling of the worth of association as such, a drive which presses toward this form of existence and often only later calls for that objective content which carries the particular association along" (Simmel and Hughes 1945, 255).

This objective may also be the reason people-on-the-move find such comfort in making new associations – because these associations help them feel this connection to the whole. As the chapters on the technologies of friendship and mobile emotion will explain, the intimately mobile ultimately connect to others in order to experience this connection to the whole, or "union with others."

Another attraction of meeting others in foreign, mobile settings may be the possibility of "reconstructing the self." Erving Goffman explained that social theorists "fail to recognise that in all times and places human agency is the product of social relations. The self refers to the powers an individual can have in a specific set of social relations. The self is only assumed to be an independent and stable entity because in contemporary western society most humans live in relatively stable social environments which continually support the concept of a coherent self. Their social relations are regular enough to affirm the individual as a stable agent (King 2004, 201).

Goffman explained that people prepared themselves for a social encounter by examining themselves in a mirror. As they did so, they were not consulting some individual essence which instructed them how they should look. On the contrary, people attempted to take on an appearance which fitted the social role which they wished to adopt (Goffman 1974, 1982). Unlike in the perspective of humanist-driven psychology (see Fromm 1949), where an individual is driven by an inner spirit, and inner 'truth,' Goffman explained that,

> ...all the time in the background, a person's social contacts are looking over their shoulder effectively instructing them how they should look; and how, subsequently, they should behave. In other 'private' spaces exactly the same social rituals are occurring, each individual accompanied in their imagination by members of their social group. The most apparently private and intimate essence is in fact a public product. In a different culture, where social relations are conducted in different ways on the basis of alternative understandings, the kind of self the members of a society impute to themselves will be different: the culture itself [prescribes] what sort of entity we must believe ourselves to be (Goffman 1974, 573-74).

For Giddens on the other hand, interaction coincided with the production and reproduction of encounters, where actors displayed an anchoring in what he called a 'practical consciousness' which was the reflexive monitoring of conduct in day-to-day life. While warning that terms such as "'purpose' or 'intention', 'reason', 'motive' and so on had to be treated with caution, since their usage in the philosophical literature has very often been associated with a hermeneutical voluntarism, and because they extricate human action from the contextuality of time-space" (Giddens 1984, 3), Giddens tried to show how an analysis of motivation, as developed in relation to routinization and the unconscious, could bring out the systematic character of Goffman's work more fully. He stated, "Goffman's emphasis on trust and tact strikingly echoes themes found in ego psychology and generates an analytically powerful understanding of the reflexive monitoring of the flux of encounters involved in daily life" (1984, xxiv).

Bauman explained that more than anything else, "globalization" means that our network of dependencies is quickly acquiring a worldwide scope (Bauman 2001, 97). Certain settings presented an opportunity to behave in a certain way, and mobile encounters at such a mass scale, in mobile online/offline settings resulted at a much later time than when Giddens was writing his theory. These mobile encounters and settings were investigated by Bauman, in order to define the social consequences of nomadic, liquid modernity. A person could be attracted and motivated to become a nomad through a process of reflexive monitoring. Bauman provided an example of this by stating that the "sole attraction of the self-chosen exile is the absence of commitments, and particularly long-term commitments of the kind that cramp freedom of movement in a community with its 'messy intimacy'" (2001, 53).

Mobile spaces

Yet what adaptations are then necessary when we inhabit both a virtual and new physical space? What are the impacts on interaction? How do people renegotiate their sense of safety? Closeness? Intimacy or trust?

Such intertwining of virtual and physical space includes internet use in public spaces as well – creating "hybrid" spaces. Some researchers explored the way in which relations between people can shift due to "practical accomplishments such as a Wi-Fi network in a public park" (MacKenzie 2005, 17), and some suggested that there is a tendency for "less social interaction to take place in the areas immediately around a cluster of wireless Internet users" (Hampton et al. 2010, 714).

Perhaps the strongest evidence of bringing networked communities into hybrid spaces (offline/online) is the emergence of hybrid-reality (location-based mobile) games – multiuser games played with cell phones equipped with location awareness. These games are often also settings, practices where strangers meet strangers, where shared goals, trust and intimacy have to be negotiated, and oftentimes, where virtual connections translate into physical proximity. Other scholars who started researching mobile gaming and other social network tracking devices that use both virtual and "real" spaces to interact showed that the distinction between virtual and "real" interactions is becoming blurred when using such devices. Milgram and Colquhoun created the term mixed reality to define situations in which it is not clear whether the primary environment is "real" or "virtual" or when there is no predominance of "real" or "virtual" elements in the environment (Milgram and Colquhoun 1999). One underlying difference in these hybrid-reality, multiuser games was that meeting-ness was not a goal in itself – meeting physically was sometimes actively avoided.

Thus, in multiuser games, the everyday space which people inhabit is virtual, and is software based (Thrift and French 2002, 309). As a consequence, de Souza e Silva explains that the main question from the past decade regarding cyberspace, is, not only "how does it create individualized networks," but also how physical space is being "re-conceptualized by the connectivity of digital mobile media and internet connections" (de Souza e Silva 2006, 269). Additionally, "how does the mobility of users influence the construction of mobile spaces?" (de Souza e Silva 2006, 270).

While CMC research and other research on communication interfaces is helpful in understanding the role of the virtual in creating ties, research focusing on CMC with the focus of meeting offline calls for a separate research agenda. Internet initiated relationships lead to a number of other research questions relating to trust, co-presence, and self-disclosure that the CMC research does not address. Intimately mobile interactions are those which involve the latter – CMC research is not as pertinent here because it relates to issues of online trust, social presence (Short et al. 1976), online interactional cues, identity creation, and other linguistic issues involved in interaction in a person-computer-person configuration. The anonymity of CMC "is a special and important difference between it and other forms of social interaction" (McKenna and Bargh 2008, 64). Internet initiated interactions are never anonymous, and the face-to-face is the main method of interaction and relationship development. As I shall outline, the technologies of friendship and hospitality that the intimately mobile use to interact with other another are only initiated online, yet quickly migrate offline. Thus, this creates a research gap between those issues focusing strictly on CMC and the development of online spaces and interactions, and the way interaction is initiated in an online platform with the intention of migrating offline. I argue in this book that CMC is only a partial element in relationship development.

The intimate people

Despite the onset of these CMC technologies to create new ties or to maintain old ones, research uncovered that there is still a compulsion to be proximate through face-to-face interaction through sensory richness that the face-to-face provides, (Boden and Molotch 1994), and because of certain social obligations to be physically at a family event like a funeral or wedding (Mason 2004).

Intimacy in this work is not defined as a sexual intimacy, but rather as a closeness, or a "willingness to disclose personal statements to another" (Jamieson 1998, 1). Under this definition, 'disclosing intimacy' "requires the mutual and routine revelation of one's inner thoughts and feelings: it is an intimacy of the self rather than an intimacy of the body" (Jamieson 1998, 1).

Intimacy, or high levels of self-disclosure in face-to-face relationships is a central issue in this work. The intimately mobile often talk to, and become close with, other strangers they meet via various technologies, and the more they use these technologies, the more skills they develop to become close. These "skills" to become close, and the ability to enter into a conversation and talk to, and feel comfortable listening to, close and personal topics has been discussed previously in a limited number of psychological and socio-psychological studies. Within studies of personal relationships and self-disclosure, Miller et. al. termed extroverted people who easily divulge personal, intimate, information about themselves as "openers" - differentiating high openers from low openers in their tendency to elicit intimate disclosure from others. Their study explained that "the extent to which an individual discloses intimate information about herself or himself in a dyadic exchange may depend not only on that individual's tendency to reveal but also on the tendency of one's partner to elicit intimate disclosure within a particular situational and interpersonal context (Miller et al. 1983, 1238). High openers, they explained, were "able to elicit more disclosure from their low-disclosing partners" (Miller et al. 1983, 1242), and that "high openers may have more close friends than low openers" (Miller et al. 1983, 1241).

Other studies suggested that relationships developed to a point of intimacy as the level of closeness, or in other words, "social penetration" increased (Altman and Taylor, 1973). Social penetration did not have to develop over a long period of time - Vittengl and Holt's study showed that relationship facilitation at the level of a single, brief conversation was accompanied by an increase in positive emotions (Vittengl and Holt 2000, 62). People felt closer to those they were talking to as they disclosed more intimate and personal information about themselves, and they expected their partners to do the same.

Social penetration theory among "high openers" had been addressed in relation to CMC in the context of self-disclosure. In McKenna et.al.'s study, CMC, they explained, was just not enough to experience the face-to-face and intimate self-disclosure. "The relative anonymity of internet interactions greatly reduces the risks of such disclosure, especially about intimate aspects of the self" (McKenna et al. 2002, 10).

While "people can travel, relocate and migrate and yet still be connected with friends and family members 'back home' and elsewhere (Larsen et al. 2006, 262), face-to-face interaction still remained the most detailed method of interaction. As was mentioned in a previous chapter, research revealed that there is still a compulsion to be proximate through face-to-face interaction through sensory richness and the reflexivity and sequentiality that the face-to-face provides, (Boden and Molotch 1994), and because of certain social obligations to be physically present at a family event like a funeral or wedding (Mason 2004).

To some scholars, primarily those who study communication in organizations as well as psychologists, "presence" became a key concept. Presence as a sort of "social richness" is related to two concepts originally applied to non mediated interpersonal communication: intimacy and immediacy. Intimacy and immediacy is one of the key questions as people become mobile, both physically and virtually. Before the onset of CMC, which questioned how to overcome the lack of presence in an online technology and the lack of face-to-face cues and sensory experiences of being together, scholars studying human interaction also began to address the importance of proximity as communities began to disperse and expand.

The "importance and effervescence of co-presence" (Büscher and Urry 2009, 110) became a research issue long before the virtual or the onset of mass mobility. In the lengthy, charismatic preface to his text on sociometry, Moreno (1953) presented two hypotheses which are worth mentioning here as they relate to presence and mobility. Moreno believed that societies hold temporal and proximal 'laws' of human interaction:

1. "The spatial-proximity hypothesis postulates that the nearer two individuals are to each other in space, the more do they owe to each other their immediate attention and acceptance, their first love. Do not pay any attention to the individuals farther away from you unless you have already absolved your responsibility to the nearer ones and they to you. By the nearest is meant the one whom you live next to, whom you meet first on the street, whom you find working next to you, who sits next to you or who is introduced to you first. The sequence of 'proximity' in space establishes a precise order of social bonds and acceptance, the sequence of giving love and attention is thus strictly preordained and prearranged, according to a 'spatial imperative.'
2. The temporal-proximity hypothesis postulates that the sequence of proximity in time establishes a precise order of social attention and veneration according to a 'temporal imperative.' The here and now demands help first, the next in time to the here and now backward and forward requires help next." (Moreno 1953, 46).

Looking at Moreno's spatial-proximity and temporal-proximity hypotheses, we can see that the 'sequence of proximity,' which created a 'temporal imperative' has drastically changed since the 1950s. The question of who a person can owe one's immediate attention to became more pressing. This traditionally meant one's community – those who were physically close. Yet this question was not a new one in the social sciences. When Tocqueville arrived at United States in the 1830s, it was the Americans' propensity for civic association – or this sense of immediacy and obligation to those around them - that most impressed him. What was making American society work, he noted, was that people of all ages were "forever forming associations. There are not only commercial and industrial associations in which all take part, but others of a thousand different types--religious, moral, serious, futile, very general and very limited, immensely large and very minute" (de Tocqueville 1969, 513). One hundred and sixty years later, Putnam gathered evidence showing the decline in membership in civic organizations across America in order to describe the erosion of civic engagement. This decline of civic engagement directly transferred to the loss of "social capital." Putnam wrote that "networks of civic engagement" fostered "sturdy norms of generalized reciprocity" and encouraged "the emergence of social trust." Life was "easier in a community blessed with a substantial stock of social capital," but, he noted that, "every year over the last decade or two, millions more have withdrawn from the affairs of their communities" (Putnam 1995, 67). Putnam believed that the "increased use of new media technologies resulting in increased privatization of leisure time, not only decreases the degree of participation in society, but also decreases trust in fellow man and societal institutions" (Vergeer and Pelzer 2009, 189).

So in other words, nobody really cared for those around them, let alone held a sense of responsibility to those immediately near them. Moreno would have been laughed at as being a wishful thinker. "Americans have had a growing sense at some visceral level of disintegrating social bonds." (Putnam 1995, 61). Bauman would also suggest that people are becoming more isolated, self-absorbed, and individualistic when making connections, and these connections are fluid, not fixed and durable (Bauman 2003).

But if we imagine that de Tocqueville lived today, observing the technologically-advanced societies, he would still state that people are "forever forming associations" – yet associations between more geographically dispersed others. Those who Moreno was referring to as immediate would relate to those physically proximate - one's suburb, village, or apartment block. But with people, objects, societies, on-the-move (Urry 2007), the idea of immediacy, of what is local and demanding "immediate attention and acceptance" as Moreno put it, is not easy to distinguish, and something that this work aims to address.

Moreno's approach, while seldom referred to today, marked the beginning of social network analysis and touched upon a central theme I will return to within this study - the idea of immediacy and urgency in interpersonal interaction. Moreno was perhaps the first to theorize the effects of geography on social networking. I will later return to this issue as I investigate the issues of neighbourliness, geography, and imagined communities as people engage in virtual networking – trying to come to conclusions of whether or not Moreno's immediacy theory does in fact ring true today.

Yet returning to present-day approaches to internet initiated relationships - presence became the extent to which a medium is perceived as sociable, warm, sensitive, personal or intimate when it is used to interact with other people. Social presence theory (Short et al. 1976) was developed to better match communication media and organizational tasks to maximize efficiency and satisfaction. Other research cautioned that research on face-to-face interpersonal interactions have a Eurocentric bias, and that the theory of social penetration and relationship development only works for individualistic cultures and less in collectivist societies (Chen 1995).

For example, some suggested that East Asians disclose less personal information to other people than do Westerners, stating that "societies and social contexts higher in relational mobility (in which relationships can be formed and dissolved relatively easily) produce stronger incentives for self-disclosure as a social-commitment device (Schug et al. 2010, 1471). Not everybody is inclined to divulge personal information, or often may feel uncomfortable listening to personal, intimate details of another.

As the chapters in this book will show, the intimately mobile are often high openers, and the close spaces which they interact in helps foster high levels of social penetration in a short amount of time. Presence is important, and the intimately mobile often use online technologies in order to interact in a sensitive, personal, and warm face-to-face setting.

Mobile sociability

At the turn of the 20th century, as sociology was still grappling with its status and aims, Georg Simmel was publishing texts regarding various aspects of interaction. Simmel's work (1907; 1940; 1947) on interaction became the foundations on which those investigating social networks took off from.

Simmel observed the process of interaction between people as both experiential as well as functional, which he first touched upon in Philosophie des Geldes (1907). It was here that Simmel adapted the Aristotelian approach to interaction – who categorized friendship into interactions based on either utility, pleasure, or civic virtue and/or trust (Chambers 2006) – and instigated a fundamental separation within interaction analysis in sociology, explaining that certain interactions are *experiential*, meaning are meant for the process of co-presence itself, and that others are based on an *ends*, or a utility which that given interaction a utility which that given interaction brings. For Simmel, there seemed to be two main configurations in a dyad – the first, is sociality in its pure form. This type of relationship "in its pure form has no ulterior end, no content, and no result outside itself, it is oriented completely about personalities" (Simmel 1949, 255). Here, the relationship is fixed on the individual, upon the person in its totality (Simmel 1950). The purpose in this sort of relationship lay within the person themselves and not what he/she would provide. Thus, the friendship is experiential – psychologically, intellectually, or spiritually stimulating.

Simmel also led the way into investigating the socio psychological impacts of relationships and social networking. It was in his short text, *Sociology of Sociability,* that he explained the relationship between the individual 'self' and society – which later inspired others like Erving Goffman, Stanley Milgram, and Anthony Giddens. In Sociology of Sociability, Simmel saw society and the individual as being constantly in flux because of one another – the social influences the singular and vice versa.

> ... although it may be possible to explain the whole content of life completely in terms of social antecedents and interactions, this content must also be considered under the category of the individual life, as the individual's experience, as something exclusively oriented toward the individual. The two – social and individual – are only two different categories under which the same content is subsumed. (Simmel 1950, 350)

In the short text, he articulated that as social beings, people do not function as an autonomous core. "Rather, at any given moment, we consist of interactions with others" (Simmel 1950, 17). The individual is nothing but the sum of numerous senses of impressions. Moreover, for Simmel, all that was social, meaning all possible configurations between individuals, were created as a way to satisfy the intrinsic human urge to become part of the social. The results of such satisfactions were the "innumerable forms of social life," (Simmel 1949, 254). In order to understand this sort of self/society symbiosis, Simmel aimed to create a highly descriptive account of interactions, relationships, and customs between individuals, in order to deepen this understanding of the influence between self and society. Simmel understood that the self and society were mutually influential, but also, questioned the differing qualities of relationships and their manners within (see Simmel 1949), in attempts to understand the configurations of acquaintanceship, friendship and marriage. Simmel's notion of "the stranger" also helped illustrate the way in which cities can create closeness and distance at the same time: here people are close in a spatial sense, yet remote in a social sense (in Wolff 1950, 402).

Goffman's notion of a "relatively stable social environment" does not take into account the mobile reality present today. Goffman could not have predicted the mobile societies filled with mobile concepts, people and interactions that are constantly in-flux.

This flux between closeness and distance (both emotional and physical), as well as Simmel's questions surrounding the purpose of interaction (utilitarian/experiential relationships) will become purposeful later in this research when unravelling people's sense of significance in engaging in new forms of networked interaction. We shall see that this process of sociability -- the ideal type of interaction – emerges during exchanges of intimate mobility, as strangers meet and experience this strictly experiential sociality. Simmel could not have predicted the magnitude of mobile bodies that would be meeting, coordinating, and re-creating experiential sociability, and thus, Simmel's empirical and theoretical musings are useful as a basis on which to extend the empirical research of sociality today.

Some Conclusions

The purpose of this chapter was to create a crossroads between existing literature and the developments of mobile, virtual, interaction, bringing together various approaches to interaction that were also conceived before the virtual. By doing so, I attempted to focus on the way in which past researchers have discussed the way in which co-presence and face-to-face intimacy can unfold when mobile, and when using virtual technologies to create offline interactions.

Network theory seems to be one area which is 'testing new water' in its analysis of interaction today. Actors are not constituted through networks in a constitutive 'top-down' manner. Networks are emergent properties of social action and they refer to the lived practices, biographies and interactive resources that actors use in a creative and meaningful manner (Atkinson and Housley 2003). Under the presumption that people function through networks, not in isolation, SNA attempted to understand the flows of influence and power during interaction. The issue with SNA, however, is that it does not account for the strength or value of a given tie. While this approach is quite multi-dimensional, it lacks the ability to understand the actor's perceived meaning within interaction.

As this work will show, people-on-the-move distance themselves from their social contexts and are often left as free-agents, able (of course within certain socio-cultural limitations) to chose their networks based on more psychological cues than ever. A person's social contacts are now not looking over their shoulder effectively instructing them how they should look because these contacts are nowhere to be physically found – as people keep moving they inevitably abandon the person that is physically immediate to them. These choices to reunite and recreate these relationships belong to a new process of mobile sociality. There is a lack of analysis centred on the role of personal agency and choice in creating social ties as a person moves away from a stable local environment, becomes detached from their social settings, and placed in settings where they can 'recreate' themselves and their social networks. Gaps do remain, and the mobilities paradigm is also a way to study new, unchartered waters of mobile interaction. I hoped to acknowledge that the emerging temporary yet meaningful inter-human interactions of an increasingly mobile world will raise new questions on how to view this intricate web of connections currently being spun.

Chapter 4
Technologies of Hospitality: issues of interaction in planned encounters between strangers

> "This is not [about] gaining or losing...its all about sharing life with someone who has got your wavelength. A guy comes to a land where everyone is a stranger and you lend a helping hand to him. That's Hospitality, you might get that for money in a hotel but you will not get the real warmth and affection. That's what is fascinating about the work of CS, bridging minds of equal wavelength....for a traveler." 30 year old Indian male Couchsurfing survey respondent.

People are becoming mobile more than ever before[5]. And on their journeys, people inevitably meet strangers. While some of these meetings are chance-encounters, at places like bus stops, airports, or park benches, Couchsurfing.com or OHWs are allowing people to create planned encounters, en mass, between strangers. By using various online social networks, websites, and mobile devices which function in coordinated systems, people are pre-planning their meetings with strangers. Technology is "deeply involved in the way people, objects and information are more and more 'on the move'" (Pellegrino 2011, 6). These tools that allow these planned encounters between strangers are what I term technologies of hospitality: producing new rules of engagement, and new relationships that blur the boundaries between friend, acquaintance, stranger, and enemy.

This chapter will show that while mobility inevitably causes strangers to meet and interact, certain technologies of hospitality in use today create conditions for strangers to meet one another and engage in acts of hospitality – moments of intimacy, closeness, or mutual understanding. Such technologies help create net-

---

[5] international tourist arrivals have shown virtually uninterrupted growth: from 25 million in 1950, to 277 million in 1980, to 435 million in 1990, to 675 million in 2000, and the current 940 million (UNWTO 2011, http://mkt.unwto.org/en/content/tourism-highlights accessed Sept 2011).

works between mobile strangers. Yet while these new networks do foster trust, learning, and "personal growth," such closeness is not always altruistic and technologies of hospitality also allow people involved to exert their status and power during interaction, creating moments of tension, awkwardness, or distrust.

Couchsurfing as well as online hitchhiking websites are both examples of these technologies of hospitality – tools which foster acts of hospitality between two or more people. These technologies, part of a larger world of the digital and the mobile, can also include:

a. Dense migration networks which are strengthened by mobile technologies, where a migrant travels only to meet a friend-of-a-friend, whom they keep in constant contact with through mobile phone
b. Hobby-based meet-up websites (see: craigslist.com, meetup.com, various gaming websites), where people meet online in order to meet offline with the purpose of engaging in, or discussing a common hobby
c. Various dating sites, where people meet online in order to date offline

Interaction between strangers using these technologies is not clear-cut, and these types of interactions fostered through such systems often challenge and renegotiate certain aspects of the interaction process. People become closer, faster, and often for a very short period of time. People using such systems make trust judgements about one another on a variety of cues not available in other contexts. Relationships fostered through technologies of hospitality create their own rules of intimacy, and longevity, as well as power and obligation. Just as "obligations to family and friends involve very strong normative expectations of presence and attention" (Elliott and Urry 2010, 54), technologies of hospitality also create relationships between strangers, rather than family or friend, which also hold certain obligations.

Through multi-method ethnography, this chapter provides an in-depth account of the interactions being created via these technologies of hospitality. I argue that interaction among strangers who use these websites can be enriching for the host and guest, creating moments of "real warmth and affection," closeness, trust and acts of giving, yet can also be problematic, fostering moments of awkwardness, misunderstanding, distrust, and the abuse of power.

I will first define hospitality in more detail, and then move on to explain more about the way in which technologies of hospitality function. Here I will present an outline of the host as well as the guest, and the way power and control surfaces as the host takes ownership of their space. I will then outline the acts of hospitality by explaining the interaction between the host and the guest. Finally, this chapter will critically examine these technologies, taking into account new rules of interaction, as well as the power, and the illusion of control that being hospitable can foster.

Opening the doors of hospitality

Hospitality is not offered to every stranger nor does every stranger gratefully receive the gift (or debt) of hospitality. Not everyone is "empowered to be hospitable, to give hospitality to strangers" (Molz and Gibson 2007, 12).

In their edited volume, Molz and Gibson (2007) explained the social contexts and implications of hospitality. By explaining the historical roots of hospitality, they offered a new understanding surrounding notions like place-making, cosmopolitanism, and inclusion/exclusion within traditional nation states, and reflected critically upon the ethical implications including the limits and possibilities of social relations between people in "an increasingly mobile and globalized world."

To develop further on the work of Molz and Gibson, the aspect of hospitality I want to explore here is the link between hospitality and friendship-making. Travellers, migrants, business people, students-on-exchange, and nomads of all sorts are creating new ways of staying in touch with others, and creating new ties, and new friends and loved ones. In societies where meetings are increasing between the mobile and the stationary, the host and the guest, the citizen and the migrant, friendship-making often involves hospitality. The plethora of different journeys in today's mobile rich north has thus led to a diversity of hospitalities (Molz and Gibson, 2007). If 'hospitality poses the question of how to welcome the stranger" (Molz and Gibson 2007, 2), hospitality can be seen as becoming acquainted with, befriending, giving to an unknown other while hosting. Hospitality is often a crucial part of social networking. Social networking today is a different type of networking – less based on third-party referencing systems (i.e. an Aunt suggests you meet her neighbour) which functions in traditional, "organic communities" (VanDjik 2005) and more on chance meetings between strangers in mobile network societies (Larsen et al., 2008).

Meetings between strangers are thus not clear-cut. As strangers engage in meetings they engage in a form of hospitality which in turn sets out a power structure: those who have knowledge or take ownership of a particular place are the hosts inviting the others in (Simmel 1950). A host can state - "you are my guest because this is mine." Derrida (2000) stated that the act of opening oneself up or offering hospitality inevitably reaffirms: "This is mine, I am at home, you are welcome in my home" (14).

Space and place are central features of the experience of 'being-in-the-world' as an embodied subject, for embodiment is always experienced through spatial dimension. The human geographer Yi-Fu Tuan defines the emotional relationship with places or landscapes topophilia, or "the affective bond between people and place or setting" (Tuan 1974, 4). Lupton, in her theoretical investigation regarding the emotional meaning of home, stated that the perceptions of place and space that individuals gather from their senses – the sights, sounds, smells, tastes and feel of the environment – have a potentially powerful role in the production of emotion. So just as people are able to shape aspects of their physical environment, so does the environment shape subjectivity (Lupton 1998, 152). The divide following industrialization between "what has been represented as the aggressive, impersonal world of paid labour or the 'public' sphere, and the 'private' domain of the family and intimate relationships, the home has become portrayed as a place of security, control over one's environment, warmth, comfort, creativity, and freedom" (Lupton 1998, 152).

The home can be an emotionally authentic, private space, and outside of its walls, a person has to become an actor and provide a mere illusion of authenticity (Goffman 1967). Modern public life is a matter of formal obligation that "seems non-authentic to us," while "private life is the realm in which we attempt to behave in an authentic manner, to be 'true' to ourselves" (Sennett 2003, 7).

In order to show how technologies of hospitality create ties between mobile strangers, I first outline the technologies of hospitality, and also describe the forms of reciprocity which are a crucial part of hospitality, and by outlining these acts, I will show how technologies of hospitality help form social networks with new rules and obligations to follow.

Technologies of power

As part of my ethnographic fieldwork, I was attempting to get from Lancaster to Warsaw using online hitchhiking websites (OHWs). OHWs help drivers find passengers (and vice versa) to share their journey and petrol costs to a given destination. Like many OHW users going on longer journeys, I had to try a combination of sites including Gumtree.co.uk in the UK, Mitfahrzentrale and Mitfahrgelegenheit in Germany and Belgium, and CoVoiturage in France. In Europe, the most popular transnational OHWs are Mitfahrzentrale and Mitfahrgelegenheit and to increase one's chances of finding a ride, OHW users often cross check a number of sites.

I found Stephan who was driving from London to Mannheim, through Brussels, my first destination. His profile provided just a phone number, his departure time and date, and the places he was stopping. I called him a week in advance and he sounded business-like and straightforward. He also asked me if I had a driver's license and if I would mind "driving a bit." I recalled stories of other OHW users who were asked to drive the car, especially during long journeys when the driver grew tired and basing my decision on the past experiences of my respondents, I thought Stephan's questions to be quite normal. He explained that he would be doing business in Warrington, on the outskirts of London, and it would be easiest if we met there. I arrived at 3pm on Wednesday, as was agreed and waited for him at the train station.

Half an hour later and Stephan was nowhere to be seen. I had his mobile number and wrote him a text message. He didn't write back. I eventually got a phone call from him saying he would be late because of a traffic jam, and that it would be easier if I met him at the next station nearest to him. I investigated the possibilities with the train conductor, and found out that getting to the next station would be a logistical nightmare. I called Stephan back, and had to explain to him that I could not get to the next station and would wait for him at the spot we agreed upon.

Stephan arrived after 4pm in a car with two other men in their early 30s. I was a bit confused as to why Stephan was not driving, but being in the role of the guest, I did not question what was happening and got in the car. Stephan then explained that "This isn't the car we will be driving to Mannheim. This is my business partner, and this is another ridesharer. We will go pick up the other cars right now." "The other cars?" I asked a bit surprised. "Yes, well I will drive the Porsche with you, and Samuel [pointing to the other rideshare passenger next to me] will drive the BMW. I import used sports cars to Germany."

We pulled up on a main road where two teenagers were sitting in a black 1994 Porsche sports car. Behind it sat a new BMW sports car. We all got out and walked up to the two cars. My confusion grew, but I agreed to get in the Porsche with Stephan, as he showed Samuel how to operate the BMW. Once in the Porsche, the passenger window did not close, and Stephan explained that we will have to drive to his friend's repair shop. Fifteen minutes later we got to a lot on the outskirts of an unknown suburb. The large lot was filled with a number of cars, and we had to wait 30 minutes for one of Stephan's 'friends' to fix the door. We started driving in the direction of Dover at around 6pm – and Stephan explained that he just received a text message that he had won a Mercedes that he bid on in an online Ebay auction – and we would have to make a detour to a town 60 km north east of Dover to pick it up. "You have your license right? Because you will drive the Mercedes."

I did drive the Mercedes, and ended up getting to Brussels at 8 in the morning. The rest of the details are not important here, but this experience is a rather extreme example of an exchange between a host/driver and guest/passenger. While most OHWs function more in the way I outlined in the introduction, the way I reacted to Stephan's extreme abuse of OHW is a product of the roles we adopted as passenger and driver – which form power relationships within all technologies of hospitality. Stephan was offering his hospitality to a stranger –

me. But I was not just a stranger – I was Stephan's passenger. Because I was receiving his 'gift' of a ride to Brussels, I felt I had no power to reject or question his 'gift.'

What becomes problematic when using such technologies of hospitality is that there is no 'user manual' to the interactions that are being created. When previous theorists explained that certain laws of hospitality mark the limits, powers, rights and duties of the host-guest relationship, (Derrida 2000), they did not take into account the fact that physical mobility can often create its own fluid 'laws' which force people involved to renegotiate such laws. Mobile hosts like Stephan are less accountable to one given socio-cultural setting or social network, and can create their own set of rules of hospitality. A redefinition of hospitality can result in the host taking advantage of their guest (as in my case) but can also result in the host enacting their utopian ideal of closeness and friendship with another (as the following sections shall explain).

This example served to introduce the way strangers adapt to their roles when using these technologies of hospitality. Additionally, this exchange included other elements found in all technologies of hospitality:

a. Communication is initiated prior to meeting face-to-face, via mobile phone or email;
b. Trust judgements are made through cues a host or guest receives during their initial communication at-a-distance;
c. Possibly also: Intense/Intimate/Personal involvement in the host's life which can last for any given period of time. The duration of this exchange is determined by the host.

Guests and passengers: the guest

As mentioned previously, as two people interact using a technology of hospitality, they shift from being two anonymous others, and take on certain roles. These roles help familiarizing one another, creating boundaries of how to act and what roles to take on in relationship to the other. Within Couchsurfing – strangers become hosts and guests, through OHWs, they become drivers and passengers.

Like in the case of Stephan, the host/driver, guest/passenger might breach these rules of interaction, and some cases in which this has happened, the causes, and the consequences, will be explored in the following paragraphs using Couchsurfing as an example.

As I mentioned in the introduction, before arriving at their destination, a guest would first make arrangements to meet the host in a specific public place and at a specific time. The host usually has the final say as to where and when they will meet. If the time and place of the meeting does not suit the guest (e.g. the guest's train is arriving later, they have too many bags to walk to the arranged destination), the guest can make requests to change the meeting time and place but the guest must always accommodate their plans to fit their host's schedule. If the guest has other priorities beyond just being hosted (ex. The guest has an event like a conference to get to) the guest will compromise their plans or comfort to meet the requests of the host.

Often prior to meeting the host, the guest will contemplate their method of reciprocity. There are explicit and implicit forms of reciprocity within technologies of hospitality – and the explicit reciprocity can be a small gift for their hosts which can be a specialty from their home country. When guests have been traveling for some time, and do not have the means of bringing a gift from their home country, reciprocity is expressed in the form of cooking or cleaning – and when the guests are creative, they make their host a present, leave a photograph, take them on a picnic, or take them out for a meal. In the past, a French group of guests made me a cake according to their family's traditional recipe, another French group put "thank-you" letters around the house, a photographer from Los Angeles took some professional head-shots of me, a student from Philadelphia vacuumed my apartment, and a Danish film maker gave me a film she made. Couchsurfers are encouraged to foster this type of reciprocity through a built-in design feature on their online profile – a small box titled "Teach. Learn. Share: What Can You Give back to the Community"? This is a section on each user's profile which is visible to all users. Filling out this section is not mandatory, but it in essence encourages a guest to share something with their host, and vice versa, while also could be seen as allowing instrumental undercurrents to the encounters.

In the online survey I conducted, I analyzed a section for my master's thesis (see Bialski 2009) which asked: "What do you learn from your Couchsurfing hosts/guests." Out of over 3600 respondents, 3 per cent stated that they do not learn from their Couchsurfing hosts/guests, while only half answered that they do learn "all of the above" – a variety of information including travel tips, as well as life goals, passions, past experiences, as well as their religious or personal philosophy.

Implicit forms of reciprocity are when a host becomes a listener, almost adopting the role of psychotherapist, or becomes the speaker, and adopts the role of storyteller. Adam, a 24-year-old Polish Couchsurfer stayed in Geneva for three days with a middle-aged journalist. His host had a "desperate need to talk about himself," and for the three days when Adam visited him, he "stayed up almost all night to talk about his life, and was less interested" in what Adam had to say. Adam was a listener, and as a guest, felt that he could not avoid the conversation.

There is a distinct role division between listener and speaker, host and guest. Sometimes the guest retells vibrant narratives (whether true or not is another issue) about their previous travels, which acts as a form of entertainment for the host. In other instances, the visitor becomes a listener – and the host tells a story or even a confession. Kasia, a Polish Couchsurfer, was in Portugal with her partner and both took on the role of the listener:

> We were sitting around the dinner table and she started telling us that she had never had an orgasm in her life. I didn't know what to say. I didn't know what to do. It was really awkward. But because we were her guests, we couldn't say anything. We just sat there and listened to her.

As will be discussed later, this type of confession can often become problematic. Conversations are not always fully reciprocal – sometimes one party is more of a listener than speaker and this division fluctuates throughout the duration of a relationship. There are also certain situations where the guest becomes the storyteller. This usually happens in the case where the host is less mobile than their guest – perhaps has a family, a job, does not want to, or cannot afford travel. The guest-as-storyteller is one of the attractions of the hospitality network – guests represent the vagabond, the wanderer, who will bring tales of exciting lands and adventures. The host is then able to engage in an imaginary mobility (Sheller and Urry, 2006) through the stories told by the guest.

Compromise is another form of implicit reciprocity – where guests must accommodate to the schedule of the host. While Couchsurfing in Glasgow, my Couchsurfing host would not leave me and the other two guests alone – wanting to show us the city, play us a private blues concert on his guitar, and cook us dinner. As guests, we had to compromise our travel schedule in order to fit our host's plan for our visit. Depending on the demands of the host, the guests must engage in small or large compromises in order "please" their host.

Kasia, much like other Couchsurfers, had to give up her freedom to maneuver between listener and speaker. And despite not wanting to be a listener, she was trapped into that role because of her obligations to her host. The same analysis applies to Adam, who did not want to stay up all night listening to his host's confessions – but had to anyway due to his obligations as a guest. As Kasia said, "What am I supposed to do? I couldn't tell her to be quiet. It was her house, we were eating at her dinner table. It would be rude to say anything."

Adam stated that avoiding talking to his host from Geneva would seem rude. Because Couchsurfing functions on a system on a non-monetary form of reciprocity – this "reciprocity" can often be vague and implicit. Engaging in conversation often becomes a form of payment. Many of my respondents expressed the fact that as hosts, they felt their visitors were using them as a hotel if they didn't "stick around and chat" to them.

The passenger

Unlike during Couchsurfing, a passenger does not have to be the first to initiate contact via OHW. Within the Couchsurfing community, hosts rarely email users, requesting that they visit their home (these types of emails are perceived with suspicion and often happen in the case of sexual come-ons). On OHWs, both passengers and drivers can post advertisements looking for a driver/passenger for their given journey. Because the exchange is financial, where a passenger pays a set amount for the petrol costs, the need for a driver to take on a passenger is equal to the passenger's need to find a driver to take them to their chosen destination. Initial contact is made via SMS or phone and sometimes email – although all of my respondents expressed the crucial role the mobile phone plays in the coordination of the rideshare. OHW passengers take on the role of the guest in the driver's car – who is, in essence, the host for the journey.

The passenger, like in Couchsurfing, must accommodate their driver/host and coordinate their place of departure to fit the needs of the driver. The way I adapted to Stephan, the sports car dealer's needs, is an extreme example of the way a passenger accommodates their schedule to fit the needs of the driver. Once the passenger meets the driver, they exchange a handshake and oftentimes, other passengers sharing the journey meet one another. To make a profit, or to make the journey financially viable, a driver will try to acquire as many passengers as will fit (comfortably or not) in their car. This creates a case sometimes found on Couchsurfing – where a host takes on multiple guests who have never met prior to the hospitality exchange. Passengers then try to make seating arrangements – the front seat being the least desirable. Unlike via Couchsurfing, where hosts and guests are more often than not like-minded, choosing their host or guest on the basis of homophily (see Bialski, Batorski, 2009), OHW users do not know anything about one another and conversation between passenger and driver has a high risk of being undesirably awkward. Awkwardness is a product of meetings through technologies of hospitality, and this awkwardness is often a result of the power relationship between host and guest.

Passengers explained that 'the worst is having to entertain the driver for the entire ride when you just want to go to sleep.' The desire to enter into conversation does exist, and especially when a car is full, often conversations become divided between front-seat and back-seat riders. Passengers also feel at times like they do not have a way to escape bad conversations because of the lack of space to escape – a car is a physically limited space. This moment of feeling "trapped," and lacking the freedom to leave fosters the feeling of awkwardness. Where the Couchsurfing guest can leave the apartment when they feel uncomfortable or disinterested – a passenger, on the other hand, must stay in the vehicle.

Liz, a Berliner, started using the German ridesharing service Mitfahrgelegenheit to travel around Europe over fifteen years ago, and remembers the time before the service was available online. Passengers would call up the rideshare offices which were situated at many subway stations, and operators would put a passenger in touch with a driver. Liz also is a frequent Couchsurfer – and says, "I remember all of my Couchsurfers and I remember their names, and I remember even they were just staying here, and we had nothing in common, and they just slept here and I had nothing to do with them, I can remember their names. But I don't remember a single Mitfahrgelegenheit's name." She explains that it might "be the fact that I am paying for the ride, takes away the necessity for niceties...like if I pay, I don't have to be special nice. Like if I can avoid making small talk, I will. But if people are staying on my couch I have to make small talk, because you know, or at least we have something to talk about – like what shouldn't I do? What shouldn't I touch? Whereas, I've been in a Mitfahrgelegenheit were I'd just sit in the backseat."

The obligation that Kasia felt to listen to her host in Portugal is eliminated when money is exchanged. Payment changes the role of driver-passenger / speaker-listener to simply that of payee and service provider. The passenger can fall asleep in the backseat, listen to their iPod, read, or speak on their mobile phone if they want to and not feel a sense of obligation to converse.

Payment as reciprocity

Thus passengers do not feel like they are really being 'hosted' and taken care of like in Couchsurfing, nor do they feel like providing implicit reciprocity. The reason OHWs will never be defined as Derrida's absolute forms of hospitality is because of the money exchanged between passenger and driver. Money makes the exchange explicit. "There is a taboo of making things explicit. To say what it really is, to declare the truth of the exchange, or as is often said, 'the truth of the price' (before giving a present, we remove the price tag), is to destroy the exchange" (Bourdieu 1998, 94).

Despite the fact that OHW users feel less obliged to converse than Couchsurfers might, what is still evident is the fact that conversation among mobile strangers can create a sense of security and minimize physical awkwardness between the people involved. Stephan, another frequent OHW user, explains:

> If there are two of us in the car, I can't really stand silence with a person I don't know. I don't feel comfortable with that. I have to have a conversation. I get in a car with a perfect stranger and there are two things that I think about 1) I want to get to know the people I'm sharing this planet with. It's an opportunity to get to know a perfectly different life situation, different attitude towards politics or whatever, so I want to get to know what kind of universe this person is living in. The other motivation is that I want to get to know if this person is a psycho and wants to chop my head off. So I get into a conversation which at some point in time must, fade out, and I'm comfortable with that as well.

The roles these strangers adopt still help create a type of sociality not available beyond such technologies. Perhaps the sociality that emerges despite the explicit nature of reciprocity deems the conversation less instrumental, more voluntary, than the conversation and interaction in some cases during the implicit reciprocity between Couchsurfers. And also, despite this explicit reciprocity, passengers are aware that they are 'inhabiting', for a set period of time, somebody else's space. Passengers are still subjected to a set of rules they must follow and are most often aware of the fact that the driver holds the power over this space.

Spaces of hospitality: the host and their home

Adam, the same 25-year-old Polish Couchsurfer who traveled to Geneva, hosts Couchsurfers sporadically. Observing him maneuver through his inbox, I wanted to understand whom he accepts and whom he rejects as a host. Adam would click through profiles and exclaim "Yes this person looks cool." or "Oh, no, I'm definitely not hosting him!" The reasons for rejection included profile photos which looked 'weird,' not enough information filled in their profile, too much information, bad looking, too good looking, too old, too young, and interestingly enough – the fact that they were from Poland. Adam did not want to accept a Couchsurfer from his own country, stating "I'm not really into doing that. They're not different enough. I don't think I'll get anything out of that."

Prior to hosting, a host makes judgments regarding whom to host and who to reject. The Couchsurfing website calculates a user's response rate – meaning that all unanswered Couchsurfing request emails lower a user's response average. A low rating "bumps" a user to the bottom of the search list for their city – which means that Adam and other users who do reject Couchsurfers must write back to all request emails. Rejection emails usually involve excuses like "I won't be around that weekend" or "I am busy" – seldom do users explicitly state why they rejected the other user. Sometimes, yet seldom, a host makes a bad judgment, and rejects their guest upon meeting them. Oliver, a young Canadian traveler in his early 20s, described a situation to me where his host, a Turkish woman living in Istanbul, had mixed up Oliver's online profile with a profile of a Turkish user.

> She thought I was Turkish, and thought I was lying to her about being from Canada. And I showed her my passport, and I don't sound very Turkish. But in the end she kicked me out at 11pm at night in a dangerous neighborhood in Istanbul...

Hosts abide by their own set of rules of safety. While some can superficially reject a host based on their personal interests, hosts often make a risk assessment online, and reject those users who look potentially unsafe. Once a host has met their guest, they also judge what is safe, right, wrong, appropriate, or unacceptable to do in their own home, and these judgments may not always coincide with a guest's values – which, like in the case of Oliver, causes conflict and sometimes places the guest in risky situations. Moreover, introducing strangers into one's private space can cause unease to those who normally have a lot of control over that space. During Oliver's first Couchsurfing experience:

> It was her first time hosting anyone. So she met me at the train station at 7am which was really nice. And then she dropped me off at her house and she gave me a little bed. And what she didn't tell me is that she hadn't explained to her grandmother who was living there that I was going to come. And her grandmother couldn't speak any English or French. And so she left to go to work, and her grandmother woke up and hour later and she saw me, and she started having like this heaving fit. Like the [demonstrates] and apparently she has this breathing disorder. But I thought that she was going to take the big one right there from me not being able to explain who I am and I'm just this strange person in her house. And so I tried to explain through hand signals which just didn't work. And the I was just like, time to leave, I'll just come back later. So I went to lock the door behind me because she [Maricka, the girl I was staying with], had given me a key. And the grandmother saw me and came up behind me heaving and grabbed the key and went back into her room... And later on when Maricka explained who I was the grandmother was very happy to see me. Patting me on the head.

A stranger like Oliver can represent a loss of control for an individual-in-control like the Turkish host, because she could not control or predict his actions due to lack of information about him, personal history, or sense of familiarity. If this host had a lot of personal history or information, Oliver would be rendered predictable, and therefore a person who would be safe and controllable in this private space.

Yet hosts adopt certain expectations of how their guest should and should not act in their home. In many cases, when asking respondents to relay a "bad" Couchsurfing experience, common statements arose such as, "I never had a bad experiences really. Just one time my Couchsurfers just slept all day," or "they used my apartment like a hotel," is also a common response. In stating that their guests "slept all day," or used their apartment "as a hotel," implies that as a guest they should *have* been exploring the city or interacting with the host more as the home's resident or new-found-friend and less as a bellboy. The emotion of disappointment follows a breach of pre-established expectations, which in this case, is for a person to behave in a certain way in this space which they are controlling. Here, the host has certain pre-established expectations of how his/her space will be used, and is disappointed when that space is exploited.

Beyond risk and rejection, the customs of hospitality vary depending on the culture. Christine, from Okinawa, explained her custom of hospitality:

> We have very different views on hospitality [in Okinawa]. We have a custom once you meet this person, treat that person like it's the first and the last time you will see that person. So you don't want to live with regret. So you would do your best for that person. To make that person's life worthwhile to spend with you. So this custom conveys the message of Japanese hospitality. Tea ceremony is also based on this custom. You try to pursue the inner connection with the people. And trust. And treat that person with maximum respect.

The challenge in hosting is also present among many other non-Japanese users – and a host often wants to be hospitable because of one or a combination of the following factors:

a. They genuinely take a liking to their guests and want to spend time with them,
b. They want to prove to their guests that the place where they live has value,
c. They have little or no interactions with anyone beyond Couchsurfing and find hospitality a chance to interact with another individual,
d. They want to make a good impression on their guests in order to guarantee that their guest provides them with a positive review/feedback on the Couchsurfing website.

The amount of value a Couchsurfer attaches to their home is socio-cultural. The significance in the exchange is the process of opening up a space to a stranger and sharing a space with a stranger. Christine explained:

> They are opening up their house. A house is the most fundamental haven for people. That's their most personal place that they can be. They're opening that up for you – for you as a stranger. And giving a place to sleep.

Oliver recalled the hospitality of his host in Belgrade:

> He was going to have me sleep on his parent's couch. Because he was still living with his parents... and so, his parents told me that was impossible. Because I was the guest. So they would sleep on the couch, and I would take their bed. How could you get any nicer than that? Serbian hospitality is the nicest that I've seen anywhere of all the countries that I've been to. It's seen as an opportunity for them – as a challenge to make you as comfortable as possible.

Sara, my host in Leipzig, lived with her 7-year-old son on the top floor of a characteristic pre-war apartment row-house. The apartment had two quite large cluttered rooms, with an even-more-cluttered kitchen. Objects, photographs, toys, or children's paintings were hung or strewn everywhere. In our discussion, she stated that:

> my private sphere has all sorts of emotions attached to it. And when I share that space with someone, it just feels more natural to be emotional and honest, and have an honest discussion. Outside, we have small talk. And small talk is not me, it's not about me. It's about nothing. But these discussions are anonymous because the surroundings, too, are anonymous.

Here, positive sociality emerges out of hospitality. The process of giving, opening up, trusting, and exchanging is already conducive to a 'pure' form of sociality – a sociality which Simmel outlined as a relationship which "has no ulterior end, no content, and no result outside itself, it is oriented completely about personalities" (Simmel 1949, 255). People open up their homes, and adopt rules to follow and roles to play which eases this type of sociality, but it is the act of opening and trusting directly leads to this pure sociality. This desire to be part of such sociality is also a primary reason one engages in Couchsurfing, as well as other technologies of hospitality, yet as was mentioned at the beginning of this paragraph, this sociality is seldom free of issues of power and control between host and guest.

In-car hospitality

The car, while not attached to as much socio-cultural and historical meaning as the home, can also provide tranquility and a sense of control over one's own environment (Bjsterveld 2010). Elaine, for the past four years, has been driving between Montreal and Toronto every two weeks and has encountered roughly 400 passengers through classified advertisement – an OHW called Craigslist. Craigslist functions like Mitfahrgelegenheit and has no profile information about the passenger or driver. The site just leaves space for a user to advertise their destination and point of departure, and a contact email or phone number. As mentioned in the introduction, OHW users coordinate their exchange via telephone. Elaine said that the initial phone call plays a crucial role in determining her relationship with her passenger – whether she will like them or not. She also explained if a passenger acts in a certain way that displeases her during the initial phone call, she can refuse her hospitality and not accept them. To date, she has rejected three people. When asked what exactly a passenger said during their initial phone call which made her reject them, she explained "They were demanding something from me as if they were doing me a favour. They would ask me to leave later. Or ask me to pick them up from somewhere downtown. And I always leave from Ste. Anne's (suburbs) so going downtown wouldn't make sense. It's the ones who have nothing to offer and just demand something. I like it when people ask me about the details, and offer to bring something, those are the people I know I'll like." This initial phone call automatically positions the driver as the one providing hospitality to the stranger – who is expected to act as a guest.

Drivers also create rules of what to do and what not to do in the car. Elaine explained: "I don't really care if someone eats in my car, but at least clean up what you've thrown on the floor! I've had a few times where I'd have to tell passengers to pick up after themselves."

At the beginning of the ride, a driver will often outline whether or not a passenger can eat in the car, smoke in the car, and play their own music. Thus, the driver, in the case of OHWs, and the Couchsurfing host, would have more power, and thus usually "call the shots" in the interaction. Why the host/driver possesses this power will be explored in a later section – yet, in the case of the driver, hospitality transpires differently than the hospitality enacted over Couchsurfing. The person being 'hospitable' – meaning the person accommodating and entertaining the other can often shift from the passenger to the driver over the duration of the ride. The reasons for this are various, and are rooted in the motivations the driver had to take on one or more passengers in the first place. Motivations can be:

a. To save on petrol costs. Drivers usually request passengers to pay around 5 Euros per 100/km, and this fee fluctuates depending on the number of passengers and the driver's own generosity. Some drivers wanting to earn money on the ride take on more passengers and charge them more per km.
b. To be entertained. Driving can be tiresome, and is often perceived as 'work.' Conversation between passenger and driver makes driving more enjoyable, more interesting, more exciting.
c. To meet new people.

Elaine, the frequent OHW driver from Montreal explains:

> I get excited before I meet my passenger. I have had really good experiences and learned a lot from the different people I meet. Because of the type of job I do, I haven't really met anybody new in a long time aside from this.

Drivers can accommodate their passengers by dropping them off directly at their destination or offer to pick them back up on their journey back. My driver who was driving to Bolzano, offered to drive me back at the end of the weekend (which was when I wanted to return) and also offered to bring me his favourite cheese back from the village where he and his wife stayed. This act of generosity arose out of the three-hour conversation we had, as he discussed his interests, his love for Italian cuisine, and his driving schedule, and would not occur if I was sitting in the backseat, listening to my mp3 player, as many passengers do. Ania, a 27-year-old Polish 'traditional' hitchhiker who never used OHWs, stated that,

> those drivers who are taking you for a short journey, 10km, through the woods or a darker area or something like that, are more the ones who are doing it just out of the goodness of their heart. Because they can't really get a good conversation out of you. They're not the ones who take you because they are bored. Drivers who take you for a longer ride want to be entertained.

The passengers have an unspoken awareness of the motivations of their drivers, an awareness which usually becomes more evident throughout the duration of the journey, or like in Ania's case, after a certain number of experiences being a guest/passenger.

A new familiarization process

Closeness does not necessarily have to mean friendship or a relationship which lasts in time. I wish to conclude this empirical section with an example of the way in which hospitality fosters closeness and intimacy. So far, I outlined the rules and regulations which emerge in the technologies of hospitality, fostering power, control, and implicit and explicit forms of reciprocity. Yet the presence of such power does not exclude the emergence of closeness and intimacy, but rather forces such closeness and intimacy to emerge.

Based on my empirical work, I observed that moments of closeness embed the host or guest in the psyche of the other. This is the moment where closeness/intimacy is negotiated between two people. In the second chapter, I introduced the notion of "social penetration" (Altman and Taylor, 1973) – that can help in describing the development of a bond between two people. And, social penetration does not have to develop over a long period of time – a single, brief conversation can be "accompanied by an increase in positive emotions" (Vittengl and Holt 2000, 62). People felt closer to those they were talking to as they disclosed more intimate and personal information about themselves, and they expected their partners to do the same.

This model is also true for OHW users and can be applied to all technologies of hospitality where ties are being created. What I present here is based on Luhmann's model, who discussed a 'process of familiarization' (1990) stating that there are certain factors which imprint a person onto the minds of another. This will be mapped out by both showing how the process of familiarization works and how it differs in the context of the hospitality networker, where both time and norms usually found within friendship shift due to various factors which shall be discussed. By doing so, I wish to show how acts of hospitality foster a closeness which gradually develops between the host and guest.

The first acts of hospitality can be categorized into an 'introduction stage', where the guest and host meet in a public place or simply at the front door of the host's home, embrace and/or shake hands. In the case of Couchsurfing, the guest enters the private space of the host's home, the host shows the guest their bed/floor space/mattress/etc., gives him/her a tour of the house, and then they sit down to dinner or leave the house together and start 'touring.' This is where the initial verbal exchange is initiated, as the host and guest take turns giving a sort of self-description, drawing out their biographical sketch. This stage can contain a true level of verbal intimacy if one or both individuals feel like delving deeper into a biographical discussion, although it usually takes the host or guest to the second stage of friendship development (see next paragraph) in order to achieve this level of intimacy. After initial small-talk, the first common biographical question observed is centered around place, such as "what brings you to Warsaw?" Or the guest can ask "how long have you been living here?"

Discussing physical place within this introductory dialogue is so common for various reasons. Mainly, discussing space is a safe subject for both the host and guest, especially in the cases of hospitality technologies like OHWs, which lack any design elements which can provide personal information about the host or guest prior to meeting face-to-face. Specifically, at this stage, both host and guest have very little in common, other than perhaps their age range or gender. The one common element during this stage of introduction is the space. Both the host and guest are, presumably, situated in the same apartment, in the same city. While the guest is transient, just passing through the given location, and the host is a permanent resident, the common element the two share at that moment of introduction is their physical location. This initial process of familiarization usually refers to space - and is engaged upon due to the fact that it is based on a common subject among the two strangers.

The second stage, the 'insight stage', is the time in which the host and/or the guest provide some insight into their own life, the lives of others around them, their personal history, their experiences, their problems, or their failures. The one common theme in this stage is the presence of insight, which in turn raises the level of intensity of a conversation, thus raising the intimacy of the exchange. As Vittengl and Holt suggested in their study mentioned above, people felt closer to those they were talking to as they disclosed more intimate and personal information about themselves, and they expected their partners to do the same (Vittengl and Holt 2000).

The insight stage can, but does not have to, include an exhibition of emotions, but it always includes a sense of trust between one or both parties. Eye contact and close, personal, spatial proximity (which will be discussed more in the chapter on mobile homemaking) is present. This process can last anywhere between an hour and several days, depending on how long the individual surfer stays with the host. It is worth noting, that it is the Insight stage which produces the close personal connection which my respondents such as Anita (who craved intensity), Simon (who craved personal growth), longed for. It is within the Insight stage that they learn, and their realities become intensified. Michael, an American in his late 20s, stated that on the "number of occasions" in which his hosts told him their life story, he could tell that doing so was "exceptionally personal to them," and that they're "very involved in it." This discussion, to Michael is for him, "part of what makes this whole experience seem so special. These things which come across as very emotional and very personal to the other person, just get given out as gifts to the stranger that comes by."

The third stage, termed here the 'embedding stage' in where the guest has to leave to his/her next destination and both the host and guest are faced with the decision of whether or not to keep, or embed, this new friend into his/her network of friends. This decision is based on the intensity of exchange during the insight stage, and the amount of intimacy, insight, or "social penetration" (Altman and Taylor, 1973) experienced by both parties. Michael described many of his conversations as "special" or as a "gift." And it is my argument that the bigger the "gift" is, meaning the more the host/guest opened up to the other, the more likely the person will be embedded within their memory. This process of embedding is not at all physical – it is not about scribbling a name down in an address book, or adding an email address to one's email account. The process of embedding a friend is a decision which is completely new, and is a contract with oneself which states "Yes, I will keep in contact with this person on a regular basis." According to my online survey, Couchsurfers keep in touch with 50 per cent of their hosts/surfers. While I admit that "keeping in touch" and "regular basis" are fairly unspecified concepts, this can give a general outline as to how often one chooses to embed or not embed a new contact. Within this process, the introduction stage must occur in some shape or form. Yet as my empirical observations and responses suggest, the absence of an introduction stage still means that an insight stage and embedding stage can occur – especially for the "high openers" (Miller et al. 1983) who find personal disclosure quite natural. It is the insight stage which gives all value for the embedding stage. The embedding stage is only as great as the value of the insight – when there is no insight the receiver has no value to embed. Moreover, the greater the insight, the greater the embedding value.

Discussion

This chapter explained the way in which technologies of hospitality create conditions for strangers to interact. Such technologies propel strangers into close, intimate, emotional settings that engage the two or more strangers into an interaction ritual. As we have seen, as within any form of hospitality, strangers adopt certain roles which help position them during the interaction ritual. Strangers strip away their status as strangers, and become passengers, guests, hosts, or drivers and these roles help create meaning within a relationship which can be closeness and intimacy. Certain products of such technologies help foster these relationships. Topophilia (Tuan 1974) helps foster a close, intimate, sociality between strangers. The affective bond between a host and their space also transfers meaning to anyone sharing that space. Oliver in Montreal explained, "anyone who's willing to invite people that they don't know into their own house, they're in general very generous and very open minded, and very extroverted to start with." Secondly, "fantasies of control" (Molz and Gibson 2007, 9) also becomes a product of such technologies of hospitality – where the host who "has both the power and the property to give to the stranger" (Gibson 2007, 169). As an individual takes ownership over private space they attach value to their private space. The feeling that one is the host who has more knowledge, possesses more, and holds more rights to a given space, can in turn, reject another from entering that given space.

As was explained, the more these technologies advance their design and help people browse profiles before meeting face-to-face, gaining detailed information regarding their host or guest, the easier it is for the host to engage in these 'fantasies of control.' The decision over which guests will or will not be welcomed can only be made once the host has gathered certain information about the guest. Couchsurfing offers users to create an online profile with over a dozen variables to fill in details about oneself. A user must fill in their age, gender, and country of origin as well as occupation, but also space to describe their favourite moment in life, their life mission, or their personal 'philosophy.' This level of detail provides a potential host with a number of justifications to either accept or reject that guest. With 'blind' forms of hospitality like in the case of OHW, where users do not provide any details online, drivers (hosts of their car space and journey) who invite passengers have no room to engage in these 'fantasies of control' as Gibson articulated.

With the feeling of control over certain spaces, hosts also place certain expectations on how their guests can, in fact act in that given space. For example, a common expectation of a host would be for the guest to be active – which often means both physically active (eager to tour, often independently), as well as mentally and emotionally active (inquisitive and open for dialogue). Elaine, the driver from Montreal, had the power to refuse hospitality – giving her a 'fantasy of control' where she could choose who to be hospitable to. A similar fantasy was displayed in Adam's judgment system when choosing his guests based on compatibility and his own subjective preferences. A hospitality technology can saturate its users with a plethora of personal information on which to base one's judgments and engage in these 'fantasies of control.' The online profile offers hosts the power to choose one member over the other – and the host chooses the visitor (and vice versa) based on the perceived ease of interaction. Thus, the profile helps a) a guest or host to express who they are, and b) allows the host or guest to discern if the given person will be someone they want to interact with. This control – what Derrida defined as the key deterrent in executing absolute hospitality – begins prior to the face-to-face meeting. The more space a technology of hospitality provides for the user to express personal details about themselves, the more room a host has to engage in a fantasy of control. Thanks to the detailed design aspects of certain technologies of hospitality, hosts are able to subjectively choose whom give one's hospitality to. Jason, an American Couchsurfer once asked me, "What if somebody homeless just joined Couchsurfing? And asked me to stay on my couch? It's hard, but there are limits. I don't think I'd let them in." Fantasies of control situate strangers into certain roles – where one holds the power and the other must comply.

Beyond the fantasies of control, technologies of hospitality also hold rules of explicit and implicit reciprocity. "Everything at present is a misfortune because, in the final analysis, it must be reciprocated… the initial act is an attack on the freedom of the one who receives it (Bourdieu 1998, 94). Those who engage in technologies of hospitality engage in forms of "symbolic violence" (Bourdieu 1998, 9) which also help provide meaning to any given relationship, but also strip away the notion of altruistic, absolute hospitality as mentioned earlier. Yet another product of interaction that occurs within technologies of hospitality is the act of explicit and implicit reciprocity. As we have seen, conversation becomes a form of implicit reciprocity within technologies of hospitality where money is not exchanged. Yet, once money enters the exchange as in OHWs, a guest feels that he/she has reciprocated, and does not have to engage in a form of implicit reciprocity.

Lastly, acts of hospitality found through reciprocity, the hosts connection to space, and one's expression of control, place the host and guest into situations where conversation becomes central to their interaction. Such conversation can often become close or emotional. Common human emotions, independent of their culture of origin, are relayed through narratives, such as memories of pain, love, fear, or loss. Ashley, a Couchsurfer, explained that "one of the most intimate things that you can do with someone is tell somebody a story. So if you want to be closer with people, if you want to grow from them, get a story." Intimacy and closeness between host and guest has the potential to be engaged in quickly because the host/guest relationship is not locked in a strict location, and therefore, is fleeting. Ulla, a Finnish respondent, stated:

> Of course the process has to be quicker because they're only staying for a while so it's more intense, deeper than it would be when meeting random strangers on the street...But with Couchsurfers it would be more intense... it's just because you only know that they're going to be gone soon. When I talk to people I do not wish to discuss the superficial things like 'what went on in the football game' or 'which model has the biggest boobs,' so with Couchsurfer there's an excuse to avoid all that stuff because they're only there for a short time. So you get closer faster.

The fact that the guest will be "gone soon," or "fleeting and transient," also seems to instigate an urgency to speed up the familiarization process or social penetration, still creating "social relations of ephemeral but intense encounters" (Wittel 2001, 72).

Conclusion

This chapter explored the tensions found in the act of hospitality, and explained how such acts of hospitality are coordinated through technologies of hospitality, underlining that meetings between strangers who use such technologies also differ from meetings-at-random. While one cannot deny the fact that there are cases in which strangers meet during chance-encounters and become acquainted with one another, sometimes befriending, trusting, comforting, understanding, and supporting one another, technologies of hospitality foster closeness between strangers due to the roles hosts and guests and drivers and passengers adopt, and the settings in which these strangers must be hospitable.

Both these roles and settings are part of the acts of hospitality. During mobile encounters, often one party has to listen while the other speaks, and the person with the most power in the relationship has a choice of whether or not to be the speaker or listener. Creating new links in one's social network is also about understanding the way in which to interact with strangers. There is a level of cultural capital needed in order to be mobile and hospitable. Bensman and Lilienfeld have stressed the growing concern to achieve intimacy in modern societies, stating that 'the demand for intimacy persists to the point where it is virtually compulsive.' They explain this situation in terms of the alienating effects of the development of large, impersonal organizations in the modern world. Much of social life becomes run along impersonal lines... A flight into intimacy is an attempt to secure a meaningful life in familiar environments that have not been incorporated into these larger systems (Bensman and Lilienfeld 1979, 94).

The following chapter will continue to explain the way in which intimacy, and specifically the feeling of home and familiarity is achieved among the intimately mobile.

Chapter 5
Rituals in mobile homemaking:
Food, dwelling, and talk

> "Floors need to be mopped, cupboards polished, beds made, dishes washed, and linen bleached. Everything should be clean and tidy and ready for use...the doings of the occupants of the house are embedded in this firm foundation" (Cieraad 1999, 19).

Rituals of home-making, or patterns of regular "doings," help situate people in space and time, and allow people to form attachments to places, people, and physical objects. Yet becoming part of the home-making process becomes problematic when constantly on-the-move. As Molz also describes, "physical migration and international travel, virtual and mediated mobilities, and the global distribution of capital and commodities threaten to undermine the geographical boundedness and emotional groundedness that we tend to associate with home." (Molz 2008, 325). In the past, popular culture has depicted the business traveller or the backpacker of today's hyper-mobile society as a lone nomad, travelling alone, eating alone, living in hostels or hotel rooms. In his text on home territories, David Morley underlined that in recent years, theories in postmodernity painted the image of supposedly de-territorialised culture of "homelessness: images of exile, diaspora, time-space compression, migrancy and 'nomadology' (Morley 2000, 3). According to Morley, the concept of home often remains as the "uninterrogated anchor or alter ego of all this hyper-mobility" (Morley 2000, 3). Place itself, or "the seeking after a sense of place, has come to be seen by some as necessarily reactionary" to the "geographic fragmentation, the spatial disruption, of our times" (Massey 1991, 4).

The previous chapter discussed the way in which hospitality is exchanged, often within the home and through sharing the process of home-making. What I wish to show within this chapter is the way in which the Intimately Mobile gain access to spaces and recreate the feeling of home and community while on-the-move through everyday rituals and practices in homemaking. By interacting with locals and engaging in everyday rituals like cooking, shopping, and cleaning, the intimately mobile gain a sense of a "mobile homemaking," through certain "patterns of regular doings" (Douglas 1991, 287).

The traditional private home setting is highly significant as a temporal and cultural construct and studies have suggested the importance of a relationship between the host and the home setting (Lynch 2003; 2004; 2005). That being said, the concept of home is very lightly investigated by the literature in hospitality (Lynch 2004). As Tim Putnam notes, the home is a "prime unexcavated site for an archeology of sociability" (Putnam 1999, 144).

Through respondent's insights and the ethnography, I have come to realize that the intimately mobile have developed ways of battling the loneliness of mobility and the impersonal nature of dis-locality by creating a variety of mobile rituals that help them recreate their sense of connection, community, and safety. I will show how the rituals around food, dwelling, as well as talk help build a sense of privacy, security, family, intimacy, comfort and control – all part of research into the meaning of home. Moreover, I will also explain the way such rituals are creating a global 'family' among strangers – one where strangers can feel familiar and engage in acts that can simulate a 'family' life.

This chapter is therefore not about the current practice of manufacturing and consumption of a globalized sameness. Here, I show that a feeling of home and connection while on-the-move is based on the mobile person's intimate rituals they engage in. The thesis here is that the feeling of home among the intimately mobile is not captured through the consumptions of standardized coffees and hamburgers. Rather, home and community is reproduced through rituals of cooking, dwelling, and conversing. While being in Beijing or Reykjavik, it is not Starbucks that will create the sensation of home for the Intimately Mobile, but rather a morning coffee made by a local host. This chapter helps explain how the intimately mobile recreates the feeling of home and security through participation in and co-creation of a variety of rituals. Rather than through strict consumption, participation and creation help root mobile people in the communities they move through. Instead of feeling displaced and homeless, these rituals of participation and home-making create belonging and ownership while away from home. I aim to answer a question posed earlier by Molz: "How can we understand the ongoing significance of home in people's material and emotional lives, even as the concept of home is being destabilized and redefined by new patterns of international travel, transnational migration, global media, and mobile communication technologies?" (Molz 2008, 326).

Global communities

As we are beginning to understand, the increase in mobility today does not come without certain social and interactional side-effects. Some state that mobility is creating a "crisis of place" which, as certain scholars explain, is in fact linked to a "crisis of community" (Beatley 2004, 3). As Trafford further explains, while there are "many forces and impulses driving us (literally) apart, we can experience emotionally rich and gratifying lives only through deep personal interactions with other human beings. The evidence of our need for others, of our need for close and direct personal contact, is considerable. People with more extensive social networks and friendships are known to be healthier, and some state that such networks and relationships are essential for surviving life's problems (Trafford 2000).

Mobility across spaces "becomes a core category that structures the social life of peoples claiming to embrace the global as a new home and reference" (D'Andrea 2006, 97). Today's globals, "operating in an institutional context of fast-paced networking and mobile life, are for the most part, relatively unconstrained by nations, national societies or communities" (Elliott and Urry 2010, 67). People increasingly find themselves "belonging" to flexible, mobile, de-territorialized, transnational and virtual communities (Molz 2005, 517). But with "impulses driving us literally apart" as Trafford explains, how are people creating happy, healthy relationships essential for "surviving the buffering waves of life"?

Some researchers expressed that happiness will not be achieved in online contact. Those tackling the issue of community in a mobile age began to question the idea of civic engagement and belonging. Krueger and Best suggested that given the inelasticity of time, use of the internet likely will displace traditional offline social interactions (Krueger and Best, 2006: 396). Several studies demonstrate that the more people use the internet to view web pages and communicate with previously unknown internet users, the less they interact with offline friends, family, and other members of their residential community (e.g., Kraut et al. 1998; Nie 2001). Still other scholars claim that the internet neither increases nor decreases social and civic engagement but instead works to supplement it (e.g. Wellman et al. 2001; Wellman et al. 2002). As Wellman explained, "Rather than being exclusively online or in-line, many community ties are complex dances of face-to-face encounters, scheduled meetings, two-person telephone calls, emails to one person or several, and broader online discussion among those sharing interests (Wellman 2002, 339). What my ethnography pointed towards was something in between – that mobility can create closeness, intimacy and meaning rather than alienation, but only if ties are rooted in daily activities and rituals. And as a person becomes mobile, people can meet online in order to meet offline, but local rituals created online as well as offline help people identify with one another, trust one another, and feel connected, rooted and safe.

These moments of feeling rootedness – when people slow down in their mobility, are very significant in understanding the needs that people develop when mobile, and help outline the significance of stopping. Mobility "cannot be conceived of without its opposite, that means immobility" (Pellegrino 2011, 9). As Urry explains, "it is the moorings that enable movements. And it is the dialectic of mobility/moorings that produces social complexity" (Urry 2003, 126). People stop at certain sites, and it is these sites that "host ritual practices that express and constitute forms of subjectivity, intimacy and sociability imbricated with hypermobility" (Urry 2003, 114).

From the perspective of the humanist psychologist Erich Fromm, all human beings must satisfy not only specific physiological needs (eating, drinking, sleeping) but also special psychic needs unique to the human being. He terms these as existential needs, and include the need for relatedness, the need for rootedness, the need for a sense of identity, the need for transcendence, and the need for a frame of orientation and an object of devotion. These needs, which are seen as universal for Fromm, must always be satisfied by every human being in every culture (Fromm, 1949). While Fromm's definition of such needs coincides with the narratives of my respondents, naturally, there are numerous possibilities for the satisfaction of these needs, and satisfying them while mobile helps create the cultural practices among mobile people. The moments where a mobile person satisfies their need for rootedness should be pinpointed in order to help precisely uncover this culture of home-making.

It is also worth noting that the practices and rituals which provide a mobile person with a sense of rootedness and connection is just beginning to be uncovered. These rituals can, in other words, be identified with home-making among the mobile, or ways in which people establish a sense of home in the unfamiliar. In the past, research in this area focused more on migrants and the way in which they sought to recreate a sense of home.

For example, research on the way rituals create stability is more often done around the assimilation and integration of migrants into a host country. In a separate ethnographic study conducted with the geographer Nick Gill (see: Gill and Bialski, 2011), we observed, among other things, how Polish migrants created a feeling of home and belonging by attending Polish mass, buying familiar goods at Polish stores, and attending school or creating friendships with other Poles and "locals."

Our research also drew from Rabikowska and Burrell, who placed emphasis on the way in which migrants reenact their sense of home in the UK through

Polish food consumption. "The feeling of home stems from the [Polish] shop's position as a place where products, language, people and characteristically Polish design all merge to create and experience which resonates very intimately" (Rabinowska and Burrell 2009, 219). Their analysis is useful here, as it underlines the role that objects play in evoking certain sought-after emotions when mobile.

What is relevant here in this chapter is not whether migrants assimilate into northern English society or create cultural ghettos, but rather how people's participation in rituals help them feel stable, safe, and at home. For answers, I will turn to my ethnography of Couchsurfers and OHW users, which suggests that similar participation and creation of rituals are created by the intimately mobile. The distinction between a stable, familiar, and organic community and a temporary, unfamiliar, and fluid community is not so clear-cut. Yet it seems that the Intimately Mobile have ways of seeking out the meaningful in the unfamiliar, the organic in the fluid community.

Turning to the research, a 27 year old Mexican survey respondent explained that he uses Couchsurfing because it provides him with "a familiar face to see when you are out of your home visiting another city," and another 35 year old French male survey respondent explained that he uses the service "to find a place where I will feel really comfortable and home." Another 55 year old American Couchsurfer explained that Couchsurfing allows him to feel "at home in their environment, seeing their part of the world through their eyes."

Another Irish survey respondent explained: "These are great people (as we all are if we let go) they have knowledge of other ways of life, of looking at the world and I love having the chance to tap into that, learn about other cultures, history, what they eat for dinner, their favourite movies, everything, it makes me realize that I am part of a much larger community and I never want to loose that." The "chance" of "tapping into" the daily practices of other cultures/communities is all based around participation and not just strict observation or consumption of these rituals. There are certain rituals of homemaking which the Couchsurfer participates in that must be explained in order to understand the way in which mobile homemaking is negotiated.

Home Rituals: food

One central ritual within Couchsurfing is eating, meal-making, creating a meal either for a host or between a guest and host together. On one hand, the intimate tourist yearns to become part of an intimate ritual, not just to observe a culture, but also to 'feel' a culture. One of the easiest ways of 'feeling' another culture is through taste. "I want to see but I also want to feel. And getting out into the world, the rest of the 6 continents, I try and take the same kind of vibe. I want to see what people are doing. What they eat for dinner. What's on the table and how do they put it there" (27 year old male American survey respondent).

These types of host-guest exchanges become what intimate tourists feel is unique to their experience – "You can't pay for that kind of experience to learn how to make pasta with an Italian family. And to wake up and have breakfast with them and see how they live and what they eat" (Michael, American respondent). Yet on the other hand, the intimate tourist becomes part of ritual creation and participation, and as we shall see, grocery shopping, using a kitchen, meal making, and eating are all central in this participatory culture, and create a ritual that helps establish the feeling of home in an unfamiliar for the intimate tourist.

On my three-day Couchsurfing stay in Stockholm, my host Bjorn was at work all day. A friend of mine and I were left with the keys to the apartment, and the freedom to use and eat anything in the kitchen. We browsed through his refrigerator, and then decided to go out to a grocery store, purchase ingredients to make him a salmon pasta dinner for when he came home. This gesture already helped us feel at home in a foreign environment because it consisted of a variety of familiar rituals we both would do at-home:

a. *Grocery shopping* – the act of shopping at a grocery store denoted usually that you have to cook for yourself, something that tourists seldom have to or want to do. Intimate tourists avoid being catered *on* and rather like catering *for* their hosts or 'friends' they created while in new place, and the ritual of grocery shopping allows them to do so. While the intimate tourist browses for local ingredients, they recreate meals that are familiar to them help establish a sense of home. Globalized meals like pasta dishes, casseroles, baked dishes, or soups are quite common because the ingredients are usually available in the 'foreign' supermarkets. Picking up a shopping basket, orienting oneself in the store, browsing, picking-and-choosing, comparing prices, and interacting with the store clerk at the checkout counter are all part of this process of grocery shopping. While the products, the prices, and the language in which the store clerk speaks in are unfamiliar, the act of shopping is one of the ways in which the intimate tourist gains a sense of control while away.

b. *Using house appliances* – the use of house appliances abroad, as a tourist, is quite rare. Having access to a local's home, through Couchsurfing or any other similar means of tourism where one is being hosted by a local, oftentimes means that the visitor has access to the host's kitchen appliances, refrigerator and cooking space. The guest who buys groceries will store their food in their host's refrigerator, and use the host's cooking equipment. As guests in Stockholm, we used the host's knife to cut vegetables, his pot and frying pan to heat the pasta and create the pasta sauce, and his bottle opener to open wine, and drink from his glasses.

c. *Meal making* – both creating a meal, and serving it to one's host becomes a process in which the visitor appropriates a foreign kitchen, creates a meal of one's own or participates in the creation of a meal, and serves it to one's host and/or other guests. Setting the table, deciding which course will be served first, the process of pouring drinks, and handling the food are all decisions which become part of the ritual of meal-making.

d. *Eating* – playing background music, using cutlery, the sounds and gestures involved in eating, the conversation and eye contact are all part of the valuable process of ritual of eating as a social event.

We can now note that these gestures and actions that encompass all the senses of the intimate tourist allows them to feel independent and in control of the space around them. While tourists are dependent on the tourism industry and often feel disoriented, creating meals that are familiar, in a way that is familiar to them, using familiar ingredients, helps establish a sense of home and a sense that they are independent and can orient themselves around a new environment. In the case where the host cooks for their guests, guests can also feel familiar being the recipient of such a gesture, simulating situations when their family members made home-cooked meals for them. The type of food being served, even the most foreign or strange, can be secondary to the familiar feelings evoked in being the recipient of such a gesture.

Moreover, the process of cooking means having access to the kitchen. This space is very intimate – a place where tourists seldom gain access to while visiting another place, but a place where local meals are made and a person enacts their daily rituals, from making coffee to a large celebratory meal. Touching the appliances that the host uses on a daily basis somehow seems to join the two together.

Meal-making is also a ritual that allows the visitor to feel at home, and for a period of time, feel in-charge or in-control of an intimate space. Participating in a familiar ritual allows the visitor to both feel in-control just as they do at home, as well as feel accepted into the home of another. This simulation of being accepted into a certain space is in fact the way in which the illusion of familiarity and home is felt. This can work both ways – the visitor can create a sense of home through a variety of familiar rituals or can also participate in existent rituals that are being enacted by the host. While hosting two French travelers from Annecy and Lyon in Warsaw, Quentin and Jerome literally "took over" my kitchen and made me a French apple tart. On their way out, I made them a few sandwiches with Polish ham to take on their train journey to Moscow. In both instances, the guest French travelers, and the host (me) took turns in creating food and giving food – rituals which helped all of us feel at home with one another.

Cooking and food culture while mobile also endows the intimately mobile with a sense of nostalgia – an emotion that connects a person to a certain place and provides a sense of meaning.

The intimately mobile person is a traveler with skill, and the ease by which the intimate tourist shops at a local grocery store, reaches into cupboards for the right house appliances, prepares a meal, and serves a meal, all come from the confidence to do so which is based on past experiences with mobility.

Dwelling, Locking, Grooming

In the chapter on technologies of hospitality, I dealt with the way in which a guest and a host interact in a home environment in order create a sense of closeness and generosity. Here, I wish to show what rituals are enacted in the home which creates a sense of belonging, security, and control for the intimately mobile. As I will show, the guest engages in a variety of rituals of dwelling – sleeping in beds or on couches, opening and closing doors, showering – because the host gives them access to these daily rituals. The act of giving access to these objects is deeply rooted in trust which also helps provide meaning to being in a certain place.

Goffman (1953) studied a small hotel in the Shetland Islands and concluded that homes are organized on a front – back axis. He suggested that people put on a performance, acting differently in different places of the house. In a more recent study on "commercial homes" – cozy houses which are rented out to visitors much like a hotel room would be, Sweeney and Lynch explained that some hosts feel that "there is trust only when the guests handover their credit card details "it' s an exchange of trust between the person booking and me, I mean I trust them if they have the keys to my house and they have to trust me with their credit details." (Sweeney and Linch 2007, 105).

As I mentioned, my host in Stockholm worked for most of the day, and one of the first things he did after showing us around his apartment was to hand us his spare key to his apartment. He showed us how to open and lock the door, and gave us the code to the front gates of his apartment building. I put the key on my keychain not to lose it. I learned how to open his door, and came in and out as I pleased. Key-giving is the general Couchsurfing practice – if a host has spare keys to their apartment, they will give these keys to their guest. This gesture is not without meaning for the intimately mobile, and for their method of homemaking when mobile.

Keys are highly symbolic. "With the turn of a key, we can unlock certain aspects of self and ways of thinking. We can expose ourselves to rooms filled with animate and inanimate objects that... trigger mentalities, thoughts, and behaviour" (Nippert-Eng 1996, 574). While placing my host's key on my keychain, I felt a sense of security – I have access to a 'home' in Stockholm. While in possession of this key on my keychain, I am able to access this 'home' whenever I want. While this sense of security through key-possession leaves me the moment I give back my key to my host in Stockholm, I am confident I will receive another key in my next destination.

For the intimately mobile, keys symbolize a sense of security and access to shelter and a feeling of 'home.' Possessing a "spare" key, and not relying on one's host to give them access to the home provides a sense of control over the space. Not reliant on one's host for access to this shelter, I could enter and exit the home as I pleased. This is a rarity – to be able to access a 'home' and not a hotel room or hostel, while being in fact, in a foreign place.

The act of grooming is a highly intimate matter – and the intimately mobile are suddenly confronted with the idea of showering, shaving, changing, teeth and hair brushing, peeing and defecating in the bathrooms of their hosts. This is not without meaning – these bathrooms are not public spaces, and the experience a Couchsurfer has with a bathroom further envelopes them in to the intimate sphere of their host. Because this space is so intimate, and often houses certain objects (perfume, toothbrushes, hygienic products, medicine) and ranges in levels of cleanliness, a Couchsurfer must "fight" for their own intimacy. In order to do so, they colonize the bathroom or toilet space with their toiletry products and objects. They often place their shampoo near the bathtub, their toothpaste and toothbrush in the toothpaste holder, or hang their towel on the rack. It must be said that due to the level of intimate objects and intimate narratives linked to the bathroom, many Couchsurfers find it hard to negotiate a sense of home in this space, and most of the time the act of homemaking is negotiated in moments of interaction with the host or other guests through various exchanges, which also can be conversational.

The Good Conversation

The image that to converse means to talk, to exchange ideas with another person, emerged between the sixteenth and the eighteenth centuries. Before that time, and throughout the middle ages, conversation was a state of being or a way of life. To converse was to "commune" with God or other people, particularly in the context of religious communities (Furey 2003, 71).

Furey explained that sixteenth-century Christians transformed conversation from 'togetherness' to 'dialogue'. Based on a series of letters written by Venetian ambassador and cardinal Gasparo Contarini between 1511 and 1517, Furey demonstrates the historical shift in the methods to 'communicate friendship' - specifically the role of dialogue in relationship. Through Contarini's letters, Furey explores how early modern Christians might have experienced and promoted the 'spiritual significance of talking.' Their practice constructed a type of lay piety in which conversing with friends was a way of living with God.

What is valuable to note is the fact that Contarini, through his letters, voiced a conviction that proximity and dialogue were crucial - and letter writing could not reenact the crucial dynamic of conversational exchange. We can also note that emphasis on interpersonal relationships, defined not by organizational structure, social obligation, or kinship but rather by bonds of affection, was a predominantly upper-class phenomenon - although this may be impossible to historically confirm without access to the oral exchanges among illiterate people (Furey 2003, 77).

A study that goes some way toward mitigating these difficulties through the examination of a wide variety of sources and a close analysis of public ritual is Trexler's Public Life in Renaissance Florence (cited in Furey 2003, 77). Here, he argues that vernacular letters exchanged among the artisan classes display the intertwining of interest in social ritual, utility, and coercion. Friendship, like every other kind of social relationship, was characterized by a dialectic of form and content, sentiment and society.

Talk can be highly sociable and pleasurable; "in purely sociable conversation the content is merely the indispensable carrier of the stimulation, which the lively exchange of talk as such unfolds" (Simmel 1949, 259). "Research helps us understand the many sources from which we derive our emotional commitments to place, including genealogical and family ties to place, religious or cosmological attachments, pilgrimages to places of personal importance, and narratives or the telling of stories that connect people and communities to the land (Beatley 2004, 31).

The importance of conversation in friendship-development was explained the previous chapters, yet here, I wish to show the way in which the intimate tourist becomes embedded in a "home" by engaging in rituals of storytelling and talk, as both a listener and a storyteller, with both their host as well as others dwelling in the shared home.

Up until now, I have described the intimately mobile as people seeking out interpersonal connection - creating interactive dyads, where a guest creates connection with a host and vice versa through discourse and other means of friendship-making. Leaving my explanation there would not be painting a full picture. The intimately mobile also become connected to a certain space, and create connection with certain people by dwelling in that space, and become part of rituals of conversation and storytelling beyond their own choosing. The visitor, dwelling in the home, or riding in a car, can become engaged in conversation that moves beyond what they planned on.

My host in Stockholm could have brought home their girlfriend, brother, or friend, and I would have to engage them in conversation as the temporary 'host' of the evening. While in Madrid, my host took me to her friend's 30th birthday party. We travelled to the suburbs of the city, and in a small apartment I suddenly was drawn into conversation around a dinner table. This conversation was not at all centred around "tourist" topics like the Madrid architecture, or fun places for me to go to. By listening to a variety of stories, I learned about the history of a couple's relationship, why they moved to Madrid, the type of work they did, and why it was important to them.

I had no choice but to engage in this birthday ritual – for an evening, the friends of my host treated me as a friend-of-a-friend, and I felt I was doing something "normal" as any citizen of Madrid does on a Saturday night – I was spending time with friends, talking and listening to stories. These stories narrated the weekly rituals of these people, and listening to these rituals provided me with a picture of what these people did, and embedded me in their weekly narrative. Through participating in this conversation, I became part of their life, and I would imaginatively exist in their lives even after I was gone – I became that Polish girl who came to their birthday party. I was an extraordinary part of their ordinary ritual – and becoming part of this ritual embedded me in their understanding of reality, and my understanding of the reality in Madrid.

Conversation helps cement the intimate tourist into the memories of the hosts. The rituals of story-telling are not only part of the act of hospitality, and are not only done so because it is 'polite' to keep up conversation between host and guest. I would like to underline that a guest wants to engage in the ritual of conversation because it is a familiar ritual that links them with a sense of home, amicability, and being loved and accepted. Both listening and being listened to is a comforting feeling, and is meaningful because it helps connect a person to a given place.

Participatory culture

Kingsley Dennis examined a "global participatory culture that is diverse, interrelated, interdependent, and connected by dynamic, often unstable, networks and relations" (Dennis 2004, 373). Here he explained that "emerging networks of technologically-mediated communications are enabling dispersed and distributed users to engage and participate in complex social webs of presence and action" (Dennis 2004, 272). In cooking, dwelling, and engaging in discourse, the intimately mobile are participating in home rituals. This participation is creating a type of participatory culture that has not been discussed before – this is a participatory culture not in a public sphere, but on a private, home-scale. The intimately mobile want to participate in everyday culture and not be treated as outsiders - "I don't wanna be treated as a tourist no longer, I'm a traveller and participate in daily live when I'm Couchsurfing" (28 year old German female survey respondent).

"I think meeting people from the world is a great way to achieve personal growth because sharing experiences and knowing lifestyles or just lives is how we learn about it. And if I have something to share I'm happy to do it with other persons so this way everybody who participates in this great project will have a little of the experiences of each Couchsurfer so everybody will be one step closer to be a great person" (20 year old Chilean male survey respondent). Here, "experiencing" a "lifestyle" of another person directly helps in development of the self (Goffman 1974), becoming involved in a culture of personal autonommy and self-actualization (Elliott and Urry 2010). "Participating" in these rituals and "lifestyles," experiencing the detailed sights and sounds of a place, is what seems to help fulfil the desire of self-actualization:

"I enjoy to experience new things, participate in other cultures and to form relationships with people from other places. I feel this is an integral part of self development" (24 year old British female survey respondent). Another respondent explained that they "hope to see the sights and sounds of the location in which I'm travelling and supplement that with close personal friendships made with interesting people local to the area, or people who are also travelling and exploring this world. I usually travel away from home alone, but find that I will meet friends to travel with along the way. This is the best part of my travel experience" (31 year old Canadian survey respondent).

Native to somewhere

Place "arranges patterns of face-to-face interaction that constitute network-formation and collective action" (Gieryn 2000, 473). Beatley explains that grasping the "seriousness of reality" by living in "real communities" which "nurture an ethic of care" is about being "native to somewhere" – or becoming connected to a local place – "places that are genuine and authentic, not replicas or copies of developments and communities across the region or across the continent." (Beatley 2004, 23). The rituals that the intimately mobile participate in, which help them connect to a specific place, help blur the lines between native and stranger, between those who have access to "real communities" and those who inhabit a temporary, inauthentic world. As one Couchsurfer explained, "when you meet new people - it's always exciting and new. I like to hear other people's stories, learning from their experiences, successes and mishaps along the way, and growing through them. People enrich my life, and have become my focus in my life, to be good to my friends and family, being the person and friend in their lives I would want them to be in mine. Plus, it never hurts to have friends from all around the world, it gives you a different perspective on global issues like Israel, Iran, North Korea etc. that we may not get through our media back home in the US" (24 year old American male survey respondent). The way in which this respondent feels that they gained "new perspectives" through these "enriching" "friends" allows the mobile to see, experience, and participate in a "back-door" reality that was once distant or out-of-access. As Beatley explained, "We don't see these people, and we don't grasp the seriousness and reality of these problems; the people and issues are abstract and remote, and consequently we don't care about them" (Beatley 2004, 6).

But the participatory community model that such technologies like Couchsurfing provide help create what Beatley terms "real communities" which offer the "great promise of nurturing an ethic of care and responsibility." As a respondent explained, "meeting people with different perspectives on the world broadens the mind of the individual and also tightens the global community. Peace, love, and harmony are what I hope to gain by finding common ground with all types of people" (19 year old American female survey respondent). While the way in which the ideology and idealistic practice of 'global community' engender complex unintended consequences is discussed in a later paragraph, Couchsurfers would also agree that it is also part of difficult to ignore community needs, individual and family suffering, when they are attached to recognizable names and faces" (Beatley 2004, 6). A 37-year old journalist from India explained that she "learns how people from different parts of the world live and think -- which makes me feel more of a global citizen than a person rooted in one culture." Another responded stated that, "Sharing my home and culture with someone else and gaining from their life experiences, culture. I get a good sense of Global community when I surf/share" (53 year old British female survey respondent).

Some intimate tourists engage in mobile home-making – recreating the home while away, while others search for home, and are unable to recreate a sense of home mainly due to their lack of any sense of home in the past. Those intimately mobile who come from "broken homes," who feel alienated in their family or community of origin, who travel to escape their past, who have been mobile their entire lives – these are all people who feel that engaging in intimate mobility creates rather than re-creates a sense of belonging.

Familiarity, home, and community

Van Dijk, when discussing social networks, explained that "our own familiar environment offers opportunities of interaction and information by means of intensive ties and high-quality communication," which Van Dijk calls 'organic communities' (Van Dijk 1999, 31), which was derived from Durkheim's idea of organic solidarity, based on high interdependence between community members (see Durkheim 1973). Yet while an organic community is based on insensitivity and quality of communication, it seems that the intimately mobile do indeed find organic communities in unfamiliar environments. What this chapter hoped to show was that certain rituals of homemaking help create the sense of community, familiarity, and membership in an organic community. While communities are stretched out geographically and socially (Larsen et al. 2008), access to these communities is aided through the practice of, and participation in, a variety of rituals.

Benedict Anderson coined the term 'imagined community' to account for the mystery of self-identification with a large category of unknown strangers with whom one believes oneself to share something important enough to make one speak to them as 'we' of which I, the speaker, am a part. (Anderson 2003).

This belief in the possibility of a 'global community' is what drives the supermarketization of friendship, engagement in confessional culture, and notching up the isolation of networked individualism by collecting exotic intense but short friendship and cultural experiences. As intimate tourists explain, "opening one's home" to someone helps create a sense of a global community, interacting beyond the computer screen, and focusing on the richness of face-to-face communication (Boden and Molotch 1994). "With the power of the internet and today's communication systems making the world 'smaller' we seem to sometimes loose the value of interpersonal relationships. It's easier to shoot off an email, rather than write a personal note, have a chat over IM instead of a phone call, etc, etc. Opening your home to someone is so very personal (at least to me) and through that I hope to nurture a greater respect and knowledge of this global community in which we reside." (31 American female survey respondent).

Through the repeated narratives of being "all connected" to the "global collective" or "global community" of my respondents are linked to the participation in the rituals of homemaking in which both the host and the guest are involved. Homemaking for intimate tourists is not an individual process. Through a variety of homemaking rituals familiar to the intimate tourist, the sense of home is achieved while away. Yet the mobile homemaker is in constant dialogue with the host: in cooking with them, sharing their toothbrush holder, attending family events, buying groceries, or making coffee the guest is not just re-creating a sense of home to feel secure, but is sharing a home with their host in order to establish themselves into the narrative of the "global community." The following chapter will look deeper into the host-guest relationship, exploring the ways in which Couchsurfing or OHWs not only provide hospitality, but also become technologies that aid friendship-making between mobile strangers.

Chapter 6
Technologies of Friendship

While conducting ethnography in the fall of 2009, I found a woman who put up an advertisement of mitfahrgelegenheit.de for a ride from Frankfurt to Brussels. I emailed her my request two days before our ride would take place, and she replied back, confirming my spot in the car. I didn't check my email for one day, and once in Frankfurt, I sent a text message to the driver hours before our departure, double-checking if everything was going smoothly. The driver replied that she gave my spot away to somebody else a few days ago. I was more than annoyed. I had to be in Brussels that evening, and keeping up with my mission to rideshare, I had little choice – I could pay over 70 Euros to get to Brussels and walk to the nearest train station or become a hitchhiker and get in the first car that came along. I decided to hitchhike the 200km distance to Koln, and then open the laptop I was carrying with me and search OHWs once in Koln using a wireless network.

I stood by the side of a gas station off-ramp waiting for someone to pick me up. I had no control, no choice over which car will offer me a ride. Within 10 minutes of waiting, one dodgy male construction worker took me 20 kilometres to a better spot on the highway towards Koln. Then, after another 10 minute wait, three 70-year-old retirees driving to Holland for a friend's 70th birthday party picked me up and drove me to a gas station outside Koln. We exchanged cordial small-talk for a few minutes, but the rest of the two hour drive went by in silence.

Once in Koln, I logged onto mitfahrgelegenheit.de and found a driver going from Koln to Brussels just hours later. The driver, Katherina, was a 27-year-old outgoing female lawyer who was doing her bi-weekly journey to visit her boyfriend in Brussels. The other passenger sharing our car was another ridesharer like myself – also an outgoing girl around my age who was, coincidentally, also going to visit her boyfriend in Brussels. The three of us spoke in English, and we instantly hit-it-off, discussing relationships, travel experiences, studies, and our life goals. I found out Katherina's approach to relationships with men, and discussed the other passenger's spiritual experiences at her recent Buddhist retreat centre in Colorado. For the two hours between Koln and Brussels – the car was filled with conversation. We exchanged email addresses and days later added each other to Facebook, (a social networking site).

The two hitchhiking experiences, in the same day, in the same area of Germany, were drastically different. While in both situations, I was forced to accept whoever offered me a ride – the difference was that with the online ride-sharing website, I 'hit it off' with the other person. What circumstances led to this compatibility? Was it just simply age, or something else? How do social networking sites help mediate interactions between others? Help people avoid standing at the side of the road, blindly waiting for anybody to cross their path? Moreover, how do such websites help discern compatibility between two people?

Today, the issue surrounding interactions concerns the degree, medium, and frequency of connectivity (Dennis 2006). The average user of a social networking website like Facebook has 130 friends, and Couchsurfing states that the community as a whole creates 317 "real-life introductions"[6], or people who meet-face-to-face every hour. As underlined in previous chapters, the increase of such connectivity is due to the increase in physical and virtual mobility. This new mode of connectivity is reconfiguring our sociality. It could be said that "the internet with its dazzling array of human and non–human intersections — may provide a template for re–imagining social relations in a new figuration" (Sterpka 2007).

In the last chapters, I discussed technologies of hospitality – how certain websites create conditions for people to share each other's home, as well as what processes in the home help provide the intimately mobile with a sense of home-making and feeling of being part of a "global family." This chapter addresses networking technologies which increase the frequency and degree of connectivity today and foster compatibility and friendship between two people. In this chapter, I will go a step further and show how certain technologies in use today help some people not only share the spaces they inhabit, but the lives they live, the experiences they have lived through, and the personalities that make them 'individual.' In the previous chapter, I used Couchsurfing.com as well as a variety of OHWs as examples of 'technologies of hospitality' – websites that foster hospitality between strangers. Here, I will show how the internet allows people to create, experience, and maintain new friendships.

---

6   Www.couchsurfing.com homepage accessed March 2011

Fluid friendship

It is crucial to discuss the technologies of friendship present today because, as this chapter will show, they provide a shift in the act of connecting, creating, and maintaining friendship in our society. There is a vast amount of written knowledge regarding the history of telecommunication networks and the development of a global 'networked' society ranging from social network studies, complexities studies and cultural and geographic history which helps us understand that friendship-making does not look like it once did. A Canadian anthropologist helped illustrate the change in sociality today. The following is an outline of criteria that Du Bois termed useful for identifying friendship:
1. closeness of physical proximity, amount of touching;
2. movement together;
3. co-ordination of eating, drinking and other activities (fishing, for example);
4. sharing of scarce resources;
5. relaxed gestures;
6. communicatory style well co-ordinated;
7. long duration of eye-contact;
8. absence of aggressive and avoidance behaviour;
9. presence of "play" rituals, including special terminology for verbal play (Du Bois 1974, 40).

Dubois believed that the "systematic collection of data along lines such as these might eventually yield differences between some kind of raw friendship and pseudo-friendship, and between raw friendship and the innumerable normatively sanctioned role relationship within cultures" (Du-Bois in Leyton 1974, 41).

Online ethnography conducted during the initiation of online social networking communities in the mid-1990s (see Adams 1998) suggests that friendships can develop in different circumstances than those proposed by Du-Bois. Adams suggested that friendships will be more likely to develop in communities without, for example, a shared territory. The technologies that help these friendships occur,
1. facilitate repeated interactions between participants,
2. have differentiated meeting places reflective of the diversity of the participants,
3. encourage contact among participants outside the setting
4. allow for shared experiences that lead to increased
5. solidarity,
6. are characterised by norms and beliefs that encourage pleasant interactions among participants,
7. have members with values, beliefs, lifestyles distinct from

8. those of the mainstream of at least similar to each other's and
9. create an atmosphere of trust and respect (Adams 1998, 167).

Online networks can affect the overall structure of people's friendship networks. Being added to a network connects a person not just to another person, but into their network of friends, as - for example in Facebook - people are shown as friends of friends. At the same time, being networked can change offline relationships - providing friends with information of events and encounters experienced by the other since the last meeting.

Not only are the forces of modernity causing a shift from a small amount of contacts based in a concrete local spatiality to a large amount of contacts which are spaced out across the globe, these contacts are often fluid, often momentary (Gergen 2002). Boase and Wellman argue that since the industrial revolution, the rise of mass transit and telecommunication systems have allowed a shift in the nature of social relationships, especially in urban areas where these kinds of systems tend to be more readily accessible. Wellman argues that this shift, which he calls "networked individualism," has at least three important characteristics: 1) Relationships are both local and long distance. 2) Personal networks are sparsely knit but include densely knit groups. 3) Relationships are more easily formed and abandoned (Boase and Wellman 2004).

Moreover, if social networks are supported by new technologies like smart phones, networking platforms, and other software, these media networks (VanDijk 2005) are increasingly being accessed by people on-the-move. Thus, networking is in fact being created while rooted or uprooted. As Barnabas explained, "to describe society we must dress the links of the social network with actual dynamical interactions between people (Barabasi 2003, 225). It is the issues surrounding compatibility, homophily (similarity), the formation of closeness and intimacy, that will help describe the degree and dynamics of interaction that both Dennis and Barabasi question today. Some researchers suggest that new studies "must determine what proportion of online relationships actually develop into friendship and whether these relationships supplement or replace those acquired offline. It is possible that online interactions increase the number of acquaintances, but not the number of friends" (Adams 1998, 171).

In accordance with this claim, networking will be strictly examined here within the domains of the practice of friendship, acquaintanceship, and familiarization. Thus in this section, I will not be delving into the historical background of sociality, but rather focus on the culture of friendship-making today. By providing examples from my ethnography as well as my online Couchsurfing survey, I will explain the change in patters of friendship.

In order to do so, I will clarify how technologies of friendship: enable strangers to meet, give people the choice of whom to meet, provide people with an opportunity to become friends, help people define their relationships, and help people maintain their relationships by "storing" their connections in a database.

After explaining the way in which technologies of friendship foster closeness and disclosure, I will also offer a critique of such websites. This critique looks at how friendship engineering looses the spontaneity of friendship-making, and the choice of friend creates a consumer-oriented friendship market.

The excitement of chance

The way in which encounters happen in OHWs was explained in the introductory chapter – with the lack of online profiles, two strangers – a driver and a passenger – contact each other through the OHW and then coordinate their meeting using a mobile phone, email, chat system, or other social networking technology. Before this meeting occurs, a passenger or driver often sense a feeling of excitement, curiosity, or eagerness to meet a person they will be sharing the journey with. Because of the lack of online profiles on most OHWs – the driver and passenger seldom are able to view photos of the other party, seldom know what their occupation is, their age, or any other characteristic that might help them make a judgement about them. This element of surprise is what Elaine, a 25-year-old frequent driver who is based between Toronto and Montreal, gets excited about most when meeting her passengers: "I get excited before meeting the person I'll be giving a ride to. I have had really good experiences and learned a lot from the different people I met."

This moment is similar to what Simmel called an adventure, where the moment – "...is just on the hovering chance, on fate, on the more-or-less that we risk all, burn our bridges, and step into the mist, as if the road will lead us on, no matter what" (Simmel 1950, 249).

People on-the-move are in essence stepping into many unknown territories, encountering people in public and private spaces that they could never have planned on encountering. This anticipation for not only unknown spaces and unknown climates, but also unknown encounters between unknown people is what makes mobility an adventure. These are "airplane seat" moments – filled with the same anticipation some feel when receiving their airplane ticket seat assignment, and wondering what strange or annoying person was "chosen" to sit next to them. This sentiment cannot be overlooked – it is a product of the increase in the meetings of mobile people present today – crossing and intersecting each other within mobile spaces such as airplanes, subways, train stations, and conference halls, during events like weddings and funerals, conferences and festivals (Sheller and Urry 2006). The potential that the passenger sitting in the adjacent seat will either positively or negatively impact the other passenger or driver's lives is something that feeds the excitement among the mobile. I could not have predicted the negative impact the 'dodgy' construction worker would have on me as he offered me a ride to the highway from the outskirts of Frankfurt on my hitchhiking venture. I also could not have predicted that I would, hours later, exchange a warm conversation with two young women in a car from Köln to Brussels – two women who I still keep in touch with. Without the aid of a mediator or third-party, neither Elaine from Montreal, nor I, nor any other mobile person can predict the type of person one will meet along the way.

As a mobile person wonders about the potential person whom they may meet while mobile, they are enacting their own beliefs in the connectivity of the world, the people living in it, and their own feeling of agency over their own lives. Certain studies explain that "people often intentionally seek certain types of experiences, but the persons who thereby enter their lives are determined by a large element of chance" and that these "chance encounters" play a "prominent role in shaping the course of human lives" (Bandura 1982, 747).

Certain respondents described themselves as being 'lucky' with the people they meet – having the 'luck' of always "getting" interesting people as co-passengers, or interesting characters. Others, like Kasia, a 25-year-old Polish driver living between Warsaw and Frankfurt, think it is a completely random process: "It's like, you're not going to start talking to everyone you meet at a bus stop. These are just random strangers. Some people are more interesting than others. You just never know."

Because of this 'randomness,' not all meetings are good meetings, and not all conversations are 'good conversations' as she explained. I drove with Kasia alone for 7 hours between Warsaw and Berlin, and the two of us had an intense conversations covering various topics from life in Warsaw, her family, and thoughts on relationships. Kasia commented that she values people with passion, and that people who are daring enough to meet strangers are usually "ones with passion" (field notes, October 2009).

Within OHWs, coming into contact with a potential friend is much like winning the lottery – some explained they were 'destined' to win, others believe they are lucky, and some think that they randomly won. A similar sentiment is felt with mobile meetings – encounters become ways in which people experience and place value on the world they are living in. These experiences are not always positive and some people avoid rather than seek meeting somebody new.

Missed opportunities

While I will deal with the escape from intimacy in a following chapter, I wanted to underline here that the "airplane seat" anticipation before two people collide while mobile may be frequent among most mobile bodies (and especially the intimately mobile), not everyone will feel like they won the lottery when sitting next to a fascinating person. Only those who engage in the lottery get excited in anticipation to win. For the business man who drove me and Jessica, another OHW ride-sharer from Heidelberg to Berlin, his eyes red from tiredness, thinking of his business meeting in Berlin, making a 'friend' was the last thing on his mind. For him, silence, and not friendly chatter, might have been his definition of winning the lottery. "We are all born with that appetite for contact. How much of an appetite – the extent to which we can and do reach out to others – is an individual matter depending on a host of circumstances" (Brenton 1974, 41). For others like another 24-year-old American male survey respondent, meeting new people is "always exciting and new. I like to hear other people's stories, learning from their experiences, successes and mishaps along the way, and growing through them. People enrich my life, and have become my focus in my life, to be good to my friends and family, being the person and friend in their lives I would want them to be in mine."

Stephan from Berlin also explains that he has to "have a conversation...My social environment is quite homogeneous. So that's a really great opportunity to find out more about [other people]." Stephan's use of the term 'opportunity' with these meetings helps underline the notion that a conversation with an immediate stranger is an act that one must engage in, in order to avoid missing chances of friendship, information, advice, anecdotes, and intense moments that may 'enrich' their life experience (Bandura 1982). Another 46-year-old Canadian female survey respondent believes that,

> we are here on this earth to learn some valuable lessons that we can only learn with the interaction we share with one another. I believe if we allow ourselves to connect on a deeper level with others, then we have the ability to close the gap where ignorance lives. I believe we have the power to change the world one person at a time. I am working on a mission of peace at this time. Every time someone comes into my life I share my views and challenge them to be open to finding that place where we all have common ground. We all want to be loved, respected and accepted for who we are. I hope to touch others and be touched by others to becoming everything we are meant to be.

This is the approach of the intimately mobile – whose objective is to engage in such interpersonal experiences and 'opportunities' of friendship. Many Couchsurfers and OHW users expressed that mobile meetings are opportunities to meet 'more interesting people,' meaning those people who provide more intensity, excitement, or are from a less homogenous crowd (as Stephan expressed) than the people they meet at home. For others, mobile meetings are the only opportunities people have to make friends at all. Elaine from Montreal also expressed these meetings as the sole means by which she can meet new people:

> Because of the type of job I do, I haven't really met anybody new in a long time aside from this. Because I work with the same people. And if I go out for a walk or somewhere, I always have my phone or iPod, and I'm not talking to random people. This is the only time I do meet random people.

This is a clear paradox – the fact that local contacts who surround Elaine on a daily basis are avoided by putting on her iPod earphones, and contact with random others is only possible while away from home and mobile. What Elaine enacts and experiences is a clear example of how relationships are shifting from being based locally to dispersed, networked, and individualized (Wellman 2002). Moreover, the idea of 'randomness' in mobile meetings also offers people the opportunity to diversify one's friendship network, and hear stories, outlooks, and ideas that may be different than the everyday. As Wellman explained, this type of diversification of one's social network is a product of our networked societies, where "boundaries are permeable, interactions are with diverse others, connections switch between multiple networks, and hierarchies can be flatter and recursive... Communities are far-flung, loosely-bounded, sparsely-knit and fragmentary...rather than fitting into the same group as those around them, each person his/her own personal community" (Wellman 2001, 227). Yet how "diverse" a social network can be challenged here, as people who use technologies of friendship have ways of choosing whom to interact with.

The three German elderly drivers going to a 70th birthday party may be an interesting experience for me – but because of the language and age barriers, and the fact that I did not meet them using a technology of friendship, 'filing them away' for future reference becomes more difficult. These people are less likely to stay my friends and be embedded in my permanent personal network than a Couchsurfing guest or host who willingly chose to host/visit one another based on a variety of cues they gained from one another's online profiles. This decrease of 'randomness' using such technologies is what increases the opportunity for two people to be compatible, and create and maintain a friendship. What makes technologies of friendship distinct is that they take connections between people from being chance-enounters to choice-encounters. The following section will delve more deeply in to the way in which such networking technologies create compatibility, and thus, create more functional technologies of friendship.

Choice encounters: online profiling

As Delille once stated, "fate chooses your relations, we choose our friends." (in Duckett 2007).

Couchsurfing.com, as once defined the founder of the website, is a social networking platform that enables people to create "long-lasting, meaningful connections between people" (Couchsurfing.com 2009). The design of such a website takes into account that the process of self-presentation online is an important aspect in relational development offline.

In order to join the community, a new Couchsurfer must establish an online profile of themselves, and this profile communicates information which is crucial in creating a sense of the other person, which influences familiarity. These features in the profile are what I will call affordances – properties of the environment that offer actions to appropriate organisms (Gibson 1977, Gaver 1992). The Couchsurfing profile offers certain affordances, which influence the way a user is perceived by other community members. The profile also plays a crucial role in a user's social navigation through the website, and enables a user to specify who they want to initiate contact with. In order to relate this to the process of social navigation, let us consider that just as "The number of cars parked in front of a restaurant is an indication of its popularity as is the length of the waiting line before a theatre," (Dieberger 2000), the number of photos, friends, references, travel experiences, etc. on a couchsurfer's profile, can have a deep impact on the way in which we perceive another user, as we shall see in the following paragraphs. Goffman's work on self-presentation explains that certain individuals may engage in strategic activities ''to convey an impression to others which it is in [their] interests to convey'' (Goffman 1959). As the average age of Couchsurfers is 27, and 70 per cent of users are from Europe or North America, most new Couchurfers have a high level of media literacy and are proficient at navigating through websites.

The design of this virtual community helps create affordances for its members to communicate a sense of trustworthiness, friendliness, and compatibility to another community member. When one person believes the other is compatible, they subjectively must discern this compatibility from a variety of cues. To become part of the online Couchsurfing network, a new user fills in a variety of boxes that ask for:

1. their personal description
2. their level of Couchsurfing participation
3. their Couchsurfing experience
4. their interests
5. their philosophy

6. their favourite music, movies and books
7. the types of people they enjoy
8. what they can teach, learn, share another guest or host
9. one amazing thing they've seen or done in their lives[7]

For example, a personal description can state that a person is "Open to every and anything new, warm hearted, interested in all possible aspects of our universe, photography, music, politics" (Couchsurfing profile of a 25 year old German male). Under "philosophy," one could write: "constantly trying to promote peace and respect among each other, indifferent of culture, skin colour, ethnicity, religion, sex, sexuality or background" (Couchsurfing profile of a 25 year old German male).

Dan, one of the founders of the website, explained that the profile questions are structured in such a way that "it brings out the essence of people. And when people's essences are visible, it contributes to the building of trust." This makes us assume that trust is dependent on the level of self disclosure, and trust is dependent on the levels of homophily (similarity) between users. Therefore, if a virtual community like Couchsurfing wishes to create trusting virtual relationships, they must provide enough space in order for the user to disclose who they are to the rest of the community.

When someone like Nana builds their first profile, a webpage flashes in front of them, suggesting that the more information a user provides, the more trustworthy they will appear to other users. This process was explained in detail in the introductory chapter (see pages 18-20), where I described the process of creating an online profile. Once the profile is created, "those viewing your profile get a better idea of who you are. This helps others understand who you are based on the content of what you write, and also how you write it."[8]

A section of the website is devoted to answering questions regarding first time interaction between potential host and guest. The following is an extract from a page found on the website, outlining the precautions new Couchsurfers should take when hosting or surfing.

> When you receive a couch request, try to get an idea of who is writing to you. Is it clear that they have read your profile? Are they interested in meeting YOU, or does it seem like they are just looking for a free place to stay? Who are your Surfers?[9]

Here, Couchsurfing is implicitly stating that the website is designed to help familiarize users with one another through their online profile. As I mentioned previously, "getting an idea" of someone else is nearly impossible on OHWs

---

7   Couchsurfing profile, www.couchsurfing.com, (accessed July 2011).
8   Couchsurfing profile, www.couchsurfing.com, (accessed July 2009).
9   Couchsurfing profile, www.couchsurfing.com, (accessed October 2008).

because of the lack of such a profile. The administrators of Couchsurfing.org explicitly state that users can 'find out' what 'kind of person' another is through an online profile which serves as a medium by which people can acquaint themselves with one another – perhaps further creating a supermarket atmosphere, where one can pick and choose one's product before buying it.

Not only do Couchsurfing users "find out" about the strangers they have the potential to meet, they must indicate whether or not to accept or reject a visitor or host. Providing space for a user to place a variety of personal information in the online profile (photos, personal descriptions, narratives) allows viewers (other users) to accept or reject that specific user or not. Accepting or rejecting meeting somebody is an essential part of using technologies of friendship, and I wish to specifically deal with the rejection of unknown others in the following chapter.

These certain online affordances which I outlined here help users specify who they wish to interact with, and help users feel that they are interacting with people they chose to interact with – not people they had to interact with out of sheer necessity (as in the case of hitchhikers, for example). As such technologies provide the means of discerning the characteristics of another person, not only can people feel more safe and trusting (because there is less risk of the unknown), but people are able to discern if the other will be compatible with them or not. We trust (and help) people with whom we are familiar... and with whom we believe to be similar to ourselves (Staub 1978), and this "similarity may elicit trust and other forms of help because the truster has an empathic relation to the target" (Cook 2001, 100).

Couchsurfers want to predict trustworthiness in order to reduce the physical and financial risk of hosting or visiting a stranger. While trust is an essential requirement for such websites to function (see Bialski and Batorski 2009), I argue here that technologies of friendship not only help predict trustworthiness but also help predict compatibility. Technologies of friendship reduce the "randomness" that exists among mobile encounters. Hitchhiking or sharing an airplane ride lacks a third-party mediator like Couchsurfing.org or an OHW to help one person select another. A 25 year old American male stated that,

> It's always a bonus to be able to 'be with your own people' (those who both share your interests and share new ones that are accepted positively) and the surprise and common good nature in making that connection.

The anticipation of the encounter that some OHW users experience is still present among Couchsurfing members – the main difference is that there is a greater likelihood of compatibility, or "being with your own people" as the previous survey respondent stated. There is also a greater likelihood that the encounter will turn into a friendship. A 28 year old Norwegian female Couchsurfer explained that "...the possibility to view profiles makes a good match more likely..." These affordances that I just outlined – the online photos, the friendship links, the personal statements, etc. -- that the technologies of friendship provide allow users to reduce their fears that the other person will be strange, awkward, or even dangerous. A 28 year old female German survey respondent explained: "Meeting new people is one of the most exciting and enriching things is to meet someone who is "on your vibe"...you meet people you have no relationship with at all before you meet. No "sister of a friend" or so..."

Users of technologies of friendship do not question the outcome of the forthcoming encounter by asking, "Will I be annoyed/threatened by the person I will encounter on this journey?" Because these users engaged in the affordances the technologies of friendship provided them with, they made a choice-encounter rather than a chance-encounter with good "matches," their "own people," "on their vibe." So rather, users of such technologies question the nature of the encounter and ask "What will I experience with this other person?"

Homophily and compatibility

The fields which are filled in by each user not only allow them to familiarize themselves with another user, but also allow her to discern whether or not the other user would be a compatible person. This decision is quite subjective, and often based on homophily – or an attraction to those who are similar. Among all the users in Stockholm, Nana found a woman her age who, like her, is interested in creative, adventurous, and open-minded people. Similarity instantly connects Nana to this stranger – and in this case, this sense of compatibility is based on the stranger's worldview described on their profile. This user in Stockholm has now shifted from being a stranger, to being a familiar, like-minded individual – all before any verbal dialogue was exchanged. The design of Couchsurfing enabled this connection to take place.

Despite the range in demographic profiles, as Nana logs into her account and chooses a couch to stay on, she will be more likely to visit someone who has a greater similarity to her. Ziegler and Golbeck (2007) explained that dependencies between user similarity and trust exist when the community's trust network revolves around a common goal or particular application, and when the individuals trusting each other share similar interests or traits. Trust, therefore, is positively related to homophily. In order to understand this among the intimately mobile, we can take into consideration an analysis carried out on 221,180 friendship dyads registered on Couchsurfing in February, 2006, which include various variables such as the origin and the duration of acquaintanceship, as well as how strongly the individuals trust one another on a scale of 1-6.

Using this data, a study I conducted with Batorski (2010) showed a higher tendency toward trust occurring within homophilious relationships according to age and country of origin, and a slightly lower tendency towards trust is found in same-gender relationships. These dyads might have had more opportunity to strengthen their relationship offline, in a variety of contexts, compared to the other relations who only know each other through the Couchsurfing system. The study also showed that if dyads share the same country of origin, they are more likely to trust each other. This can be linked to a feeling of national identity or the perception of gaining a common understanding which can be linked to a lower sense of risk which facilitates higher trust. Therefore, it seems that people in homophilious relationships tend to trust each other more than those in heterogeneous relationships. Moreover, we can also see that technologies of friendship help discern homophily, and that people are more likely to host/surf one another if they are more similar (see Bialski and Batorski 2010, 191).

Homophily and friendship

If two people are similar or seemingly compatible, that does not necessarily mean that they will become friends. The outcome of the large-scale network data analysis conducted with Batorski is that those relationships which last longer are indeed more homophilous than those relationships between people who know each other for a shorter period of time. Thus, compatibility impacts the durability of a relationship. Closeness also depends "on the length of stay of course... the longer the stay the deeper the connection" (42 year old female American).

During my interviews, Couchsurfing respondents stated that they kept in contact with their hosts/guests after the Couchsurfing exchange occurred. Results from my online survey show that half of all Couchsurfers keep in touch with their hosts or guests. Some found good friends, others found partners. OHW users are less likely to stay friends with somebody they meet through a ride-sharing website. One of the main reasons is the purpose of such websites – which function in order to save people costs on fuel and, in the case of the German OHWs – to offer an alternative to the expensive train system, where a 300km journey between Berlin and Hamburg can cost between 50 and 70 Euros. Liese, a Berlin-based OHW user and Couchsurfer explains:

Mitfahrgelegenheit is something I do not choose for the social factor – I choose it for the money factor. And that makes a huge difference from Couchsurfing...And it's just one of those things – It's completely cost related.

While OHWs exist mainly to save people money, only 5 per cent of all Couchsurfers think that making long term friendships is not the purpose of Couchsurfing. Of those 5per cent, most discuss long-term friendship as a 'bonus' of Couchsurfing, but that intense momentary encounters are more frequent on Couchsurfing. Momentary "friendliness" and compatibility is what is valued, and, as a 31 year old Finnish male survey respondent stated, "Long-term friendships are a possible by-product of Couchsurfing." Another 22 year old Australian male survey respondent explained that "Couchsurfing is an experience be it good or bad, a place to stay, an insight into another's life, part time friends... Long term friends are just a bonus."

Part-time friends

Friendship, then, in the case of the technologies of friendship, cannot be defined as a long-lasting durable relationship in which two people confide in one another on a regular, ongoing basis. Many of the characteristics of friendship that was outlined by the Canadian anthropologist Du Bois in the introductory paragraph of this chapter could not be met by the relationships created via this technology of friendship. On the other hand, these relationships cannot be defined as regular "acquaintances" in the traditional sense of the word. Georg Simmel, who wrote extensively on the subject of socialization and interaction, believed that mutual "acquaintance by no means is knowledge of one another; it involves no actual insight into the individual nature of the personality. It only means that one has taken notice of the other's existence, as it were (Simmel 1949). Yet, Simmel, writing at a time when online socialization was nonexistent, did not take into account the virtual phenomena of online profiles - when strangers could gain information about one another through their online identities and, before meeting each other in person, create an illusion of closeness, familiarity, and compatibility.

So neither defined as true long-term 'friends' and neither as acquaintances, Couchsurfers use the term 'friend' despite the lack of longevity of these relationships. Rather than gauging their new connections as lasting reliable friendships, users of such technologies use adjectives like "brief," "intense" and "exciting" in order to define their new connections. A 30 year old American male explains that "Long term [friendship] is certainly possible and desired, but short intense friendships are what I usually encounter." A 32-year-old Indian female explains that she

"just lost touch" with her previous guest. "But I know if/when we meet again, we'll hug each other like long lost sisters." Another 23-year-old American female survey respondent explains, "sometimes you just have a good few days and then you drift out of contact. I do feel like I could resume communication at anytime with everyone I have had a Couchsurfing experience with."
Another Couchsurfer stated:

> I am fascinated by encounters with new people, especially people who are instant friends and kindred spirits. Some of my most magical moments in foreign places have been these sorts of instant, lovely friendships. I don't think these friendships lose anything by being "in the moment" and not continuing - sometimes those brief moments are all you need for a person's life to touch your own. (26 year old American female survey respondent).

These 'moments of friendship' are for some people just 'moments' which are also highly valued. "It's great when [friendship] happens, but random brief encounters are wonderful too" stated a 30 year old English male Couchsurfer. "Sometimes you just need to take these encounters as once in a lifetime experiences" 27 year old American female. Another 21 year old Canadian male survey respondent stated that, "Sometimes friendships are brief but exciting, this is not bad, after all it is impossible to keep in touch with everyone you ever meet in your life."Some, then, do not create 'lasting friendships,' and rather treat their connections like a pause-and-play relationships, where constant mobility brings them together into moments of closeness and intimacy, but then their mobility is what separates them. Their relationship is then not completely stopped but rather 'put on hold' and can be resumed at any time in the future when the two decide to come together again. Putting somebody "on hold' can mean writing down somebody's email, Skype login, or 'friending' them on a social networking site. This type of friendship is also termed a "latent tie: a tie for which a connection is available technically but that has not yet been activated by social interaction" (Haythornthwaite 2002, 398).

Conclusion

An investigation into the culture of certain new technologies like OHWs and Couchsurfing.org allows us to define the way patterns of acquaintanceship and friendship-making are being reorganized and restructured among mobile individuals today. These technologies of friendship are creating personal communities which allow the individual to specify who they wish to interact with. Moreover, the social culture around creating sparse personal networks of ties which range from both formal to very informal and last throughout time suggests that there is a reduction of the feeling of strangerhood between highly mobile people. Choice and individualization of one's personal network is what propagates the popularity of technologies of friendship. As Fischer pointed out,

> The lowering of social and spatial barriers and the consequent increase in the freedom to choose social relations have not led to less communal social ties. And it may just have led to the opposite. The disintegration of the monolithic community has perhaps led to the proliferation of many personal communities, each more compatible and more supportive to the individual than ascribed corporate groups (Fischer et al. 1977, 202).

These compatible, personal communities are being created among the intimately mobile, and my respondents have suggested that they feel even more part of a global community, even more connected to a community across social and spatial barriers.

Ride-sharing seems to offer more heterogeneity in its match of driver and passenger than Couchsurfing does because a user is not able to specify who exactly they want to encounter. For example, I did not learn anything about the three 70-year-olds who drove me to Koln, nor did I feel a close, personal bond with them (nor vice versa). I did not meet these people using a technology of friendship, nor were we at that point a group of intimately mobile people. Thus, we were less likely to feel a bond or sense of 'learning' in our meeting. This can be problematic – there is a chance that listening more and trying harder to find commonalities during a live conversation between a 70-year-old and a person in their 20s may become much more difficult the more people get used to technologies of friendship and the conveniences of the various 'match-making' compatibilities they provide.

In this chapter, I used OHWs and Couchsurfing to show that while both may provide hospitality, only certain websites like Couchsurfing.com can be defined as 'technologies of friendship.' Other websites like OHWs, provide certain conditions for strangers to connect, yet a variety of design features are not taken into account for friendship or compatibility to occur. While many social networking tools are present today which allow strangers to meet online with the purpose of meeting offline, only technologies of friendship provide users with *choices* of whom to meet. Technologies of friendship which provide users with a sense of choice of whom they meet, increase the chance of compatibility between users, and in turn, increase the chances of long-term friendships to occur. The fact that people are meeting online and offline in closed, intimate spaces does not necessarily mean that they will become friends. The creation of friendship is not a requirement between two people using technologies of friendship, yet it is a possible product of such technologies. I compared OHWs and Couchsurfing to show that the likelihood that a friendship will occur depends on the design of the technology – meaning the more detailed and individualized each personal profile is, the more choice and perceived compatibility a person can have with another, and thus, the higher the likelihood that the two will get along and be friendly.

This chapter attempted to answer the call for further investigation into "conventional notions of what it is to be close (Larsen et al. 2006, 7). The following chapter will now take into account that closeness is not always the product of mobile interactions. There are moments where isolation from others is preferred, and the ways in which solitude is negotiated will be explored.

Chapter 7
The Avoidance of Intimacy:
escaping interaction on-the-move

> Taking joint spontaneous involvement as a point of reference, I want to discuss how this involvement can fail to occur and the consequence of this failure. I want to consider the ways in which the individual can become alienated from a conversational encounter, the uneasiness that arises with this, and the consequences of this alienation and uneasiness upon the interaction. (Goffman 1967, 114)

While the past two chapters shed light on the way amicability and friendship are fostered through new technologies, intimacy and closeness is not always desirable. "The relations of co-presence always involve nearness and farness, proximity and distance, solidity and imagination" (Urry 2002). The culture of acquiring friends, network-building, connecting, linking, friend-ing, and all other types of mobile intimacy I described in the last chapters are a product of an increased mobility of people living in the rich north. But the increase in mobility does not only foster these new forms of friendship and compatibility, but also the way in which people avoid such friendships and the way in which incompatibility is negotiated.

"Modern society is to be distinguished from older social formations by the fact that it affords more opportunities for impersonal and for more intensive personal relationships" (Luhmann 1998, 12). This opportunity for impersonal contact is an important part of mobile sociality. So too is the way in which a person distinguishes between their impersonal and intensive opportunities to be social – "We are all born with that "appetite" for contact. How much of an appetite – the extent to which we can and do reach out to others – is an individual matter depending on a host of circumstances" (Brenton 1974, 41). While these individual circumstances will not be outlined, this work shows that people 'have an appetite for some people and not for others,' and will focus on the way in which people withdraw themselves from interaction, rejecting some strangers and not others by using a number of excuses available to us when on the move.

Mobility among those living in the rich north forces people to accept certain strangers into their lives and reject others. Interactions enabled through various forms of mobility, urban life, and a multitude of communication technologies, mean that people are not just engaged in amicable discussions with others, but that they are also negotiating solitude, rejection, de-friending one another, distrusting, and dodging each other in a number of mobile situations. What I encountered through my participatory observation as well as through my respondents' experiences is that not all mobile people are intimately mobile, and not all intimately mobile are friendly with everyone they meet. So who are these people rejecting, why are they rejecting them, and how do they go about doing so?

There is a growing amount of scholarly analysis surrounding the issues of interaction when mobile - outlining the strengths and weaknesses of CMC, the impact such communication has on face-to-face encounters, and the way real relationships use technologies to supplement their interaction at-a-distance (Walther 1996, Adams 1998, Uslaner 2000, Wellman 2001, Bargh and McKenna 2004, Elliott and Urry 2010). And as outlined in the theoretical chapter, the negative personal impacts of CMC use has also been more recently outlined among social researchers (Dunbar 2010, Turkle 2011), and the popular media.[10]

Returning to the ethnography of hitchhiking – I encountered people while mobile that I hoped I would never meet in my life again. People meet others (not through technologies of friendship or hospitality) that they do not "hit it off with," or worse, feel threatened by, disgusted by, or annoyed with. And as outlined in the last two chapters, there are moments where people use technologies of friendship or technologies of hospitality to strategically choose certain people to share one's mobile life with – either for a couch to sleep on or for a lifelong friendship. Certain technologies help produce these intimate relationships.

Yet the harsh reality is that when choosing whom to interact with, people avoid certain strangers, in order to get to those they truly want to socialize with. What I hope to uncover in this chapter is that the more people one encounters, the more chances they have to experience positive interactions, while at the same time increasing the amount of people they avoid to get to these 'positive' experiences. In other words, the oversaturation of faces, voices, gestures, and narratives forces people to select those they want to create and maintain contact with. This chapter will describe this process of avoidance – and in doing so, will create an ethnography of mobile contact which helps describe not only the pro-

---

10   See: http://www.bbc.co.uk/news/magazine-11465260 or
http://www.bbc.co.uk/news/magazine-14202981(accessed July 2011)

cess of acquaintanceship but also the acts of rejection and avoidance of interaction. Moreover, this chapter will also investigate the culture of "keeping-to-oneself" when on-the-move – specifically how people avoid contact with others through direct speech, and through the use of other media and technologies.

Saturating the self

Before describing the processes of interaction avoidance, it is worthwhile to examine the possible sources causing alienation when mobile. Ethnography with Couchsurfers and OHW users led to the creation of two possible causes of interaction avoidance - one, being an oversaturation of people resulting in a need to be alone, and the second being the expectations of amicability and 'deeper connections' with others resulting in boredom or dislike of those who do not fulfil these expectations.

In the early 1990s Gergen (1992) observed that the accumulation of twentieth-century communication technologies, including (but not limited to) radio, television, the internet, the World Wide Web, and cell phones has created a dramatic expansion in the range of relations (real, virtual, and imagined) in which the individual is increasingly engaged. He calls this process the 'oversaturation' or 'overpopulation' of the self (Gergen 1992). This condition of saturation leads to a receding sense of authenticity, and a diminishing in the time and attention devoted to any particular relationship.

The oversaturation of people can occur in both the public and private dimension of a person's life. As people become physically and virtually mobile and encounter a multitude of people on-the-move, there is a chance that we will taste too much, that our sensitivity to meeting people will diminish. Interaction with others takes effort – effort from our senses, our attention, effort to create time in our lives and effort to think of ways in which to interact with others. While sometimes, interaction with a friend or a stranger goes smoothly and is seemingly 'effortless,' there are other instances where interaction is mentally and emotionally exhausting. Efforts to explain something to somebody, to react, to listen, to smile, to laugh, to express a variety of emotions and expressions necessary to engage in face-to-face contact with somebody else is part of such interactions. Goffman's rules of interaction that he coined in the 1950s through thick ethnographic description – the process of "saving face," (Goffman 1955) and all the details inherent in gesturing, listening and responding – all engage a person more intensely the more frequently they are faced with others.

Fischer explains that "we decide whose company to pursue, whom to ignore or to leave as casual acquaintances, whom to neglect or break away from..."

(Fischer 1982: 4). Network analysis which states that that sociality is supported by making choices based on individual agency (Scott 2000, Wellman 1988, Wittel 1998), also shows the way in which people manoeuvre through their social network in order to achieve certain gains. Fischer explained that,

> network analysis stresses individual agency. Every day, we decide to see people or avoid them, to help or not, to ask or not, we modulate the nuances of our relations, we plan, anticipate, or worry about the future of those relations. We each build a network which is part of building a life. And in all this activity we make choices the best we can to attain the values we hold dear (Fischer 1982: 5).

Couchsurfers are conscious of their own network-building. When asked why a Couchsurfer has not kept in touch with their previous guests or hosts, some responded, "I only keep in touch with the people I really connected with. Have too many contacts abroad to keep contact with them all." Another Couchsurfer stated, "having a good time together does not always or necessarily imply that you become friends for life. Meeting others enrich your life in the here and now" (61 year old Dutch male survey respondent). The decisions to keep one Couchsurfer as a friend, and another to leave as 'just a [Couch]surfer" is part of what Fischer explained as the process of building a network. Another Couchsurfer explained, "Sometimes people are just a day at my place and I don't have a real connection with them, so I spend my time on other connections" (22 year old Dutch male survey respondent).

In this chapter 'agency' is seen as more relational, where individuals as well as other objects move, creating and recreating space and meaning itself through their attachments and detachments (Ahmed, 2004). It is precisely this process of detachment that will be outlined in this chapter. I wish to also outline that mobility helps enforce contact but also can divide. People can blame their choice to alienate from a conversation on by-products of mobility - a long trip may have exhausted a traveller and they close their eyes rather than talk to their driver. Or two people do not even engage in conversation, knowing that they live on separate continents and may never speak again (Adams 1998). These complexities of life on the move prevent some Couchsurfers from staying in touch with some of their hosts and guests: "Life is already too complex to add tons of new friends to your world every year!" (26 year old American female survey respondent). Another explained, "I have met a lot of people in my life - keeping in touch with all of them would be a full time job or two, so I only keep in touch with those that I like the most" (34 year old Danish male survey respondent).

These statements help illustrate they way in which "social saturation steadily expands the population of the self" (Gergen 1992: 79). Because of such high social saturation of these Couchsurfers, the respondents are forced to make choices of whom to relate to and to maintain a relationship with, and whom to reject. Thus

I outline that while people may 'build their network' as Fischer suggests, they do so as a result, and with the help of, various mobile forces which shall be outlined.

Not my cup of tea: 'faulty' interactants

Elaine, the OHW user living between Montreal and Toronto, uses Craigslist to find passengers nearly every weekend. The route from Montreal to Toronto is popular, and Elaine often gets a multitude of phone calls every week requesting a ride. When I asked her how she selects the people to ride with, she said that she always talks to her passengers on the phone prior to their trip, after a short conversation, she can tell "who is nice by their voice on the phone." Elaine explained that she does not feel comfortable with everyone and that she does not want to spend the distance between Montreal and Toronto (over 5 hours) with someone she does not like. People become part of one's journey, and annoying, strange, or awkward people make for an annoying, strange, or awkward journey. In order to avoid an awkward 5 hours of her life, Elaine cannot accept everyone she speaks to – she has to create personal standards of those she wants to interact with and those she does not. This is a personal choice, one which Elaine makes based on her attachments to various values, images, ideas, and objects, and people associated with the other she is meeting. Somebody who sounds aggressive, awkward, too quiet, or too loud over the phone to Elaine, may seem attractive to another person. When asked why one Couchsurfer did not keep in touch with his host or guest he responded, "Some people are not worth my time" (31 year old Swiss male survey respondent). People here become 'worth' the interaction or not, and these standards are discerned through interaction.

By making such decisions, "faulty interactants" as Goffman explains (see following paragraphs in this chapter), or undesirable interactants, can be avoided before the physical encounter takes place. A mobile phone conversation or glance at an online profile prior to the face-to-face meeting gives interactants the opportunity (like in Elaine's case) to discern if the stranger is a faulty interactant. If none of these opportunities are available, the chances are higher that a meeting will occur and one or both interactants will feel a level of alienation. In this case, the relationship has no longevity, and the two people never make any effort via online communication or other communication technologies to interact with one another again.

One Couchsurfer stated that "some people you just don't 'click' with, so you say thanks and adios" (29 year old Australian male survey respondent). Another Couchsurfer explained that "there have been some surfers who just didn't click with me, in other words, weren't 'my kind of people'" (29 year old American female survey respondent), and another stated that the reasons that she did not keep in touch with her host or guest was because she felt their "personalities didn't match" (20 year old Latvian female survey respondent). Creating a good 'match' or somebody to 'click' with was a common reason to avoid an interaction. "They weren't my cup of tea: too young, too green, too republican, you get the idea" (33 year old American female survey respondent).

Some people are just fucking boring" explained a 22 year old Australian male when asked why he doesn't keep in touch with certain people after Couchsurfing with them. The purpose of asking this survey question was to find out specific characteristics of 'faulty interactants' that Goffman refers to when describing the interaction ritual.

The individual recognizes that certain situations will produce this alienation in him and others, and that other situations are quite unlikely to do so. He recognizes that certain individuals are faulty interactants because they are never ready to become spontaneously involved in social encounters and he will have "folk-terms such as 'cold fish,' 'kill-joy,' 'drag,' 'wet blanket' to refer to these refractory participants" (Goffman 1967, 129). While the term 'faulty' can be misleading and suggest that there is something wrong with the interactant – for the purpose of this chapter, it is worth expanding on Goffman's term and replacing 'faulty' with 'undesirable.'

My Couchsurfing respondents use certain terms to evaluate the strangers they do not like. Terms like 'annoying' or 'boring' are used more often to describe certain hosts or guests. In the case of the OHW driver Hakan, a Turkish teacher living between Frankfurt and Warsaw, a passenger he did not like was a young Berliner who "talked too much" and was annoying (field notes, November 2009). Usually 'annoying' strangers are those who talk too much, and 'boring' strangers are those who do not know how to, or do not want to, engage in spontaneous involvements and say little or nothing at all. The perfect balance between these two extremes must be achieved in order for a conversation to become a euphoric interaction (one which is filled with intensity of positive emotion and eye contact), which captures the attention of both participants. "Weird" people can be those who are either annoying or boring, and more often than not they are those who do not know how to become "spontaneously involved" in the interaction. "They were weird" (25 year old Australian male survey respondent) was one reason for not keeping in touch with one's host or guest.

Ideal interactions

Yet, if some people are not 'worth' interacting with, what standards are these faulty interactants not meeting? Before understanding what a bad interaction looks like, it would be worth presenting the opposite extreme - an ideal form of interaction. Goffman explained interaction as this sort of merging – "joint, spontaneous involvement is a unio mystico, a socialized trance" (Goffman 1967, 113). Many Couchsurfers explain their best encounters as spiritual, mystical, magical, or intense. Unio mystica refers to a "Mystical union; the merging of the individual consciousness, cognitively or affectively, with a superior, or supreme consciousness."11 This hope to create a mystical union with a community of strangers seem to be one of the main goals of the intimately mobile.

As explained in previous chapters on friendship, mobility narratives engage the mobile in the promise of finding romance, amicability, and 'mystical encounters' with strangers. When asked what she learns from other Couchsurfers, a 33 year old female Couchsurfer stated that she learns "mystical connections of chance, timing, fate that can change your life and others forever. Taking nothing...and turning it into positive energy. And of course, reinforcement that we are not alone in our quest for compassion, connection, and understanding. I could go on and on..." (Couchsurfing Survey 2006). When this socialized trance does not happen, when the moment of 'unio mystico' does not occur between two people, the communication is rejected, the interaction may be awkward, embarrassing or just not stimulating. A 23 year old Australian explained that she does not keep in touch with certain people because she is "not interested in just everyone - if there is no kind of 'spiritual' connection, why should I keep in contact?" Other responses help illustrate the search for elements of mystical spontaneity:

> With the power of the internet and today's communication systems making the world "smaller" we seem to sometimes loose the value of interpersonal relationships. It's easier to shoot off an email, rather than write a personal note, have a chat over IM instead of a phone call, etc, etc. Opening your home to someone is so very personal (at least to me) and through that I hope to nurture a greater respect and knowledge of this global community in which we reside (31 year old American female survey respondent).

> If we have a reason to talk we will, but sometimes distance and the possibility of never meeting again, prevents the effort to forge a long-term and long-distance relationship if there isn't a strong connection (22 year old American female survey respondent).

Expectations of finding this unio mystica in an interaction while on-the-move is a common desire for many Couchsurfers. The idea that mobility will bring engaging 'life-changing' connections is also a reason to become mobile for many Couchsurfers. To illustrate this - 56 per cent of survey respondents said that they travel in order to experience personal growth, and nearly 20 per cent of respondents' sole motivation to travel is to meet new people.12 42 per cent of respondents

---

11   http://www.encyclo.co.uk/define/unio%20mystica (accessed July 2011)
12   Out of 8 possible answers regarding the respondent's 'primary motivation to travel': Seeing interesting sights of the world 14.19per cent, Personal growth/personal

feel that they have empty, superficial relationships or friendships in their life (Couchsurfing survey, 2006). What this indicates is that interactions or connections that do not fulfil these various expectations are not fulfilling interactions and mobility then, become a disappointment rather than a success.

Goffman and forms of alienation

Almost 50 years ago, Goffman gave social science a description of mores inherent in face-to-face interaction in American society. Many of the encounters described which are sought by couchsurfers could be classed as "euphoric interactions" - interactions where participants 'click', and extraordinary emotions or sociability are experienced. Now describing the mobile society of the rich north, the following extract helps to poignantly summarize the "euphoric" interaction (see below) of the intimately mobile, but it also explains that failure in interaction happens when people fail to fulfil the obligations inherent in conversation. For Goffman:

> Many social encounters of the conversational type seem to share a fundamental requirement: the spontaneous involvement of the participants in an official focus of attention must be called forth and sustained. When this requirement exists and is fulfilled, the interaction "comes off" or is euphoric as an interaction. When the encounter fails to capture the attention of the participants, but does not release them from the obligation of involving themselves in it, then persons present are likely to feel uneasy; for them the interaction fails to come off (Goffman 1967, 135).

With his thick description he deconstructed the way meetings and interactions succeed, and the places where they go wrong. Yet while similarities exist, sociality in rich, mobile societies today has changed since Goffman's first texts appeared. As argued in previous chapters, in highly mobile societies, conversations are happening more often, both online and offline, meetings are initiated online and offline, and strangers are colliding more than ever before. Meetings are also accompanied by a variety of technologies like mobile phones, Mp3 players, laptops, and other personal digital assistants (PDAs). While the magnitude and way in which people negotiate their coordinated and spontaneous meetings has changed, Goffman's ethnographic descriptions help map out the mobile interaction ritual today which will

---

development (learning about yourself and the world around you) 56.21per cent, Meeting and building relationships with people from around the world 17.78per cent, To relax 1.56per cent, To escape daily responsibilities 1.12per cent, To see family 0.41per cent, For business 0.61per cent, and other 7.21per cent.

especially help unveil the dysfunctions of such interactions, the way in which alienation happens, and how people negotiate solitude.

In Interaction Ritual, Goffman focuses on conversations as a "conjoint spontaneous involvement." A conversation, for Goffman, has a "life of its own and makes demands of its own behalf. It is a little social system with its own boundary-maintaining tendencies; it is a little patch of commitment and loyalty with its own heroes and its own villains" (Goffman 1967, 113). In conversations, Goffman notices that meetings between people are not always harmonious, and amicability and mutual understanding is not always present. Goffman observed that "joint involvement" is a "fragile thing, with standard points of weakness and decay." It is "a precarious unsteady state that is likely at any time to lead the individual into some form of alienation" (Goffman 1967, 113).

Goffman explains that there are many forms of alienation which mainly occur as a result of the obligatory involvement of a conversation. Conversations for Goffman are never without rules and regulations, and people involved hold expectations that certain obligations of interaction will be fulfilled. In the previous chapters, I described the culture of hospitality, and the etiquette inherent in being a host or guest. For example, the expectation that a driver will be 'entertained' on a given trip, and that the passenger will 'liven' up the ride by telling stories is often present during OHW but something that fails to be achieved. Passengers sometimes go to sleep in the back seat, or if there is more than one passenger, they sometimes talk amongst themselves, ignoring the driver. When these obligations of interaction are not fulfilled, the driver can become frustrated and unhappy with the conversation.

"Conversational encounters in which participants feel obliged to maintain spontaneous involvement" (Goffman 1967, 130) increase in frequency as a person collides with unknown others through physical mobility in densely populated areas. These types of encounters between people happen in homes and cars when using hospitality networks or OHWs, as well as in airplane seats, riding the metro, waiting for a bus, or standing in line for a ticket. Goffman explained that "Conversational encounters in which participants feel obliged to maintain spontaneous involvement and yet cannot manage to do so are ones in which they feel uneasy, and ones in which they may well generate uneasiness in others" (Goffman 1967, 130). Forms of alienation therefore, "constitute misbehaviour of a kind that can be called 'misinvolvement.'" This is important to my analysis because the ways in which people "misbehave" during interaction takes on a new form as people are mobile and use new technologies.

This uneasiness is also becoming more frequent, and the increase in failure to create spontaneous involvement within conversational encounters significantly impacts people today. The ways in which mobile people try to deal with situations of social alienation and interaction with 'undesirable interactants' is worth outlining because it affects the overall happiness, positive satisfaction, or positive connection a person has with the rest of their society. An excess of awkwardness and faulty interactions can force people to distrust or escape from others in a variety of ways. The ways in which distrust and alienation manifests itself will be described in this chapter.

This issue will be examined by analysing mobile encounters found within Couchsurfing and OHWs, and applying them to the four forms of conversation alienation outlined by Goffman. When mobile, people can alienate themselves from a conversation through:

1. External preoccupation - where one moves their focus of attention to something that is not being talked about.
2. *Self-consiousness* -- where the failure of conversation leads the individual to focus more attention than he ought to onto himself.
3. *Interaction-consciousness* – where "a participant in talk may become consciously concerned to an improper degree with the way in which the interaction, qua interaction is proceeding, instead of becoming spontaneously involved in the official topic of conversation."
4. *Other-consciousness* – encompass a variety of other distractions that may alienate an interactant (Goffman 1967).

My research suggests that new forms of interaction are emerging - and I will attempt to update the interaction ritual written before mass mobility by outlining the failures in interaction among mobile and immobile people. I will explore how mobility presents new obligations of involvement and with that, I will come to conclusions on the ways in which mobile people who come into contact with a multitude of unknown others negotiate distance and solitude. Based on survey and interview responses from Couchsurfing and OHWs, I will explore the way in which mobility creates new rituals of interaction, specifically focusing here on matters of alienation and the avoidance of intimacy.

External preoccupation

Travelling from Toronto to Warsaw on a 9-hour flight, I had the 'luck' to sit next to a man in his mid-20s. He was a theatre student and clearly liked the medieval period and English folklore with long stringy hair tied into a ponytail, black jeans a black leather vest and many silver chains hung around his neck. He was very eager to talk about his passions – theatre and multiplayer online role-playing games (MORPG). I was tired and had no interest in either of his passions, but by the intonation in his voice and body language, he communicated to me that avoiding him would not be easy. Especially given his physical proximity. In order to escape the conversation, I used what Goffman describes as "external preoccupations" -

The individual may neglect the prescribed focus of attention and give his main concern to something that is unconnected with what is being talked about at the time and even unconnected with the other persons present, at least in their capacity as fellow-participants (Goffman 1967, 117).

This can be done by initiating "side-involvements, such as leafing through a magazine or lighting a cigarette" (Goffman 1967, 127). When technologies of friendship fail to create homophilic matches between people, and people are forced to engage in more spontaneous interactions like in OHWs or other mobile spaces like an airplane, the first method of alienation from an unwanted conversation is through external preoccupation. I took out the in-flight magazine and flipped through it, and when that did not work and my seat-mate continued talking to me, I put on my iPod earphones and started listening to my own music. The types of side-involvements which foster external preoccupation today have extended beyond print medium and cigarettes (which are less common). Today, new technologies of external preoccupation can include other mediums like mobile phones, laptops, iPods or a variety of other PDAs.

Objects of preoccupation

A limited amount of ethnography has arisen in the past years on the use of such technologies. Bull is one who explains the way personal music players create privacy in public spaces. He states that "Mediated sound reproduction enables consumers to create intimate, manageable and aestheticised spaces in which they are increasingly able to, and desire to, live" (Bull 2004: 1). An increasing number of us demand the intoxicating mixture of noise, proximity and privacy whilst on the move and have the technologies to successfully achieve these aims (Bull 2004, 2).

Goffman stated that "the object of the individual's preoccupation may be one that he ought to have ceased considering upon entering the interaction, or one that is to be appropriately considered only later in the encounter or after the encounter has terminated" (Goffman 1967, 117). A prophetic statement from Goffman, who seems to be writing about PDAs or, more commonly, mobile phones. A mobile phone is often today the object of preoccupation and serves as an excuse to detach from conversation at any point. Note that in most cases the standard etiquette among interactants is to set aside one's mobile phone when interacting face-to-face. A person 'ought to have ceased' using a phone upon entering interaction. But when a conversation with a stranger holds a risk of being dysfunctional, a phone can become a method of escape from unwanted conversations. Faking urgency ("I just have to take this call! It's from someone important") can be another way of escaping an unwanted conversation. "I have to make an important phone call" has become the keyword of alienation from dysfunctional conversations among mobile people.

The process of putting on my earphones communicated to my seatmate that my music, and not his voice, was my listening priority. This technique is also employed in other mobile meetings. Liese, a frequent Couchsurfer and OHW user explained that when she is not interested in the discussion with her driver, she also puts her earphones on and listens to music on her mp3 player. Couchsurfers often travel with laptops, and when they are tired of their conversation with their host or guest, they explain that they have to "check their email" or "call their family member" on an online telephony service like Skype.

The downside of these types of external preoccupations is the explanation needed when employing them. Making up these explanations and excuses is another example where the intimately mobile must organize their actions and interactions in order to function in their surroundings. Garfinkel termed this "accountability" (1967), where people organize their everyday actions and interactions. For Garfinkel, it is an inescapable fact that our actions are accountable and obligations to account for actions are implied in social situations.

When wanting to engage in my external preoccupation to avoid talk with the amateur actor on the plane, I had to explain to him exactly what I was doing in order to minimize being offensive. By telling him that "I will listen to my music now," I reduce the confusion of why exactly I escaped the conversation. This only works in spontaneous mobile meetings which hold little or no obligation to keep the conversation going. Meetings of friends or family hold certain inherent obligations which make external preoccupation more tricky. For example, meetings between a daughter and a mother, two neighbours, or a teacher and their student all hold specific rules of interaction with their own specific obligations of involvement. I argue that mobile interactions between strangers have little obligations of involvement because of the lack of social pressure to keep up the interaction. Mobile people have more choice to become involved in conversation with another mobile person because they have less socially-constructed obligation to interact when being on-the-move.

"I don't always click with everyone in a way that would make a long term relationship worthwhile, sometimes things are best left, even if positive, as a once off" said one 26 year old survey respondent from New Zealand. Another explained that they are "lazy and sensitive to whom [they] build relationships with" (46 year old male survey respondent who did not provide his place of origin). This sort of approach is specific to new relationships with strangers which hold no previous history, and have no socially-constructed obligation to interact. Couchsurfers and OHW users can return home and never 'have to' interact with their host or driver ever again. Geographic distance absolved interactants of any responsibility to that other person. As one Couchsurfer explained, when "you just know you won't see someone again, and you only knew them for a day or two, so it's just not worth all the effort." Another stated "sometimes distance and the possibility of never meeting again, prevents the effort to forge a long-term and long-distance relationship if there isn't a strong connection" (22 year old American female survey respondent).

Blame mobility

But if we return to the conversation - methods of escaping interaction also become more available to mobile people. This is what I term "blaming mobility" – where interactants blame a variety of objects of mobility, mobile settings and mobile situations for their alienation from conversation. This can be, as was discussed in the previous paragraph, objects of preoccupation like mobile phones or the internet. Terms like "I have to make a phone call" express to another person that they have to escape the conversation with their Couchsurfer to urgently call somebody at-a-distance. The interactant feels that they are not to blame, but rather their mobility, and the fact have to 'be here' at a time when they should 'be there.'

Also, when wanting to avoid explaining the reasons for escaping a conversation, mobile interactants can blame their escape on their physical space. As I mentioned, seating arrangements often bring people together, but also help separate them. I could have avoided interaction with the Viking-actor by moving airplane seats – complaining that my seat was 'too close to the washroom' or 'did not have enough legroom.' Jessica, a Berliner who I shared the backseat with on a journey between Heidelberg and Berlin, stated that the "backseat is the preferred spot" because you can always "doze off, put your earphones on and avoid conversation" (fieldnotes, February 2009). Again, the interactant absolves themselves of the guilt of escaping a conversation by blaming mobility – here the physical space as well as the objects found in that space are to blame for having to escape the conversation. Instead of communicating, "I don't want to talk to you," an interactant escapes by communicating "I don't want to sit in this seat because my legs are cramped" or in the case of Liese and many OHW users "I can't talk to you because I can't hear you from the back seat."

There is a list of ways interactants can "blame mobility" which can be added to Goffman's list of external preoccupations when avoiding interaction. Other ways of "blaming mobility" for ending an unwanted conversation is blaming a scheduled departure or arrival or all activities related to transportation. "I have to catch my flight" or "I have to check if my friend's train arrived" or "I have to go call my rideshare driver" become ways of blaming mobility for one's alienation. Confirming meetings ("I have to text her the time I'll be at the restaurant"), checking travel arrangements ("I have to check my email"), activities linked to geographical orientation ("I have to check google maps" or "I have to buy a map"), or purchasing equipment related to mobility ("I have to buy a German SIM card") also become methods to 'blame mobility' for one's alienation.

The offensiveness of preoccupation

Possessing the means to distract oneself from an unwanted conversation does not automatically free a person from the feeling that he or she has caused the other interactant offence.

The offensiveness of the individual's preoccupation varies according to the kind of excuse the others feel he has for it. At one extreme there is preoccupation that is felt to be quite voluntary, the offender giving the impression that he could easily give his attention to the conversation but is wilfully refusing to do so... (Goffman 1967, 117).

Yet the feeling of causing offence is tied to the notion of obligation to another, as I mentioned previously. The notion of obligation is tricky and its origin is not clear cut. What makes these obligations when on-the-move so complex, and how are these obligations being transformed? One can feel general obligation not to cause offence to another human based on moral or religious grounds. In this case, the obligation to be good is not dependant on the other interactant, but rather on a general feeling of obligation to all of mankind – which also shows the way in which the ideology of Couchsurfing is practiced and takes shape in interaction. Specific network obligation is one in which a person feels obliged to interact in a certain way due to social pressures. Here, obligation to interact in a certain way is in fact dependant on the other interactant. In this case, a person feels that they give attention to another interactant because they are friends with them, because they are a friend of a friend or family member, because they care about what the interactant will think, and what they will tell a third party about them. These interactants are often seen again and a person has a certain relationship with them.

The feeling of obligation is dependent on a person's perceived longevity of any given relationship. Mobility deeply impacts the perceived longevity of a relationship, and thus, also affects the "offensiveness of the individual's preoccupation" (Goffman 1967, 119) because often a person does not feel any remorse in causing offence if they do not ever plan on 'keeping in touch' with the interactant again. Who cares if a person is offensive and retracts from a conversation if the interactant they are conversing with will never see them again?

Chatroulette.com is an example of such blatant offensiveness and rejection. The website uses a simple structure – a webcam and chat system where a user clicks 'play' and the system randomizes a partner to chat with. The catch is that this partner can be anybody in any part of the world. If you do not want to chat with the given stranger you find onscreen, you can press 'next' and automatically your screen shows another random stranger, the previous having been lost forever. Rejecting somebody (colloquially termed 'nexted') is remorse-free, because you will never see the person again.

A 31-year-old male Couchsurfer expressed in my online survey that he does not keep in touch with other Couchsurfers because "It's just often the human character - out of sight, out of mind." Mobility inevitably brings people close together, but inevitably and quite rapidly, creates geographical distance between those who have once been close. Distance abolishes a person from the feeling of responsibility to another. This lack of responsibility to another that many intimately mobile people experience is a product of our times, as Bauman (2002) suggests. Liquid intimacy, friendship, or love, is favoured above the messiness of real intimacy. People today favour "lightness and speed" (Bauman 2002, 49), and the inability to commit to those immediate can be a side effect of a mobile life. Moreover, while the offensiveness of retracting from a conversation may be as present as it was 60 years ago when Goffman wrote his ethnography, mobility abolishes people from any direct consequences of their offences.

Interaction-consiousness

The judgement statements my respondents made about the way in which their hosts and guests interacted as well as my statements about the over-eagerness of my airplane seat-mate are part of another form of conversation alienation – known as "interaction-consciousness" – where, "a participant in talk may become consciously concerned to an improper degree with the way in which the interaction, qua interaction is proceeding, instead of becoming spontaneously involved in the official topic of conversation.... A common source of interaction-consciousness is related to the special responsibility that an individual may have for the interaction "going well," i.e. calling forth the proper kind of involvement from those present." (Goffman 1967, 120).

Some respondents said that they did not keep in touch with their hosts or guests because of the lack of topics to talk about - "She's a middle aged woman, I'm a college student. Not much to talk about." Another survey respondent explained that she did not keep in touch with her host because "His place was very dirty and he was boring to talk to." Couchsurfers often "want to learn how other people think and why" and "want to expand [their] view and have a better understanding of the world around." Engaging in spontaneous interaction through talk helps "expand that understanding, and [couchsurfing] does it faster than I do on my own" (30 year old American male survey respondent). Faulty interactants therefore, do not fulfil these needs to "expand" their "understanding of the world" and thus, time spent with them becomes disappointing. Interactants with "nothing to talk about" beyond small-talk are thus considered boring.

And once people enter a conversation they are obliged to continue it,

> until they have the kind of basis for withdrawing that will neutralize the potentially offensive implications of taking leave of others. While engaged in the interaction it will be necessary for them to have subjects at hand to talk about that fit the occasion and yet provide content enough to keep the talk going; in other words, safe supplies are needed. What we call 'small talk' serves this purpose. When individuals use up their small talk, they find themselves officially lodged in a state of talk but with nothing to talk about; interaction-consiousness experienced as a 'painful silence' is the typical consequence (Goffman 1967, 120).

Spontaneous interactions while traveling last the duration of one's travel period – this may be two hours (like during some OHW rideshare trips between cities) or a few days (like a stay with a Couchsurfer). These situations tend to "lodge" two people in a state of talk without the possibility of leaving the interaction. This is mainly because the priority in interaction becomes the journey, getting from point "a" to point "b," and the two interactants must complete their journey no matter how awkward the conversation is. This gives no room for either party to escape the conversation. An interaction becomes compartmentalized into a given space until one party is able to leave. This compartmentalization is due to the physical space which the two interactants find themselves in, but also, due to the power relationship between the two interactants. As mentioned in the previous chapter on Technologies of Hospitality, there is an uneven power relationship between a host and a guest, where the host, in return for providing a 'gift' of accommodation, or a ride to another destination, is able to determine the topic or duration of conversation.

If a OHW passenger has a 'boring' driver and sits in the front seat during a 4 hour ride, they cannot just step out of a driving vehicle. And if they have no "basis for withdrawing that will neutralize the potentially offensive implications of taking leave of others" (Goffman 1967, 120), like an object of preoccupation as Goffman explained, they will find themselves lodged into a state of interaction with their driver without possibility of escape. To reiterate, when interacting on a journey, people lack the freedom to leave the physical space, as well as the social space of the conversation.

Self-consiousness

Another form of conversation alienation can be self-consciousness. Goffman explains this type of alienation as a redirection of focus on oneself rather than the interactant. Both the host and guest, placed in an unnatural situation of physical closeness for the duration of a trip, will feel additional awkwardness or embarrassment if the conversation does not go well. If there are no available "objects of preoccupation" as described in the previous paragraph, a person will alienate themselves from the interaction by analyzing, deconstructing, and stressing over the way the given interaction is proceeding instead of becoming spontaneously involved.

> Self-consciousness for the individual does not, it seems, result from his deep interest in the topic of conversation, which may happen to be himself, but rather from his giving attention to himself as an interactant at a time when he ought to be free to involve himself in the content of the conversation (Goffman 1967, 117).

One cause of self-consciousness is when the failure of conversation leads the individual to focus more attention than he ought to onto himself. For example, the guest could start talking for hours about their private life to their guest, not listening to what their host has to say. This process is similar to interaction-consciousness, as both forms of alienation are evoked by the feeling of embarrassment or awkwardness that result from the conversation. The difference here is rather than blaming a poor conversation on a faulty interactant, the "self" is now the person to blame for the conversation not going well. In the instances of conversations during OHWs or Couchsurfing, hosts or guests can ask themselves a variety of questions while conversing – which alienates them from the conversation and its content. Some of these questions can be related to the host and their personal space like – "Is my car big enough for these passengers?" or "Does my house look clean enough?" Other forms of self-consciousness when mobile can be related to a host's feelings of obligations to entertain. Questions like "am I a good tour guide? Are my guests having fun in my city?" or "how am I driving?" can be also part of the process of self-consciousness. A guest, on the other hand, can worry if they are being too imposing, what objects or part of the house or car they can touch, or what they can and cannot say. Online profiles can also evoke self-conciousness offline, as strangers who meet face-to-face can often ask themselves, "am I who they thought I was on my profile?" or "what if I made myself look better than I do in real life?"

Note that self-conciousness is a much more complex issue when two strangers meet in intimate spaces. Two old friends have presumably established a relationship of trust and acceptance. Strangers meeting in places as hosts and guests feel many new obligations, insecurities, risk of rejection, and social disharmony which can add to a feeling of self-conciousness.

Other-consciousness

There are, of course, other sources of alienation during a conversation, and a handful of those Goffman terms as 'other-consciousness.' An interactant is not able to fully engage in a conversation because of a variety of external distractions – Goffman explains that this can be strange physical or speech features of the other interactant. Another source of other-consciousness is "over-involvement" where one party becomes much more eager or involved in the conversation than the other party. Goffman explains that "during any conversation, standards are established as to how much the individual is to allow himself to be carried away by the talk, how thoroughly he is to permit himself to be caught up in it... We are to see that over-involvement has the effect of momentarily incapacitating the individual as an interactant; others have to adjust to his state while he becomes incapable of adjusting to theirs" (Goffman 1967, 123).

This readiness to become over-involved is a "form of tyranny" suggests Goffman, practiced by "children, prima donnas, and lords of all kinds..." (Goffman 1967, 123). Yet such "tyranny" can also develop between a host and a guest. More often than not, such tyranny is practiced by the host or driver, who exudes his power of hospitality (as I described in my previous chapter) and gets "carried away" with the opportunity of conversation. This can manifest itself in various forms. Adam, a Polish Couchsurfer described a situation in which he travelled to Geneva for three days on a conference, and stayed with a Couchsurfer who would keep him up until 3:00 a.m., talking about his personal life. Not only did Adam feel obliged to listen to his host, but he also did not feel he made a connection with his host because of the one-sidedness of the conversation (interview notes, 2006). Adam was "incapacitated" as an interactant, and the conversation failed to be a process of "joint spontaneous involvement." This type of alienation that Adam's experienced is one of the most common sources of alienation during these types of mobile meetings. This was the main cause of complaint among Couchsurfers and OHW users – that their host or guest was too involved and talked too much about their lives. The other Polish female Couchsurfer who I mentioned in a previous chapter felt alienated from a conversation when her host started discussing her sex-life over dinner. Kasia explained, "I could not believe that my host started telling me such personal things. I felt really awkward" (fieldnotes, 2009). Goffman's statement that "what is one man's over-eagerness will become another's alienation..." could not be more fitting for these situations. (Goffman 1967, 122).

This type of alienation is linked to my discussion of power between the host and guest in my chapter on technologies of hospitality. This is a relational power, when the host feels that in exchange for providing hospitality, they are able to disclose as much information as they wish, taking away their guest's time and energy to listen to them.

Additionally, this type of over-eagerness is easy to employ when mobile, and more difficult when interacting with people whose opinion and presence matters to us. Mobile people have the freedom to engage in any opportunity of involvement that arises on their journey (a conversation in a plane, a Couchsurfing meeting, a discussion at a bus stop) and the promise of never seeing the other stranger again provides them with new ways of interacting; without being constrained to the way in which their social network identifies them at 'home.' Not only can one interactant say anything they want to another without the fear of rejection, they can also say as much as they want, for as long as the journey allows. Additionally, as was already mentioned, mobile spaces like cars or planes trap two people into a given space for the duration of their journey, and an interactant who feels alienated cannot escape until their journey is over. Thus, one can argue that those who become alienated from interaction when mobile can become more affected by the over-involved "tyranny" of their interactant, because of this inability to escape the interaction.

Conclusions

This chapter dealt with the issue of friendship-avoidance – the way in which people negotiate rejection – using geographical space, time, and our own personal psychology as catalysts.

By using Goffman's theoretical approach to the interaction ritual, I hoped to explain that within interactions, or "conjoint spontaneous involvement in a topic of conversation" (Goffman 1967, 130) alienation from such interaction is quite common, even among the intimately mobile who travel in order to interact and create 'mystical' or life-changing connections. These meetings filled with moments of learning, harmony, and complete amicability common to the intimately mobile have, as Goffman had explained, "standard points of weakness and decay" (Goffman 1967, 117) and are often precarious and unsteady. As I explained, these moments of unease during conversation will lead the individual into some form of alienation. Thus, an alienation ritual has developed among the mobile. Some conclusions regarding the processes of alienation include:

a) Interactions or connections that do not fulfil expectation of 'unio-mystica' or joint spontaneous involvements are deemed as failures or disappointments.
b) Blaming a variety of objects of mobility, mobile settings and mobile situations for alienation from conversation is what I term 'blaming mobility.' By blaming mobility, an interactant is absolved of the feeling of guilt or remorse in rejecting or ignoring another interactant.
c) Mobile interactions between strangers have little obligations of involvement because of the lack of social pressure to keep up the interaction.
d) Mobile spaces enable individuals to exert 'tyranny' on an another person, trapping them into interactions the other wishes to avoid.

This chapter helped indicate that people who are mobile have a heightened sensitivity to strangers – developing skills to judge who is trustworthy and friendly, and who isn't. Mobile individuals are selective, judgemental, and sure of who they like and whom they do not wish to interact with. Often the highly mobile know how to network, how to discern who is trustworthy and who is not, and create homogenous social networks. The consequence of creating a homogenous social network is often linked to the avoidance of conflict. The 'messiness of real intimacy' as Bauman explained (2002), is not avoided, but rather more easily achieved. People know how to "grow closer, faster" as Ulla suggested in an interview. This can possibly lead to a sort of sensitivity and sensibility to interaction with strangers – sensing whom to avoid, whom to interact with and whom to trust. In order to understand this process of trust and alienation, more investigation is needed to discern if people who are mobile have developed a sensitivity to strangers – enabling them to more precisely and more rapidly discern who they want to interact with and whom they want to avoid than somebody who does not travel.

As consumer life favours "lightness and speed" (Bauman 2002, 49) the inability to commit to those around us can be a side effect of life in such societies. The increase in the sheer number of people a given person encounters when mobile may invite people to look at their relations as if they were consumer objects. "This networking we might view as a major component of global consumerism, that at least for the rich third of the world, partners, family and friends are a matter of choice and increasingly a choice spreading itself around the world. There is a 'supermarket' of friends and acquaintances" (Urry 2007, 89). Just as we do not have time or room in our stomach to taste every yogurt in the supermarket shelf at one time, people are forced to become more discerning by rejecting the "boring" and desiring the "exciting" strangers. An example of this was the statement made by Adam, mentioned in my previous chapter – when not wanting to accept a Couchsurfer from his own country, stating "they're not different enough. I don't think I'll get anything out of that." Based on survey and interview responses from Couchsurfing and OHWs, I used Goffman's ethnographic approach to the interaction ritual in order to outline the way in which people enforce distance between themselves and the stranger.

More research within mobilities calls for investigation into the settings and situations which foster alienation. By stating this, I do not wish to argue that alienation can or should be minimized or avoided. Rather, I aimed to highlight the processes of selectivity and rejection among the mobile in order to unveil the negative forces urban life and mass networking have on sociality. The processes of rejection, loneliness, alienation, distrust and feelings of awkwardness and isolation are also part of mobility and social networking and must be discussed in order to grasp the entire picture of mass mobile sociality. The following chapter will look at the opposite – the way in which various positive emotions and feelings of "growth and learning" that accompany the intimately mobile while on-the-move help ignite rather than extinguish their desire for to be mobile.

Chapter 8
Sentiments of Mobility

The past three chapters dealt with the way mobile people encounter others and create ties, acquaintances and friendships, or attempt to avoid such ties. Patterns of sociality which emerge from such mobile meetings were also presented. When investigating the shift in interactions and friendship-making as people become mobile, this analysis should not overlook the emotional aspects motivating meetings and encounters to happen or reoccur. As people meet one another, emotions such as love and hate, or feelings of compassion and joy or unease and suspicion can arise, defining these encounters.

Some researchers feel that they "have been forced to confront the glaringly obvious, yet intractable, silencing of emotion in both social research and public life" (Anderson and Smith 2001, 7). As recent research in the area of mobilities and material culture has shown in particular, there is a crucial conjunction between motion and emotion, movement and feeling (Sheller, 2004). In light of this, scholars like Mai and King recently advocate for an "'emotional turn' in migration and mobility studies which explicitly places emotions, especially love and affection, at the heart of migration decision making and behaviour" (Mai and King 2009, 296).

Additionally, as Mai and King point out, decisions to migrate or to avoid migration are contingent on emotions, and one of these instigators of a variety of our emotions are the people we meet when mobile - significant strangers, loved ones, and new acquaintances. By accepting Mai and King's call for an 'emotional turn' in mobilities research, an explanation of Intimate Mobilities cannot overlook the emotions that are at the heart of the decision to move.

My analysis in this chapter focuses on studies in mobile culture where attention is given to embodied emotions and privileges a human subject, while still "allowing for a degree of intercommunication between human and non-human, social and material, cultural and corporeal" (Sheller 2004, 228).

Indeed, the space people move through, the technologies that help people move, and the objects and people encountered while on-the-move are all part of the emotional culture of mobility. As mentioned in earlier chapters, individuals and objects move, creating and recreating space and meaning itself through their attachments and detachments (Ahmed 2004). In what way then, does space, technology, as well as objects and people evoke certain emotions among the intimately mobile which helps propel or deter future mobilities?

This chapter coincides with other studies on emotion that do not try to answer whether sensation precedes emotion or the cultural organization of emotion precedes the embodied feeling, but rather how sensations, cognitions and feelings arise together out of particular orientations toward the material and social world (see Sheller 2004, Ahmed, 2004).

Here, I demonstrate that encounters between people take on a certain emotional character and the character of encounters can affect a person's motivations to be mobile, as well as their route of mobility. Moreover, I will show that emotions are central to defining one's encounters. Through respondent commentary, I will show that rather than using terms like friend or boyfriend, people while mobile are rather labelled using a variety of emotional descriptions. This chapter will also point at the centrality of emotions in defining our mobile encounters by showing that emotions are also intimately tied to experiencing new people.

The origins of the sociology of emotions

One of the first to compile theories on the 'sociology of emotions' was Thoits who outlined the ways in which sociologists can tackle the issue of emotions, stating that emotions "are not simply innate, biophysiological phenomena" but rather "culturally delineated types of feelings or affects" (Thoits 1989, 318). Specifically, Thoits outlines emotions as:
a) appraisals of a situational stimulus or context,
b) changes in physiological or bodily sensations,
c) the free or inhibited display of expressive gestures, and
d) a cultural label applied to specific constellations of one or more of the first three components (Thoits 1989, 319).

The notion of 'affect' as outlined by Heise explains that "events cause people to respond affectively...event responses and anticipations develop out of feelings about the separate components of an event – actor, act, and object in particular" (Heise 1979, viii). The sociology of emotion focuses on "the sociocultural determinants of feeling, and the sociocultural bases for defining, appraising and managing human emotion and feeling" (Hochschild 1998, 5).

Most sociologists assume, either explicitly or implicitly, that "feelings motivate subsequent behaviours, but attempts to specify which emotions lead to which behaviours are rare" (Thoits 1989, 328). While emotions are felt in and through the body, they are constituted by relational settings and affective cultures; Emotions, in this chapter will be explored as not simply 'felt' and 'expressed', but also "elicited, invoked, regulated and managed through a variety of expectations, patterns, and anticipations" (Sheller 2004, 7).

Sheller's work in mobilities studies linked automobility and emotions, and addressed the ways in which "feelings for, of, and within cars come to be socially and culturally embedded in embodied sensibilities, in familial and sociable practices of car use, and in entire regional and national car cultures that form around particular systems of automobility and generate different aesthetic and kinaesthetic dispositions toward driving" (Sheller, 2004: 2).

Other scholars who dealt with "affects" rather than emotions were Conradson and McKay. They explained that affects "are created through social interaction and movement... affect is an embodied, physiological state that emerges through relational encounters whether through engagements with the environment or other people" (Conradson and McKay, 2007: 171). For them, transnational mobility may be implicated in the generation of certain affective states, whether broadly positive or negative. For "scholars of transnationalism, this raises the challenge of producing intercultural and cross-cultural accounts of emotion and intimacy" (Conradson and McKay, 2007, 170).

The culture of being on-the-move generates it's own affective states that are characteristic to being on-the-move and not stationary, rooted in one's own 'home.' If we accept that many of the events and communities that shape our senses of self are connected to particular places (Conradson and McKay, 2007: 168), emotions can be viewed as constitutive features not of individuals but of relationships (Gergen 1997, 210).

Mobility thus provides opportunities for new forms of subjectivity and emotion to emerge, whether broadly positive or negative (Sheller and Urry, 2006). Conradson and McKay employ the term "translocal subjectivities in order to describe the multiply-located senses of self amongst those who inhabit transnational social fields" (2007, 168). They argue that affect and emotion are central aspects of mobility. I introduce the notion of affective states as meetings in cars and apartments between mobile strangers help people create certain sentiments and purge others. As this chapter will explain, various affective states – creating and purging of emotions – instigates and hinders future patterns of mobilities. This chapter thus draws attention to the important role a variety of emotions play in mobile interactions.

Emotional space

People create meaning and make sense of the world "as they move bodily in and through it, creating discursively mediated sensescapes that signify social taste and distinction, ideology and meaning" (Büscher et al. 2011, 6). Perhaps through an "exploration of diverse senses of space, we could become better placed to appreciate the emotionally dynamic spatiality of contemporary social life" (Davidson and Milligan, 2004: 524). To first discuss the emotional landscape of mobility, it is worthwhile to borrow from cultural geographers – who stress that moving through space, land, and various environments evokes a myriad of emotions that have socio-cultural consequences. Urry highlighted that emotions are intimately tied to experiencing new places (Urry, 2005). But not only are emotions inextricably linked to experience, Davidson and Milligan explained that emotions themselves are only understandable in the context of particular places. As such, there is an "emotio-spatial hermeneutic: place must be felt to make sense. This leads to our feeling that meaningful senses of space emerge only via movements between people and places." (Davidson and Milligan, 2004: 524).

One Couchsurfer explained that the very process of mobility, of "being on the road" becomes "a quick way to cut to personal extremes in emotion, in desolation, in ecstasy, and interpersonal connection" (21 year old Irish male survey respondent). This response captures what many mobile people explain to be their main motivation to become mobile – the promise that life will be different than it is at "home," or when stationary. New spaces create new sensory stimuli which can provoke, as it did for this Couchsufer, a heightened emotional state.

The dichotomy of home/away in itself evokes emotion – at one point or another, the Intimately Mobile will associate home with emotions of confinement, the lack of fulfilment, the absence of freedom and other emotions from their childhood. The familiarity of their home space creates a stagnancy in emotion – little if no new emotions are evoked, life at home is familiar, nothing is a "discovery." Another survey respondent (24 year old American male) explained that on the road, they feel an "illusion and actualization of 'freedom'...in contrast to the feeling of confinement (no matter how slight) that I feel when I have to be in a preordained place i.e. 'home' or squat." The home keeps "some routines that monotonously eat away the very fabric that is the perception of 'free spirit' in me..." This feeling of freedom opposed to confinement is one fundamental emotion for the intimately mobile – an emotion that primarily instigates travel. The 'home' for the intimately mobile is linked to emotions of monotony and routine, and travel and mobility promises emotions like excitement and freedom.

New emotions

Travel through and to new spaces promise new stimuli which instigate new discoveries and new emotions:

> Every day that I travel I am faced with a new challenge I have to figure out how things work, whether it's something simple like doing laundry or making a train where there are no signs in English. It's amazing to feel so independent and challenged by things I take for granted at home. I am addicted to this feeling, and find it hard to stay in one place for too long. I am always wondering what is over the next hill or around the next corner (29 year old American male survey respondent).

New spaces evoke emotions of excitement, anticipation, and sometimes risk and fear, new spaces also create intimacy, awkwardness, and as I mentioned in my previous chapter on the technologies of hospitality, they also can create emotional obligation to act and respond in a certain way. Couchsurfers and OHW users feel "instant intimacy" with somebody because their mobility requires them to inhabit, for a short period of time, the private space of somebody's home or car.

Michael, one of my respondents, told me that "part of this [instant sense of intimacy] has to do with the environment fostered by staying with someone." For him, this process is kind of an "equalization process" that people go through. "You have this intimate relationship where you're sharing a physical space with someone that's very personal to you and so to equalize this physical intimacy you develop this emotional intimacy and that kind of makes people more comfortable. Because as soon as they get really close and really personal with someone they don't seem to feel that strange about how physically intimate the relationship is."

Thus, spaces not only evoke emotions because they are new, spaces are also able to create emotional closeness between two people, or build up emotional attachment, awe, awkwardness, nostalgia, or coziness due to the meaning that space signifies for the host or the mobile person.

Space and place are central features of the experience of 'being-in-the-world' as an embodied subject, for embodiment is always experienced through spatial dimension. The human geographer Yi-Fun Tuan calls the emotional relationship with places or landscapes topophilia, or 'the affective bond between people and place or setting" (Tuan 1974, 4). The emotional meaning of a home was presented by Deborah Lupton, who stated that "in contemporary western societies, the concept of 'the home' has particular resonances for the 'authentic' emotional self" (Lupton 1998, 156). The perceptions of place and space that individuals gather from their senses – the sights, sounds, smells, tastes and feel of the environment – have a potentially powerful role in the production of emotion.

So just as people are able to shape aspects of their physical environment, so does the environment shape subjectivity (Lupton 1998, 152).

Sara, my 30-something Couchsurfing host in Leipzig, lived with her 7-year-old son on the top floor of a characteristic pre-war apartment terraced house. She stated that "my private sphere has all sorts of emotions attached to it. And when I share that space with someone, it just feels more natural to be emotional and honest, and have an honest discussion." Emotional closeness between two people is thus evoked not simply because two people are together, it is rather due to the space they inhabit, and the reaction the Intimate Tourist has to their surroundings while being on-the-move.

Moreover, various forms of emotionality can heighten the authenticity of a place and the authenticity of an experience (Urry 2005). One Couchsurfer explained that meetings between host and guest shows the "places they live, their local cultures, their life perspective and understanding, their emotional states..." Seeing another person's 'emotional state' is an escape into the backstage of a stranger's life – and becomes a rare opportunity, a cherished experience which can be likened the tourist experience of seeing the 'backstage' of a city (Urry 2002). Also, obligatory for the emotional experience of place is something Urry calls the "collective tourist gaze" – which involves conviviality. "Other people also in that place give liveliness or a sense of carnival or movement. Large numbers of people that are present indicate that this is the place to be" (Urry 2005, 78).

Emotional technologies

While I already explored the workings of Technologies of Hospitality as well as Technologies of Friendship, I reframe my analysis of these online-offline social networking sites in order to demonstrate that a variety of technologies today are also designed in such a way to evoke emotion and emotional exchange between two or more people. This emotional exchange takes on a certain character – being inspiring, strange, scary or loving – and the way people experience these exchanges helps instigate further interaction and mobilities.

Features in the online Couchsurfing profile are what shall be called affordances – properties of the environment that offer actions to appropriate organisms (Gaver 1992). The Couchsurfing profile offers certain affordances which influences the way a user is perceived by other community members. The profile also plays a crucial role in a user's social navigation through the website, when he/she chooses whom to initiate contact with (see Bialski and Batorski, 2009). Goffman's work on self-presentation explains that certain individuals may engage in strategic activities "to convey an impression to others which it is in [their] interests to convey" (Goffman 1959). Dan, one of the founders of the website, explained that the profile questions are structured in such a way that "it brings out the essence of people. And when people's essences are visible, it contributes to the building of trust." Dan's use of the understanding of another person's "essence" which builds "trust" between two people is part of what is important for other couchsurfing community members.

When the design of the website provides a variety of affordances such as profile photos, space to communicate identity, stories, and personal emotion, positive, rather than negative emotions are expressed by the two parties meeting each other. Couchsurfers who chose to host/visit one another do so because they made a positive judgement about the other person. Mobility in this case is welcomed and emotions linked to this mobility seem exciting and promising. In the case of OHWs, where there are no affordances to help a user communicate who they are to the rest of the community of users, drivers and passengers have to make judgements about the other and risk more. These judgements and risks that result from the lack of transparency online often evoke emotions of fear, risk, and curiosity. And as I mentioned in the chapter on the technologies of friendship, the lack of transparency in such technologies also heightens the chance of creating bad 'matches' where two people do not 'hit it off.' Journeys are then marked by negative emotions of awkwardness, frustration, repulsion, or boredom. My drive between Warsaw and Frankfurt with Hakan, the turkish teacher (mentioned in the chapter about the technologies of friendship) at many points evoked feelings of frustration, where for 7 hours, Hakan became the talker, and I the listener. This emotion was not only evoked by our conversation, but the OHW which got me into that situation was in fact entangled in the entire emotion of frustration. Technologies of friendship and hospitality help evoke a variety of emotions among people on-the-move. Those who design such technologies create certain affordances or opportunities that help in evoking these emotions.

Objects of emotion

In her article on Polish migration to the UK, Burrell explores the way the physical practice of journeying and border crossing is not an empty act, suspended in space and time between two realities, but is a highly materialised and emotional undertaking (Burrell 2008). In a subsequent study which was introduced in the chapter on mobile homemaking, Rabikowska and Burrell placed emphasis on the way in which migrants re-enacted their sense of home in the UK through Polish food consumption. "The feeling of home stems from the [Polish] shop's position as a place where products, language, people and characteristically Polish design all merge to create and experience which resonates very intimately

(Rabikowska and Burrell 2009, 219). As mentioned, their analysis underlined the importance in evoking certain sought-after emotions.

How, exactly, can the self "use an object [either human or non-human] in such a way that the latter comes to act as a kind of emotional container for the former?" (Elliott and Urry 2010, 39). Emotions are attached to events and objects in movement, and objects enable an opening out of unconscious experience (Dewey 1895, Bollas 2009).

The main significance that objects have during mobile interactions is that mobile people use these objects to help create stability and familiarity in settings where instability and unfamiliarity is commonplace. Much like in the case of Polish food consumption – migrants recreate a sense of home in a similar way that Couchsurfers or OHW users take with them their favourite pillow or photographs of their family. This chapter focuses on the way objects are linked to emotions that evoke a sense of home when on-the-move, drawing also from Rabikowska and Burrell.

Yet what is useful to mention here in this chapter is that certain objects are a crucial part of interaction between two mobile people – and are necessary tools in stimulating conversation, or evoking emotions that help create mutual trust and understanding.

Oliver, the young Canadian traveler mentioned in a previous chapter, had to prove he was Canadian by showing his host his passport. In doing so, the passport became an object that helped pacify the host's fears. Sara, the host from Leipzig, "fell in love" with one of her Couchsurfing guests and explained that the reason she thought he felt so close to her was because of the objects in her house. She stated that their initial connection did not strictly stem from their level of compatibility, but from the opportunity to spend so much time together in her intimate space, which, she says, revealed so much about her as a person. "He got to see everything about me in just a few days, he lived here and we spent hours talking... but it was the atmosphere in which we were talking which made us so close. He saw all my things, he could look at them, touch them." She also stated that if they had met elsewhere, despite being so compatible, she did not see the connection between them as being as strong as their meeting at her home.

These objects became entangled in the emotion and connection present in interaction between Sara and her guest. In other cases, objects can evoke negative emotions – Sandra, a fellow OHW passenger who shared a car with me from Montreal to Toronto explained a negative experience. On a similar journey, the driver and his friend in the passenger seat "started doing cocaine -- they offered me some, I was so freaked out at that point." The fact that cocaine is loaded with negative sociocultural connotations is nothing new – but what is worth pointing out is that the temporary moments of co-presence that are part of mobility allows people to hide certain objects and reveal others in order to, at times, manipulate one another's emotions. In Sandra's case, the interaction between her and her driver would have gone smoothly if not for the cocaine - an object that stimulated such negative connotations and emotions for her. When interaction lasts over a period of time, there is a smaller chance that meaningful objects which are loaded with various emotions will go unnoticed. Mobile meetings can create an illusion of harmony and safety depending on the objects used and the settings in which the interaction takes place. In an alternative reality, these drivers could have been heavy drug addicts, but without presenting the object of the drug to Sandra during their car ride, Sandra would have driven 5 hours with them having known nothing about their drug addiction, felt safe and calm thinking her driver was completely sober.

Co-presence and emotion

As mentioned in the previous paragraphs, objects and spaces are part of the complex process of meetings between people (Shove 2007), and the emotions that humans attach to both these objects and spaces help define the meaning of the given interaction. Now I wish to focus on the mobile interaction itself – how it is defined, sought after, and evaluated by the people involved.

People, objects and spaces inspire a variety of emotions. But for the intimately mobile new people in particular inspire emotions. Moments of solitude are strategically dispersed between encounters that impact the traveler or the mobile individual in some way or another. The act of meeting a new person in itself becomes a sought-after emotionally-charged part of being mobile.

Not only are emotions like happiness, sadness, frustration, excitement and ambivalence that accompany mobility central to social life, these emotions "shape our experiences of the world and relations with others" (Conradson and McKay 2007, 168). Additionally, specific emotions are sought after when traveling, and often only meeting new people can fulfill these desires.

As mentioned, a dichotomy arises when mobile – where the home is seen as static and 'away' is deemed as exciting, full of "new experiences." A 23 year old American female survey respondent explained that "It is hard to grow staying in the same place because the world has so much to offer. I want to travel to learn about me and my place in the world as well as hopefully have a positive impact where I venture."

A 21 year old American female survey respondent explained that her interests are "psychological" and that her "studies at school most psychologists

I learn about study only American subjects. The world has so much more to offer." The Intimately Mobile experience interactions with people as if they were central to their process of mobility. They leave home in order to meet better and "more exciting" people than those at home. The world beyond their home has more to "offer." Johan, a 27-year-old Dutch Couchsurfer, stated: "If I look back on my friends, I've been in Holland and I think I got into more meaningful relationships with Couchsurfers than people whom I've known for years. I don't know why. I just see them being so static, as they are, they didn't get out. Even though we spent all these years together as friends, drinking together, or whatever, they still stay static, they're still in the same place, [mentally] too."

Ulla, a 26-year-old Finnish Couchsurfer explained that "all the Finnish culture and the Helsinki culture is just so closed down somehow. It's tough to break into circles and meet people for the first time.... There are people who do not understand this side of me... Couchsurfers all have the same needs to see."

In an ethnographic study regarding closeness and intimacy in the Shetland islands, Thien noted the relationship between an island native and her pen pal. Her research explained that Judy, the Shetland citizen,

> "strategically expanded her capacity for intimacy by stretching her relations beyond the limits of the community's purview. This relationship is an effective vehicle for practicing an intimacy without the obstacles that the small community engenders...her well-being is enhanced by maintaining a relationship that extends out with her community and within the self" (Thien 2005, 200).

For Judy, Nana, as well as many of the Intimately Mobile, the desire to achieve intimacy can "assume a distance covered, a space traversed to achieve a desired familiarity with another. As a vision/version of an achieved relationship [self to other]" (Thien 2005, 193).

Through this process of engagement (mentioned in the chapter on the technologies of friendship) – being mobile, meeting, experiencing and 'understanding' other people like themselves forces the mobile person to engage in a variety of emotions that, in turn, create meaning for the mobile person. This type of intimacy is the "antithesis of distance and as such the antidote to loneliness, unhappiness, estrangement and lack" (Thien 2005, 193).

A culture of of interacting

The intimately mobile share the conviction that meeting new people will 'offer' something 'new' and 'different' from their interactions at home as well as the idea that they are repeatedly able to experience a state of anticipation prior to meeting. As a 22 year old Italian male survey respondent explained that by being a Couchsurfer, they hope to gain, "personal growth, knowledge of different cultures and maybe find someone to share emotions with."

This respondent feels that they are on a search to find somebody to "share these emotions with." "An experience, a thought, everyone has something they can teach, sometimes its when to walk away, sometimes it's something small that can change your whole world, or an idea that changes how you view your world." (24 year old Australian female survey respondent).

This attitude is worth outlining for a number of reasons. The hunger for interaction is emotional – and based on the anticipation of each interaction, the emotional/sensory/spiritual experience of that given interaction and the non-material emotional/spiritual/cultural capital that is gained through such interactions. The frequent OHW driver whom I drove with from Montreal to Toronto explained that she is always curious and excited before meeting her passengers – they can be strange, or somebody she will have a close conversation with. This anticipation is part of the "fun" of being an OHW driver or passenger.

Anticipation: the first date affect

Anticipation of an interaction plays a critical role in the appeal of mobile meetings between strangers. These "new experiences" and "new emotions" are not definable prior to the meeting – all is unknown, a surprise in store. This feeling that the OHW driver explained is akin to the anticipation one feels before a first date – the butterflies, the anxiousness, the excitement – this is repeated over and over again before meeting strangers through Couchsurfing or OHWs. One of the reasons this feeling of excitement arises is that the intimately mobile feel that each person they meet might alter their lives in some way.

The anticipation of such meetings helps conjure up various forms of emotions which may become addictive. Anita, one of my interview respondents literally called herself a "people whore" who wants to meet new people because of the feelings she gains from the meeting and the anticipation of the meeting. Many Couchsurfers and OHW users also stated that oftentimes the meetings themselves are not the sole reasons interaction on-the-move becomes so addictive – the emotions experienced during the processes of anticipation also make such meetings sought-after. Emotions entangled in longing, hope, eagerness, wonder, and risk are all evoked through these mobile meetings between the intimately mobile. Immobility makes conjuring up such emotions of anticipation more difficult, because new, unknown people who help evoke such emotions are not entering into one's daily routine. It is often said that a single person has to "mobilize" themselves to find a partner – join a club, change their look, change their social circle. This constant change and new sensory stimuli are intrinsically part of being on-the-move, and anticipation of such change and new stimuli is more possible while mobile than while stationary.

The meeting: clicking with someone

As mentioned in previous chapters, when on-the-move, people 'bump' into one another by chance, or strategically plan to meet via technologies of friendship and hospitality. Meetings using such technologies are strategic, and usually based on homophily or a commonality of interests. Despite the fact that many of these people are quite similar, the intimately mobile like the feeling of anticipation, as I mentioned in the previous section, as well as the illusion of "discovering" another person.

As one Couchsurfer explained - "I'm a traveller and love to discover the world, cultures and feelings." Another survey respondent stated that they are "searching for special, new feelings all the time." People become "discoveries" and interactions become experiences. Some "discoveries" can be a source of new information and a way to gain cultural capital. One 27 year old female Brazilian survey respondent stated that "it's through the people that we can get new experiences, emotions, knowledge, about us, about life." By engaging in these new encounters, meetings become opportunities to gain or "get" these new experiences and enrich one's life. Interactions while on-the-move are ways in which a mobile person can "get" or achieve an emotional experience that is not available to them while stagnant.

Discovery of space becomes secondary to the discovery of emotion through the self and through encounters. And while the intimately mobile explore people as much as they explore touristscapes (Bialski 2008), they do not wish to discovery anybody and everybody. The most sought-after connections are those which "click.": "Meeting new people is one of the most exciting and enriching things…is to meet someone who is "on your vibe'" (28 year old German male survey respondent).

An 18-year-old Irish Couchsurfer explained that by using Couchsurfing, she hopes to gain "a new perspective on the world, on life; to learn about different things, such as, perhaps, cultures, languages; to gain an insight into the lives and thoughts of people of different walks of life; sometimes, a friend, someone I may be able to "click" with; something inexplicable."

A 26-year-old Greek female explained that "If you click with the other person you may become extremely close," yet not 'clicking' with another person – or experiencing no emotions or negative emotions – during a meeting is one of the reasons that Couchsurfers and OHW users do not keep in contact with one another. "There have been some surfers who just didn't click with me, in other words, weren't 'my kind of people'" (29 year old American female survey respondent).

Being "on the same vibe" or "clicking" with another person affirms the belief that there is "somebody else like me out there." The idea that one "clicks" or is understood by a complete stranger is part of the "imagined community" (Anderson 2003) of nomads, travellers or intimate tourists – people who identify themselves as those wanting to "discover" the world. This can help create not just an urban tribe (Watters 2003), but a feeling of a global tribe, and a connectedness to a multitude of people regardless of geographical distances.

One Couchsurfer said that they "love the feeling of the commonality of mankind" and another stated something similar, explaining that they "love to meet people learn about their lives, dreams, feelings, experiences in life, thoughts. And finding out how similar and how different all human beings are." Maffesoli would argue that there is not just one large imagined community but rather a multitude of groups which, due to various socio-cultural reasons are segregated into "neo-tribes," to which individuals become members in order to exchange the same emotions.

When Couchsurfers travel and exchange thoughts and feelings, they seldom come into conflict. Emotional exchange is an exchange of empathy, understanding, and agreement. Instead of a "rationalized social" environment, in which we see the world as a rational individual, we are witnessing an empathetic "sociality" expressed by a succession of ambiences, feelings, and emotions (Maffesoli 1996, 11). The emotions Couchsurfers wish to experience is usually an emotion of understanding and insight, but seldom conflict. Dialogue between "surfer" and "host" often involves social commentary or personal narrative which is almost always greeted with approval and "clicking" is the best way to define this exchange of emotions for the intimately mobile.

Gaining and offering

Beyond just a connection or "clicking," my respondents repeatedly underlined that people they meet always have "something to offer" and what these meetings offer are "new experiences, new learnings, new emotions" and to "see a place through another pair of eyes." Learning "what these people have to offer" (40 year old American female survey respondent) is something central to intimate mobility – and also the discourse around newness and "learning" what people "offer" can suggest again the supermarket-like approach to friendship-making. Some Couchsurfers stated that "Each person that you come across in your life has something new to offer, something different to teach!" (25 year old Greek male survey respondent). Another 21 year old American female stated that "every person has something to offer everyone else and I am eager to learn as much as I can!" And a 31 year old Austrian male had almost the exact response when stating that "Every person in this world has special things to offer, that's not limited to [Couchsurfing], but it's part of it." Another respondent explained that they "hope to get new friends, to share our emotions together, spend time discovering my or their city, share moments of joy. And create new links between our countries and cultures..." (41 year old French male survey respondent).

This search and discovery of new emotions through encounters with unknown others is the essence of the intimately mobile. Thus mobility seems necessary in order to engage in a search for what "others" and the "world" have to offer. But why do so? Emotion becomes central to mobility because it is only through emotional experience that a person feels they are alive and developing, learning, and 'being-in-the-world'. Another Couchsurfer gains "a sense of who the people really are in a country. I can learn how they feel and think and I can leave them feeling better about people from my country because they, also, will know someone (me) from my country" (56 year old female American survey respondent).

Empathy in the emotional exchange is also sought after, people seeking interactions on-the-move want to "See things through other peoples' eyes, understand their life and find ideas." The intimately mobile also expressed that these ideas, emotions and experiences "would never have thought about alone." Couchsurfing is a way to "party with simple feelings." Wanting to meet others in order to 'gain' something seems like a type of relationship centred on clearly circumscribed interests that must be fixed objectively (Simmel 1950). Badhwar termed this type of friendship as a means friendship, "a lesser friendship where the central feature is the instrumental or means value of each to the other" (Badhwar 1987, 2). An example of this sort of friendship is one in which two individuals are social as a means for further social advancement, amusement, the promotion of some cause, or even mutual edification or improvement (Badhwar 1987, 1).

Blau made a distinction here between strictly economic transactions and intimate friendships – "economic transactions are focused on benefits of some extrinsic value and on, at least, implicit bargaining for advantage, which distinguishes it from the mutual attraction and support in profound love." (Blau 1964, 112). The way the intimately mobile talk about people's "essence" as a unique selling point, how they search out for "interesting" people who have something to "offer" suggests that this technology can foster a fixation on this type of commodity culture, where people perform transactions based on an emotional currency, rather than economic as Blau outlined.

Emotional currency

Meetings that foster conversation filled with a multitude of emotions are necessary for the intimately mobile because they state that this helps them learn, grow and discover the world away from 'home.' Dialogue is a way to gain cross-cultural understanding, which is emotionally important. One survey respondent stated that Couchsurfing is "rocking the way I see the world, believing in a better world, emotional connections." Another 22 year old French male survey respondent defined Couchsurfing as a way of getting "emotional satisfaction" and "gratifying relationships."

As another survey respondent explained, emotions are also part of a process of sharing. The 22 year old Italian male respondent stated that he hopes to find somebody "to share emotions with." The process of 'sharing' ones emotions is for some the central purpose of Couchsurfing, as another survey respondent stated: "sharing feelings, being astonished, and discovering sense of my life" (28 year old French female survey respondent).

Others state that this emotionality, and "spreading good feelings" will help them "get a better understanding of the world..." which they do in the "hopes of [making] a better world" (28 year old French female survey respondent).

Here, one can see that one key characteristic of intimate mobility is experiencing the sentiments of others in order to expand one's view of the world. Moments of emotional interaction, where feelings and sentiments are shared, help intimate tourists gain not only an informational understanding of the world around them, but also an emotional understanding: "you can feel much more connected with the world around you by sharing a smile or a story...People are like a mirror, where you can see yourself... your reactions seeing different ways to think and to live, your feelings, your ability to communicate and to understand other people, that are the world around you" (21 year old American female survey respondent).

Another respondent loves "to meet people, learn about their lives, dreams, feelings, experiences in life, thoughts. and finding out how similar and how different all humans beings are" (19 year old Swiss female survey respondent). Emotion, thus, becomes a type of currency, an exchange which grows in value the larger the amount is exchanged. Interactions while on-the-move are considered more valuable the more emotion is discovered, both for the visitor as well as for the host. In this case, online-initiated emotional encounters are not just temporary, not just online and available in online chatrooms, encountered between online 'buddies' -

"Buddies, as every chat addict knows, come and go, switch in and out - - but there are always a few of them on the line itching to drown silence in 'messages'. In the 'buddy-buddy' sort of relationship, not messages as such, but the coming and going of messages, the circulation of messages, are the message... We belong to talking, not to what is talked about" (Bauman 2003, 34). This chatter is what the intimately mobile wish to avoid through tangible, all-sensory, face-to-face emotional encounters that provide "depth" and "authenticity." The intimately mobile seek a full-time intimate community (Matsuda 2005).

Eric from Seattle explained that closeness is created because "there is a certain amount of affirmation, physical contact, cooking with somebody, laughing with somebody, bonding with people on that level, and it's always new and it's always fresh. People literally come into my door and give me a hug. But there is something that feels really sincere about it. There is this joy that washes over us all, we have this smile... like old friends being reunited."

These emotional encounters achieved through technologies of friendship and hospitality like Couchsurfing are "elsewhere impossible, deeply emotional, highly teaching" as one respondent stated. It is about "sharing emotions, experiences" (43 year old Italian male survey respondent).

Emotional encounters

When on-the-move, the more the merrier – the more emotions evoked the better, which can seem like a step towards a commodification of interactions. Yet what seems to arise from my respondents' sentiments, interactions on-the-move cannot be categorized as friendships/ acquaintanceships but rather as emotional moments and encounters that one experienced or hopes to experience. Relationships on-the-move are not placed into categories of friend/non-friend acquaintance/stranger but rather associated in-time as emotional encounters that take place during one's life-course. Emotion, thus, plays a key role in cementing these contacts as "meaningful" and "spiritual" for those interacting. Eric from Seattle explained:

> We spent almost an entire night talking about our lives talking about our dreams, our past, our hopes. This is something that doesn't happen usually. If you meet someone in the street you usually don't end up doing these things – in talking in a deep way of yourself and your work...I think that part of people in the world want to carry on doing this. It is possible to trust each other. It is possible to be very genuine. It is possible to do this with somebody you don't know...mutual trust and mutual exchange of feelings and thoughts.

Bauman warned that fleeting interactions, which are often virtual are "present-day obsession" and he warns no to confuse these obsessions with "the compulsive confessions and splurging of confidences," where a person "submits the innards of the soul to the partner's inspection and approval" (Bauman 2003, 35).

Words voiced or typed, explains Bauman "no longer struggle to report the voyage of spiritual discovery" (Bauman 2003, 35).

As evident from a number of responses already presented in this work, the intimately mobile seem to rebel against the lack of depth in interaction that helps voice the "voyage of spiritual discovery." What is evident from my ethnography is that there is a vast difference between connections and 'chatter' maintained online, and connections that are instigated online for the purpose of meeting offline. The online-offline encounter creates a co-present space where interaction between strangers turns away from the "chatty" trend of a 'buddy-to-buddy' sort of interaction that Bauman described. For hosts and guests, drivers and passengers, what makes interaction more solid than liquid is that the conversation during a journey or throughout the duration of one's visit promises the purging and building of emotion that rebells against the shallow chatter of online communication. The all-sensory face-to-face communication between two strangers becomes an opportunity to anonymously yet intimately engage in emotional dialogue that can be, as Sennett (2003) described, a voyage of spiritual discovery.

Online chatrooms and the case of chat services like ChatRoulette that I introduced in the last chapter can be examples of Bauman's critique of the fluid, temporary, click-on-and-off nature of interaction online. Yet as will be explained, for people like Eric, a Couchsurfing respondent from Seattle, emotional experience is key in connecting with someone – and this emotional experience is locked in face-to-face co-presence, close contact, and intimacy.

Mobility, self-understanding and personhood

The answers as to why emotionality between mobile others is important to the intimately mobile is not clear-cut. A possible answer is the lack of family or partners/spouses which are often the source of such emotional closeness. Eric from Seattle explained: "I have such a hard time... well... I'm single... I have back luck with skills in changing that status. I live solo. And I like it, I like having the space to live solo... so this is a replacement sort of. It's like having instant friends... and both of us are showing the best sides of themselves. Which in the long run is not really an honest assessment of who I am and what they are. But at the same time, I acknowledge that that is the case. I really want to believe the best of myself and of other people."

Some theorists explained that process of establishing a close emotional relationship with another human being is experiencing a modern crisis. Highly individualistic "me-first" societies of the west have greatly increased the displacement of each individual from the rest of their surroundings. The emotional disconnectedness individuals feel towards one another on a day-to-day basis starts from childhood. Francis Fukuyama reminds us that much of the classical social theory written at the turn of the nineteenth century assumes that "as societies modernize, the family diminishes in importance and is replaced by more impersonal kinds of social ties...the hollowness of impersonal social ties has "led the individual to search for more substantial relationships" (Fukuyama 1999, 37).

Mobility, thus, becomes a method to search out these "substantial," emotional relationships and once these relationships are experienced, further mobility yet again allows people to continue their search:

> "All that coming together and drifting apart makes it possible to follow simultaneously the drive for freedom and the craving for belonging -- and to cover up, if not fully make up for, the short-changing of both yearnings" (Bauman 2003, 34).

The drive for freedom and the craving for belonging that Bauman speaks of "melt and mix in the all-absorbing and all-consuming labour of 'networking' and 'surfing the network.'" Yet Bauman also warns that the ideal of 'connectedness' so often repeated among Couchsurfers and other Intimately Mobile "struggles to grasp the difficult, vexing dialecticts of the two irreconcilables. It promises a safe (or non-fatal at least) navigation between the reefs of loneliness and commitment, the scourge of exclusion and the iron grip of bonds too tight..." (Bauman 2003, 35).

Emotions: artefacts of mobility

This chapter explained that people who experience mobility come into contact with a variety of emotions which fuel their mobility further. As interviews and survey respondents indicated, those who use Technologies of Friendship and Hospitality, interactions between on-the-move are often hyper-emotional compared to their life while stationary. This chapter showed how the intimately mobile experience mobility through the emotions that result from mobile interactions. Yet the increase in emotion while mobile is also due to a variety of other factors – the obvious being that one's senses are bombarded with new stimuli found in new environments. While new stimuli can include traditional touristscapes and experiences (Urry 2005) they must include new people and encounters that are either engaged in or avoided. These encounters produce emotions, and Couchsurfers specifically and other intimately mobile, emotionality is longed for rather than avoided.

Moreover, not only do negative emotions evoked through reading another person's profile or email deter interaction or mobility, the lack of any emotion evoked through a profile can also prevent mobility from taking place. If a person viewing another's profile feels indifferent to the other person, contact will probably not be made. Places and people which do not evoke emotion will not be visited, or will not be contacted. Emotion creates significance for the intimately mobile and the situations in which no emotion is evoked will also lack significance.

Through the description of the way in which the intimately mobile collect emotional artefacts – experiences that create meaning for them when mobile, this chapter aimed to address the way in which the phenomenon of emotion is practically achieved when mobile, addressing the importance of investigating how sense is made in and through movement (Büscher et al. 2011).

Chapter 9
Intimate Mobilities:
Consequences and Conclusions

> "CouchSurfing is not about the furniture, not just about finding free accommodations around the world; it's about making connections worldwide. We make the world a better place by opening our homes, our hearts, and our lives. We open our minds and welcome the knowledge that cultural exchange makes available. We create deep and meaningful connections that cross oceans, continents and cultures. Couchsurfing wants to change not only the way we travel, but how we relate to the world..." (Couchsurfing.com)[13]

Since I began this inquiry almost six years ago, not only have people been using computers more to coordinate meetings offline, people have also been Couchsurfing more, and using OHWs and carpooling websites more often. The couches being slept on, and cars being filled with strangers traveling to the same destination is increasing. Since I started my study in 2007, Couchsurfing has grown in size, from around 50,000 users to 3,197,842.[14] The OHW Mitfahrgelegenheit has now developed a Facebook application which is used by over 10,000 users, and developed offshoot websites in other countries in Europe like Poland, Switzerland, Greece, France, and England (carpooling.pl, carpooling.co.uk). Facebook has also become a major part of people's social lives, and "informal" couch-surfing and ride-sharing is being exchanged via recommendation systems using friends-of-friends and other weak ties.

Not only are people meeting through these websites, an increasing number of strangers are meeting and subsequently experiencing hospitality and closeness. Based on internal statistics, Couchsurfing claims that weekly, it helps create around

---

13 accessed July 2011
14 Couchsurfing statistics, www.couchsurfing.com, accessed March 2011.

40,024 real-life introductions (31,185 positive, 84 negative). In one week, 1,189,634 couches are made available and 189,879 people state that they made a close friendship connection through Couchsurfing15. The amount of new technologies that are creating close interactions offline, and enabling the coordination of people offline are growing at a vast pace. Since I began this research, social networking services like Facebook "Places" or Four Square (www.facebook.com/places, www.foursquare.com) for example engage people, their mobile devices, and the internet, in social networks which are constantly updating 'hot spots' in a certain city - places to meet, places to eat, places to dance, places to avoid dancing. Four Square and Facebook Places are recommendation systems and trust networks - where strangers help other strangers in their vicinity. With the help of such technologies, people are discovering they have neighbours who share their same interests and are willing to share their information with others.

The large body of work that has developed in recent years which focuses on the social impacts of CMC as well as the proliferation of social networking sites was introduced in the third chapter. Starting with the work of Barry Wellman and other scholars at the NetLab at the University of Toronto – which focused on various research projects involving smart communities (the impact of technology on neighbourhoods which use peer-to-peer programs, enhancing community life online and offline), the strength of weak ties in online social networking communities, as well as various other projects focusing on the issues surrounding CMC, have all been impacting this research area. A researcher which became highly influential in the area of CMC throughout the years I was completing my own work was Danah Boyd. Boyd's prolific research surrounding the sociality developing online on social networking sites, as well her co-edited *Journal of Computer Mediated Communication*, has been at the forefront in expanding this research area in the social sciences.

Although both Wellman, Boyd, and others, have been helpful to my own work, their research focuses mainly on CMCs and the patterns of interaction and the methods of sociality that develop between people virtually, as well as among already-established social networks. For example, Boyd and Ellison use the term "networking" with caution, explaining that "'Networking'' emphasizes relationship initiation, often between strangers" (Boyd and Ellison 2008, 211). Their studies focusing on social network sites (not social "networking" sites), that do not "allow individuals to meet strangers, but rather that they enable users to articulate and make visible their social networks" (Boyd and Ellison 2008, 211). These types of studies promote the notion that the "internet creates a protected environment for users where they have more control over the communication

---

15   www.couchsurfing.com, accessed September 2011

process" (Amichai-Hamburger and McKenna 2006, 825). Other studies focus on the way in which friendship is performed online, via various communication media, and the changing definitions of such ties. Few studies in the Journal of CMC or elsewhere explore the way in which online social networking sites initiate offline contact, between strangers.

This book aimed to add to a small body of work in the social sciences (McKenna 2000, Hampton and Wellman 2003, de Souza e Silva 2006, Larsen et al. 2007, Stephure et al. 2009) which treats the internet as a supplementary tool in fostering interaction between people face-to-face.

I underline that technologies of friendship and hospitality which foster intimate mobility are not virtual communities (Rheingold 2000). Note that both the empirical examples, Couchsurfing.com as well as OHWs, have little to do with online interaction after the initial contact between parties is made. Most of the interaction between people using these websites is strengthened offline. Technologies of hospitality, as were defined in this work are not part of the culture of CMC, due mainly to the fact that the act of receiving and providing hospitality is something maintained and created offline, face-to-face, and the main requirement is that the host has a space of which they take ownership of, and share it with their guest, engaging in hospitality. While the cultural, social and psychological norms, problems, and developments arising out of CMC is highly pertinent to social life today, the empirical research did not refer to a strictly 'online' culture. This worked aimed to show the process of becoming intimately mobile – the way in which intimacy, closeness, hospitality, the sense of home, and moments of friendship are achieved among highly mobile people. I aimed to show that new technologies in use today, including certain social networking websites like Couchsurfing.com, help mobile people initiate these relationships and interactions – yet these interactions are not strictly, or even in a large part, achieved or mediated online, and as such, terming these interactions forms of CMC would be misleading.

While dating or matrimonial websites would be defined as tools in fostering interaction between people face-to-face, I refrained from studying such websites. The main reason is that the act of online social networking for the purpose of finding a romantic or sexual partner has various connotations attached to its practice. Becoming intimately mobile is in no way about becoming mobile strictly to find a romantic partner, but is rather about a new form of sensitivity to interactions among strangers. Throughout the eight chapters, I described the culture surrounding new technologies which provide exchanges of hospitality and friendship and not love, romance, sex, or dating. Discussing dating websites, I believe, would call for a discourse on motivation and self-presentation which should be left for more psychological studies.

There are undoubtedly many sociological impacts of online technologies on the formation of intimate relationships, yet the main difference I wish to outline is that those studying online dating sites often define intimacy as "emotional/romantic and/or sexual relations between adults, ranging from one-off interactions to sustained offline relationships" (Barraket 2008,150). This study defines intimacy as a feeling of close familiarity to others, and focuses on the skill that is developing among mobile people to become intimate in this sort of close and familiar way. Being intimately mobile the act of experiencing a sense of closeness while on-the-move (whether it is through an exchange of hospitality or friendship).

It was also obvious when choosing my research subjects that dating websites are not technologies of hospitality and friendship simply because their main aim is not to contact two or more people in order to foster hospitality or friendship, but to foster a romantic or sexual relationship or exchange. Scholars studying online dating sites define them as "a purposeful form of meeting new people through specifically designed internet sites." (Barraket and Henry-Waring 2008, 149). While some Couchsurfers or OHW users meet others through these websites to engage in romantic or sexual relations with another, these websites are focused mainly on travel and tourism. Dating websites therefore can not be defined as technologies of hospitality or friendship, and people using such websites are not intimately mobile.

This research did not focus on all possible aspects surrounding the culture of mobile hospitality and networking when mobile, and refrained from examining the intercultural patters of friendship-making during intimate mobility, as well as the ways in which people reject or accept hospitality or friendship depending on a stranger's gender, culture, race, or socioeconomic status. Rather, this text explained the intimately mobile as an emerging practice of a global culture. I found that the gendered, age, or cultural differences that help determine the way in which people become close and intimate are not critical in explaining the general practices I found emerge through a cross section of male, female, younger and older people from a variety of nations. My research question wished to address how intimate mobility was an emerging culture on a global field (Robertson 1992), and specific tendencies of practice restricted to age, gender, or nationality were not critical in describing my research problem. Avoiding to distinguish the patterns of interaction between genders or cultures allowed me to focus on other aspects surrounding the new culture of the intimately mobile and the way hospitality and friendship is being negotiated when on-the-move.

During the course of the past years, social scientists have undoubtedly been noticing the way people do friendship using new technologies, and the way in which trust and intimacy are mediated through these new types of communication mechanisms. The spread of ICTs constitutes an intriguing phenomenon for studying the interweaving between ways of knowing, thinking and experiencing new realities (Contarello and Sarica 2007). Various studies and academic surveys have been conducted, each focusing to some extent on the impact of internet use on the quantity and quality of interpersonal communication and sociability (Nie 2001).

Other studies attempt to show the increasing civic engagement and social capital which social networks and online interactions can bring. Studies like Vergeer and Pelzer's attempt to identify relations between people's media use, network capital as a resource, and loneliness (Vergeer and Pelzer 2009) and others show the way in which the internet furthers contact between people who would normally not meet, lessening prejudice (Bargh et al. 2002, Bargh and McKenna 2004). Allport (1954) presented the first widely accepted outline of the contact hypothesis, making the claim that acquaintance lessens prejudice, and other studies apply the contact hypothesis to internet use (in Amichai-Hamburger and McKenna 2006).

Even as this book was being written, only a limited number of studies focusing on Couchsurfing (Tan 2010; Gasser and Simun 2010; Rosen et al. 2011, and Molz in Büscher et al. 2011) have been published, using the website to explore trust systems, friendship, hospitality, and methods of studying mobile social relations and interactive travel. While Molz, for example, focused on the new understanding surrounding notions like place-making, cosmopolitanism, and inclusion/exclusion within traditional nation states, as well as the boundaries of home, and the way in which strangers are welcomed and excluded, I feel the concept of intimate mobility helps further a discourse surrounding the role that friendship, closeness, and the compulsion to proximity plays in mobile interaction. The concept of intimate mobility calls for further research which would focus on various interactional patterns between cultures, genders, or socioeconomic classes – helping unveil the way in which these factors influence the way people interact while on-the-move.

The aim in writing this book was to add to the small body of work currently existing in the social sciences which describes ways in which the internet aids face-to-face intimacy between strangers. Specifically, by defining the subculture of the intimately mobile, I named the way in which highly mobile people engage in very close, oftentimes intimate face-to-face relationships with the help of the internet. In doing so, I argued that social networking websites are becoming so prolific and diverse, that in order to study the way in which people use them and describe the social as well as psychological impacts of their use, the social sciences are in need of new theoretical terms to help define such trends in online social networking. Thus, I explained that certain social networks in use today can further be defined as technologies of hospitality or technologies of friendship.

Through the analysis of mobile homemaking, emotionality, and the way hospitality and friendship is negotiated, this work also helped deepen the understanding that mobility is becoming more about sociality and less about place. Social obligations and the need for proximity to others generate tourist travel. While mobilities research has underlined that people organize co-presence with significant others (Larsen et. al 2006; 2007; 2008; Sheller and Urry, 2006; Urry 2007), this research also showed that people organize co-presence with *yet-to-be significant* others. While intimate tourists do not initiate contact between one another as a direct result of some sort of obligation to each other – oftentimes intimate tourists do come into contact with one another due to an obligation to somebody else. For example, an intimate tourist can use an OHW because they have a a wedding to get to, and then can use Couchsurfing because the bride and groom did not provide accommodation for all wedding guests. The concept of intimate mobility helps us theorize the significance of sociality in tourist travel as well as more broadly – with a view to how friendship and relationships to strangers are being reshaped. It also shows that the need for proximity to others does not only foster travel to distant friends and family, but also travel to distant strangers.

I also explained that chance-encounters differ from the planned-encounters that are happening en masse between strangers through what I termed, technologies of hospitality. A significant shift in sociality is happening today, mainly - strangers are meeting each other more than ever before and strangers are meeting for brief moments in intimate settings like the home, and the negotiation of home and intimacy between a host and guest helps these strangers become close. As I defined in this work, people are creating pre-planned meetings using various social networks, websites, and mobile devices which function in coordinated systems. The nature of these meetings also differs from meetings-at-random. As outlined in this work, certain technologies in use today foster closeness between strangers due to the roles strangers are forced to adopt, and the settings in which these strangers must be hospitable.

Thus, while mobility inevitably causes strangers to meet and interact, certain 'technologies of hospitality' in use today create conditions for strangers to meet one another and engage in *acts of hospitality* – these moments of intimacy, closeness, or mutual understanding. Technologies of hospitality enable people living in mobile network societies to strategically choose strangers to interact with, becoming closer with strangers in an unprecedented scale, and in unprecedented ways. Undoubtedly, these new forms of interactions invite further research into the conflicts and societal benefits that are arising through the use of such technologies. Further investigation into the psychological motivations of using such technologies of hospitality, the longevity of such interactions, and other socio-cultural or socio-psychological contexts must undoubtedly be explored in order to fully gain a grasp of the impacts of using such technologies.

New modes of connectivity enabled by various social networking technologies are reconfiguring our sociality. Not only do these technologies help maintain already-existing relationships, and not only do they help create hospitality but some even help establish compatibility, trust, and face-to-face interaction between strangers. These technologies are what I termed 'technologies of friendship,' and have certain design features which help create compatibility and trust between people, mediating friendly, intimate interactions between strangers.

While there are certain social and psychological benefits of such technologies, I was surprised to discover that such interactions become problematic when intimate tourists start connecting and networking en-masse. As Urry warned, networking technologies today can create a "supermarketization of friendship." I noticed that some intimately mobile engage in networking so prolifically that they are bound to create choice encounters rather than chance encounters. Technologies of friendship and hospitality can replace the spontaneity of friendship-making. People use these technologies and make choices, which allow them to feel in control over their lives, in control over their network, and whom and when they meet someone. OHWs or hospitality networks are designed in a certain way that if they have a multitude of drivers or hosts providing transportation or accommodation for their destination-of-choice, users can make decisions over who will driver them to their destination, or who's couch they wish to sleep on. The process of creating 'choice encounters' creates an individualized model of interaction which is based on gaining experiences, closeness, and various other forms of emotions as outlined in chapter 8, and can be deemed utilitarian (Bahwar 2008) and fleeting (Bauman 2003).

What I also discovered was that encounters using technologies of friendship and hospitality are not always intimate and closeness is not always desirable. What is fascinating is the ways in which obligations to one's host or guest arise and then avoidance of these obligations is negotiated. As mobile people come into contact with a multitude of unknown others, distance and solitude must be somehow negotiated as well. As was noted during ethnography, as the loners and those seeking solitude come into contact with the intimately mobile, a culture of "keeping-to-oneself" when on-the-move arises. People promote a distance between themselves and the other, casting the other primarily as the object of aesthetic. The amount and frequency of new people being met means that some intimately mobile are not morally or 'spiritually' sensing the other, but rather evaluating the other based on taste, not responsibility. I found that for some, certain people become more desirable. When rejecting the 'boring' friends and desiring the 'exciting' friends – people look at others as disposable, not needed in their social network, linking back to the point I made in the previous paragraph regarding the supermarketization of friendship that the technologies of friendship and hospitality foster.

But while the intimately mobile have the ability of creating choice-encounters, these ties do not have to necessarily be fleeting. My research also outlined that intimate mobility is creating solidarities at-a-distance. Where intimacy or friendship becomes impossible or undesirable locally, technologies of friendship and hospitality help negotiate solidarity and closeness at-a-distance. Not all young people living in cities are happy living in their "urban tribes" (Watters 2004), meaning individualized communities that are less based on kinship ties and familial obligation, and more focused on personal interests and values. Certain people like my Finnish respondent Nana, do not feel comfortable or satisfied with their social network in their home town or city and become intimately mobile in order to create global network of friends. Technologies of friendship and hospitality are part of a growing number of systems which "facilitate the personalization of networks" (Urry 2007, 17). This supports other recent studies which explained that increasingly, social solidarity between friends exists less locally (Spencer and Pahl 2006, 193, or Wittel, 2001). These studies of contemporary friendship, as well as my research in this work, argues against a strictly isolated, self-absorbed individualist model of online networking that others have proposed (Kraut 1998, Dunbar 2010, Turkle 2011) .

Various studies are explaining the benefits of online social networking. People with profiles on social networking websites have greater risk taking attitudes than those who do not (Fogel and Nehmad 2009), and friendship among people is not decreasing, but rather increasing, both online and offline, locally and globally (Wang and Wellman 2010). Technologies of hospitality and friendship, and the process of intimate mobility adds to the discourse in the social sciences that explains the ways in which the internet can create social capital, solidarity, and openness among people.

Intimate mobility is a skill that people are acquiring as mobility becomes more prolific, being able to engage in close, reciprocal interaction or 'real intimacy' with much more proficiency. Through the process of negotiating mobile intimacies, people are creating significant skills for the future culture of interaction. Car sharing communities, hospitality networks, hobby-based coordination networks that engage smartphones, and other technologies of friendship and hospitality may become more significant.

As I mentioned in the introduction, people who use these technologies frequently develop a sensitivity of intimate mobility – and upon returning 'home,' the stranger is redefined, becoming somebody closer and accessible. Negotiating interaction between strangers, hosting and being hosted, entering a stranger's private home, avoiding intimacy, anticipating closeness, becoming attached and then detached – these are all skills that people have to acquire and adapt to as they increasingly become mobile and come into contact with mobile others. As a Couchsufer aptly stated: "I believe I'm learning exactly what I intended to learn when signing up: to faster estimate what kind of person I have in front of me, how to anticipate that person and to more rapidly be able to size up whether/to what extent I can allow myself to trust that person and what it does to me" (31 year old Dutch male survey respondent). Closeness, understanding, trustworthiness, rejection, 'spiritual growth,' 'personal growth,' friends, enemies, intercultural understanding, and the feeling of a global commons are only some of the large number of artefacts that are acquired by intimately mobile upon returning, or settling home. This work showed that the process of becoming intimately mobile and the social and personal artefacts that arise from becoming intimately mobile can be seen as part of a global shift in sociality today.

Ethnographic Appendix

Hosted –
February 2005-April 2009

Arnaud – French
Aaron – American
Andor – German
Casey – American
Derek – Italian
Desneige – Canadian
Gennady – English
Iris - French
Jim – American
Josh – American
Krisztina – German
Mark and Marika - Australian
Robert- American
Steph - German
Stephan - Austrian
Tristan - French
Nico, French

Visited –
February 2005-April 2009

Andrew - Bradford, UK - 1 night
Bettina - Leipzig, Germany – 2 nights
Dane - London, UK – 1 night
Dimitris Corfu, Greece – 1 night
Erna, Madrid – 2 nights
Frank, Amsterdam – 2 nights
Jemiro, Brussels – 2 nights
Kalimona and Menelaos, Manchester – 1 night
Kinga, Gdansk - 1 night
Joris, Amsterdam - 1 night
Mario, Stockholm - 2 nights
Michael, Eastbourne – 2 nights
Ondra, Prague – 2 nights
Bill, Glasgow – 1 night
Shlomy, New York – 2 nights
Thanos, Athens – 1 night
Liese, Berlin – 3 nights
Cole, Boston – 1 night

Interviews conducted at the Couchsurfing Collective
Date conducted:
July-August 2006

Alicia, Canadian
Bobby, Canadian
Brad, American
Cari, American
Casey, American
Chris, American
Chris, American
Christine, American
Christopher, Canadian
Donna, American
Drew, American
David, American
Eric, American
Giancarlo, Italian
Heather, American
Steve, American
Ian, Canadian
Jim, American
Monika, Polish
Nana, Finnish
Michael, American
Nick, American
Nancy, American

Other Couchsurfing interviews
Date conducted: April 2009

Adam, Polish (in Warsaw)

OHW in-car interviews
as passenger
Date conducted:
August 2008-August 2009

Monika (Montreal to Toronto)
Hakan (Warsaw to Frankfurt)
Stephan (London to Brussels)
Kasia (Warsaw to Wroclaw)
Agata (Warsaw to German border)

John (Boston to Montreal)
Hans (Brussels to Bremen)
Ludwig (Heidelberg to Berlin)
Julia (Heidelberg to Berlin)
Luciano (Vienna to St. Polten)
Vladek (Kaunas to Warsaw)

OHW interviews
Date conducted: August 2008

Liese (in Berlin)
Stephan (in Berlin)
Julien (in Lancaster)

Bibliography

Abell, Peter. 1991. *Rational Choice Theory*. Aldershot: Edward Elgar.

Adams, Rebecca G. 1998. "The demise of territorial determinism: Online friendships. Placing friendship in context." in *Placing friendship in context. Structural analysis in the social sciences.*, edited by R. G. Adams, Allan, Graham. New York: Cambridge University Press.

Aday, Peter. 2006. "If Mobility is Everything Then it is Nothing: Towards a Relational Politics of (Im)mobilities Mobilities" *Mobilities.* 1:75 - 94

Ahmed, Sara. 2004. *The Cultural Politics of Emotion*. Edinburgh: University of Edinburgh.

Altman, Irwin and Dalmas A. Taylor. 1973. *Social penetration: The development of interpersonal relationships*. Oxford: Holt, Rinehart & Winston.

Amichai-Hamburger, Yair and Katelyn Y. A. McKenna. 2006. "The Contact Hypothesis Reconsidered: Interacting via the internet." *Journal of Computer-Mediated Communication* 11:825–843.

Amin, Ash and Nigel Thrift. 2002. *Cities: Reimagining the Urban*. Cambridge: Polity.

Anderson, Benedict. 2003. *Imagined Communities: Reflections on the Origin and Spread of Nationalism*. New York: Verso.

Anderson, Kay and Susan J. Smith. 2001. "Editorial: Emotional Geographies." *Transactions of the Institute of British Geographers* 26:7-10.

Ang, Jimmy and Panayiotis Zaphiris. 2009. "Social Computing and Virtual Communities." London Chapman & Hall.

Atkinson, Paul and William Housley. 2003. *Interactionism*. London: Sage.

Badhwar, Neera K. 1987. "Friends as Ends in Themselves." *Philosophy and Phenomenological Research* 48:1-23.

—. 2008. "Friendship and Commercial Societies." *Politics, Philosophy, and Economics* 7:301-326.

Bærenholdt, Jørgen Ole, Michael Haldrup, Jonas Larsen, and John Urry. 2004. *Performing Tourist Places*. Aldershot: Ashgate.

Bandura, Albert. 1982. "The Psychology of Chance Encounters and Life Paths." *American Psychologist* 37:747-755.

Bargh, John A. 2002. "Beyond Simple Truths: The Human-internet Interaction." *Journal of Social Issues* 58:1-8.

Bargh, John A. and Katelyn Y. A. McKenna. 2004. "The internet and Social Life." *Annual Review of Psychology* 55:573-590.

Bargh, John A., Katelyn Y. A. McKenna, and Grainne M. Fitzsimmons. 2002. "Can you see the real me? Relationship formation and development on the internet." *Journal of Social Issues.* 58:33-48.

Barraket, Jo and Millsom S. Henry-Waring. 2008. "Getting it on(line): Sociological perspectives on e-dating." *Journal of Sociology.* 44:149-165.

Bauman, Zygmunt. 1995. "Making and Unmaking of Strangers." *Thesis Eleven.* 43:1-16.

—. 2001. *Community.* Cambridge: Polity.

—. 2003. *Liquid Love: On the Frailty of Human Bonds.* Cambridge: Polity Press.

Beatley, Timothy. 2004. *Native to nowhere: sustaining home and community in a global age.* Washington: Island Press.

Bensman, Joseph and Robert Lilienfeld. 1979. *Between public and private: The lost boundaries of the self.* New York: Free Press.

Benson, Douglas and Hughes, John A. 1983. *The Perspective of Ethnomethodology.* New York: Longman.

Best, Samuel J. and Brian S. Krueger. 2006. "Online Interactions and Social Capital: Distinguishing Between New and Existing Ties." *Social Science Computer Review* 24:395-410.

Bialski, Paula and Dominik Batorski. 2010. "From Online Familiarity to Offline Trust: How a virtual community creates familiarity and trust between strangers " in *Social Computing and Virtual Communities* edited by P. Zaphiris and C. S. Ang. Boca Raton: Chapman & Hall

Bijsterveld, Karin. 2010. "Acoustic Cocooning: How the Car became a Place to Unwind." *Senses and Society* 5:189 -211

Blanchard, Anita and Tom Horan. 1998. "Virtual communities and social capital." *Social Science Computer Review* 16:293-307.

Blau, Peter. 1964. *Exchange and Power in Social Life.* New York: John Wiley & Sons.

Boden, Deirdre and Harvey L. Molotch. 1994. "The Compulsion of Proximity." in *Space, Time and Modernity*, edited by R. Friedland and D. Boden. London: University of California Press.

Boden, Deirdre and Don H Zimmerman. 1991. *Talk and Social Structure: Studies in Ethnomethodology and Conversation Analysis.* Cambridge: Polity Press.

Bollas, Christopher. 2009. *The Evocative Object World.* Hove, East Sussex: Routledge.

Boniface, Priscilla. 2003. *Tasting tourism: travelling for food and drink.* Aldershot: Ashgate.

Bossard, James H. S. and Eleanor S. Boll. 1949. "Ritual in Family Living." *American Sociological Review.* 14:463-469.

Bourdieu, Pierre. 1998. *Practical reason: on the theory of action.* Cambridge: Polity Press.

Boyd, Danah M. and Nicole B. Ellison. 2008. "Social Network Sites: Definition, History, and Scholarship " *Journal of Computer-Mediated Communication* 13:210–230.

Brehm, Sharon S., Rowland Miller, Daniel Perlman, and Susan Miller Campbell. 2002. *Intimate Relationships.* New York: McGraw-Hill.

Brenton, Myron. 1974. *Friendship.* New York Stein & Day

Bull, Michael. 2004. "Sound connections: an aural epistemology of proximity and distance in urban culture." *Environment and Planning D: Society and Space* 22:103 – 116.

—. 2005. "The Intimate Sounds of Urban Experience: An Auditory Epistemology of Everyday Mobility." Pp. 169-178 in *The Global and the Local in Mobile Communication*, edited by K. Nyiri.

—. 2006. "Investigating the Culture of Mobile Listening: From Walkman to iPod." in *Consuming Music Together: Social and Collaborative Aspects of Music Consumption Technologies* edited by Kenton O'Hara and B. Brown. Netherlands: Springer.

—. 2007. *Sound Moves: iPod culture and urban experience* New York Routledge

Burawoy, Michael. 1979. *Manufacturing consent: changes in the labor process under monopoly capitalism*. Chicago: The University of Chicago Press.

Burrell, Kathy. 2008. "Materialising the Border: Spaces of Mobility and Material Culture in Migration from Post-Socialist Poland." *Mobilities* 3:353-373.

Büscher, Monika and John Urry. 2009. "Mobile Methods and the Empirical." *European Journal of Social Theory* 12:99-116.

Büscher, Monika, John Urry, and Katian Witchger (eds). 2011. "Mobile Methods." New York: Routledge.

Callero, Peter. 2003. "The Sociology of the Self." *Annual Review of Sociology* 29:115-133.

Canzler, Weert, Vincent Kaufmann, and Sven Kesselring (eds). 2008. "Tracing mobilities: towards a cosmopolitan perspective." Aldershot: Ashgate.

Castells, Manuel. 1996. *The Rise of the Network Society: The Information Age: Economy, Society and Culture*. New York: Wiley.

Cetina, Karin Knorr. 1997. "Sociality with Objects: Social Relations in Postsocial Knowledge Societies." *Theory, Culture & Society* 14:1-30.

Cetina, Karin Knorr and Urs Bruegger. 2002. "Global Microstructures: The Virtual Societies of Financial Markets." *American Journal of Sociology*. 107:905-950.

Chen, Guo-Ming. 1995. "Differences in self-disclosure patterns among Americans versus Chinese." *Journal of Cross-Cultural Psychology*. 26:84–91.

Cieraad, Irene. 1999. "At Home: An Anthropology of Domestic Space." Syracuse: Syracuse University Press.

Coleman, James S. 1986. "Social Theory, Social Research, and a Theory of Action." *American Journal of Sociology* 91:1309-1336.

—. 1990. *Foundations of Social Theory*. Cambridge, Mass: Belknap Press.

Conradson, David and Deirdre Mckay. 2007. "Translocal Subjectivities: Mobility, Connection, Emotion." *Mobilities*. 2:167 - 174.

Constant, David, Lee Sproull, and Sara Kiesler. 1996. "The Kindness of Strangers: The Usefulness of Electronic Weak Ties for Technical Advice." *Organization Science*. 7:119-135.

Contarello, A. and M. Sarrica. 2007. "ICTs, social thinking and subjective well-being - The internet and its representations in everyday life." *Computers in Human Behavior*. 23:1016-1032.

Cook, Karen S. 2001. "Trust In Society ". New York: Russell Sage Foundation.

Cresswell, Tim. 1997. "Imagining the Nomad: Mobility and the Postmodern Primitive" Pp. 360-382 in *Space and social theory: interpreting modernity and postmodernity*, edited by U. S. Georges Benko. Oxford: Blackwell.

—. 2004. *Place: A Short Introduction*. Oxford: Blackwell.

—. 2006. *On the move: mobility in the modern Western world*. New York: Routledge.

Csíkszentmihályi, Mihály. 1990. *Flow: The psychology of optimal experience*. New York: Harper & Row.

Csíkszentmihályi, Mihály and Eugene Rochberg-Halton. 1981. *The meaning of things: domestic symbols and the self*. Cambridge: Cambridge University Press.

Czupryński, Jakub. 2005. *Autostop polski. PRL i współczesność*. Kraków: Korporacja Ha!art.

D'Andrea, Anthony. 2006. "Neo-Nomadism: A Theory of Post-Identitarian Mobility in the Global Age." *Mobilities*. 1:95-119.

Davidson, Joyce, Liz Bondi, and Mick Smith (eds). 2005. *Emotional Geographies*. Aldershot: Ashgate.

Davidson, Joyce and Christine Milligan. 2004. "Embodying Emotion Sensing Space: Introducing emotional geographies." *Social & Cultural Geography*. 5:523-532.

Dayan, Daniel and Elihu Katz. 1994. *Media Events: The Live Broadcasting of History*. Boston: First Harvard University Press.

Dennis, Kingsley. 2006. "New complexities: converging spaces of connectivity, communication, and collaboration." Doctoral Thesis, Department of Sociology, Lancaster University, Lancaster.

—. 2007. "Technologies of Civil Society: Communication, Participation, and Mobilization " *Innovation: The European Journal of Social Science*. 20:19 - 34

Derrida, Jacques. 2000. *On Hospitality*. Stanford: Stanford University Press.

de Souza e Silva, Adriana. 2006. "From Cyber to Hybrid: Mobile Technologies as Interfaces of Hybrid Spaces." *Space and Culture*. 9:261-278.

Dewey, John. 1895. "The Theory of Emotion." *Psychological Review*. 2:13-32.

Douglas, M. 1991. "The Idea of a Home: A kind of space." *Social Research* 59:287-307.

Du Bois, Cora. 1974. "The Gratuitous Act: An Introduction to the Comparative Study of Friendship Patterns " in *The Compact: selected dimensions of friendship*, vol. Issue 3 of Newfoundland social and economic papers, edited by E. Leyton. St. John's Memorial University of Newfoundland.

Duckett, Bob. 2007. "The Yale Book of Quotations." *Reference Reviews*. 21:6-7.

Dunbar, Robin. 2010. *How Many Friends Does One Person Need?: Dunbar's Number and Other Evolutionary Quirks*. New York: Faber and Faber Limited.

Durkheim, Émile. 1973. *On morality and society: selected writings*, Edited by R. N. Bellah. Chicago: University of Chicago Press.

Dwyer, Catherine, Starr Roxanne Hiltz, and Katia Passerini. 2007. "Trust and Privacy: A Comparison of Facebook and MySpace." in *Proceedings of the Thirteenth Americas Conference on Information Systems*. Keystone, Colorado.

Ekeh, Peter P. 1974. *Social exchange theory: the two traditions*. London: Heinemann Educational.

Elliott, Anthony and John Urry. 2010. *Mobile Lives: self, excess and nature*. New York: Routledge.

Ellis, Carolyn and Arthur P. Bochner. 2003. "Autoethnography, personal narrative, reflexivity: Researcher as subject." Pp. 199-258 in *Collecting and interpreting qualitative materials*, edited by N. K. Denzin and Y. S. Lincoln. London Sage.

Featherstone, Mike. 1990. *Global culture: nationalism, globalization and modernity*. London: Sage.

Feld, Scott L. 1981. "The Focused Organization of Social Ties." *The American Journal of Sociology*. 86:1015-1035.

Fischer, Claude S. 1982. *To Dwell Among Friends: Personal Networks in Town and City*. Chicago: University of Chicago Press.

—. 1994. *America calling: a social history of the telephone to 1940*. Berkley: University of California Press.

Fischer, Claude S., Robert Max Jackson, C Ann Stueve, Kathleen Gerson, Lynne McCallister Jones, and Mark Baldassare. 1977. *Networks and places: Social relations in the urban setting*. New York: Free Press.

Fogel, Joshua and Elham Nehmad. 2009. "Internet social network communities: Risk taking, trust, and privacy concerns." *Computers in Human Behavior*. 25:153–160.

Franzen, Axel. 2007. "Social Capital and the New Communication Technologies" Pp. 105-116 in *Machines that become us: the social context of personal communication technology*, edited by J. E. Katz. New Jersey: Transaction Publishers.

Frida, Nico H. 1986. *The Emotions: Studies in Emotion and Social Interaction*. New York: Cambridge University Press.

Fromm, Erich. 1949. *Man for Himself: And Enquiry Into the Psychology of Ethics*. London: Routledge & Kegan Paul LTD.

Fuchs, Christian. 2008. *Internet and society: Social theory in the information age*. New York: Routledge.

Fukuyama, Francis. 1999. *The Great Disruption: Human Nature and the Reconstruction of Social Order*. New York: Touchstone.

Furey, Constance. 2003. "The Communication of Friendship: Gasparo Contarini's Letters to Hermits at Camaldoli." *Church History*. 72:71-101.

Garfinkel, Harold. 1967. *Studies in Ethnomethodology*. Englewood Cliffs, NJ: Prentice-Hall.

Garton, Laura, Caroline Haythornthwaite, and Barry Wellman. 2006. "Studying Online Social Networks." *Journal of Computer-Mediated Communication.* 3.

Gasser, Urs and Miriam Simun. 2010. "Digital Lifestyle and Online Travel: Looking at the Case of Digital Natives." *Trends and Issues in Global Tourism.* 2:83-89.

Geertz, Clifford. 1973. "Thick Description: Toward an Interpretive Theory of Culture." Pp. 3–30 in *The Interpretation of Cultures: Selected Essays*, edited by C. Geertz. New York: Basic Books.

Gergen, Kenneth. 1992. *The saturated self: Dilemmas of identity in modern life.* New York: Basic Books.

Gergen, Kenneth J. 2002. "The challenge of absent presence." Pp. 227-241 in *Perpetual contact: mobile communication, private talk, public performance*, edited by J. E. Katz and M. A. Aakhus: Cambridge University Press.

Gibson, James J. 1977. "The Theory of Affordances." in *Perceiving, Acting, and Knowing: Toward an Ecological Psychology* edited by R. Shaw and J. Bransford. Hillsdale, N.J.: Erlbaum.

Gibson, Sarah. 2007. "'Abusing our Hospitality': Inhospitableness and the Politics of Deterrence." in *Mobilizing Hospitality: The Ethics of Social Relations in a Mobile World* edited by J. G. Molz and S. Gibson. Aldershot: Ashgate Publishing.

Giddens, Anthony. 1984. *The Constitution of Society: Outline of the Theory of Structuration.* Cambridge: Polity Press.

—. 1991. *Modernity and Self-Identity: self and society in the late modern age.* Cambridge: Polity Press.

—. 1992. *The transformation of intimacy: sexuality, love and eroticism in modern societies* Stanford, California Stanford University Press.

Gieryn, Thomas F. 2000. "A Space for Place in Sociology " *Annual Review of Sociology.* 26:463-496.

Gill, Nick and Paula Bialski. 2011. "New friends in new places: Network formation during the migration process among poles in the UK." Geoforum. 42:241-249.

Girgensohn, Andreas and Alison Lee. 2002. "Making web sites be places for social interaction." Pp. 136-145 in *Proceedings of the 2002 ACM conference on Computer supported cooperative work.* New Orleans, Louisiana, USA: ACM.

Goffman, Erving. 1953. "Communication conduct on an island community." *Unpublished PhD Dissertation.* Chicago: University of Chicago.

—. 1955. "On face-work: An analysis of ritual elements in social interaction." *Psychiatry: Journal for the Study of Interpersonal Processes.* 18:213-231.

—. 1963. *Behaviour in Public Places.* New York: The Free Press.

—. 1967. *Interaction Ritual.* London: Penguin University Books.

—. 1974. *Frame analysis: An essay on the organization of experience.* London: Harper and Row.

Goldmacher, Amy. 2009. "Located Mobility: Living and Working in Multiple Places." Pp. 118-127 in *Mobile work, mobile lives: cultural accounts of lived experiences*, vol. 30, edited by T. L. Meerwarth, J. C. Gluesing, and B. Jordan. New York: Wiley-Blackwell.

Goonatilake, S. 1991. *The Evolution of Information: Lineages in Gene, Culture and Artefact*. London: Pinter Publishers.

Granovetter, Mark. 1973. "The Strength of Weak Ties." *The American Journal of Sociology*. 78:1360-1380

Green, Nicola. 2002. "On the Move: Technology, Mobility, and the Mediation of Social Time and Space." *The Information Society*. 18:281–292.

Gulia, Barry Wellman and Milena. 1999. "Virtual communities as communities: Net surfers don't ride alone." in *Communities in Cyberspace*, edited by P. K. Marc A. Smith. London: Routledge.

Gustafson, Per. 2006. "Place Attachment and Mobility " in *Multiple dwelling and tourism: negotiating place, home and identity*, edited by N. McIntyre, D. Williams, and K. McHugh. Cambridge, MA: Wallingford.

Hampton, Keith and Barry Wellman. 2003. "Neighbouring in Netville: How the internet Supports Community and Social Capital in a Wired Suburb." *City and Community*. 2:277–311.

Hampton, Keith N., Oren Livio, and Lauren Sessions Goulet. 2010. "The Social Life of Wireless Urban Spaces: internet Use, Social Networks, and the Public Realm." *Journal of Communication*. 60:701–722.

Hannam, Kevin, Mimi Sheller, and John Urry. 2005. "Editorial: Mobilities, Immobilities and Moorings " *Mobilities*. 1:1-22.

Hauben, Michael and Ronda Hauben. 1997. *Netizens: on the history and impact of Usenet and the internet*. Los Alamitos, California: IEEE Computer Society Press.

Haythornthwaite, Caroline. 2002. "Strong, Weak, and Latent Ties and the Impact of New Media." *Information Society*. 18:385-401.

Heckathorn, Douglas D. 1997. "The Paradoxical Relationship Between Sociology and Rational Choice." *The American Sociologist*. 28:6-15.

Heise, David R. 1979. *Understanding events: affect and the construction of social action*. New York: Cambridge University Press.

Henderson, Samantha and Michael Gilding. 2004. "'I've never clicked this much with anyone in my life': trust and hyperpersonal communication in online friendships." *New Media & Society*. 6:487-506.

Hightower, Jim. 1994. "Roadkill On The Information Superhighway."

Hiller, Harry H. and Tara M. Franz. 2004. "New ties, old ties and lost ties: the use of the internet in diaspora." *New Media & Society*. 6:731-752.

Hochschild, Arlie Russell. 1998. "The Sociology of Emotion as a Way of Seeing" in *Emotions in Social Life: Critical Themes and Contemporary Issues.*, edited by G. Bendelow and S. Williams. London: Routledge.

—. 2003. *The Commercialization of Intimate Life*. Berkley: University of California Press.

Ishii, Kenichi and Morihiro Ogasahara. 2007. "Links between Real and Virtual Networks: A Comparative Study of Online Communities in Japan and Korea." *CyberPsychology & Behavior.* 10:252-257.

Jacobs, Jane. 1961. *The death and life of great American cities*. New York: Random House.

Jamieson, Lynn. 1998. *Intimacy: personal relationships in modern societies*. Oxford: Polity Press.

Jennings, M. Kent and Vicki Zeitner. 2003. "Internet Use and Civic Engagement." *Public Opinion Quarterly.* 67:311-334.

Jones, Steven G. 1998. "Cybersociety 2.0: Revisitng computer-mediated communication and community." Sage: Thousand Oaks, CA.

Kandell, Jonathan J. 1998. "Internet Addiction on Campus: The Vulnerability of College Students." *CyberPsychology & Behavior.* 1:11-17.

Katz, James Everett (ed). 2007. *Machines that become us: the social context of personal communication technology*. New Bruswick: Transaction Publishers.

Katz, James Everett and Mark A. Aakhus. 2002. *Perpetual contact: mobile communication, private talk, public performance*. Cambridge: Cambridge University Press.

Katz, J. E. and R. C. Rice. 2002. *Social consequences of internet use: access, involvement, and interaction*. Cambridge, MA: The MIT Press.

Kaufmann, Jean-Claude. 2004. *Ego: Sociologia Jednostki*. Warszawa: Oficyna Naukowa.

King, Anthony. 2004. *The Structure of Social Theory*. New York Routlege

Kobayashi, T, K. I. Ikeda, and K. Miyata. 2006. "Social capital online: Collective use of the internet and reciprocity as lubricants of democracy." *Information, Communication & Society.* 9:582-611.

Kraut, Robert, Sara Kiesler, Bonka Boneva, Jonathon Cummings, Vicki Helgeson, and Anne Crawford. 2002. "Internet Paradox Revisited." *Journal of Social Issues.* 58:49-74.

Kraut, R. E., M. Patterson, V.Lundmark, S.Kiesler, T. Mukopadhyay, and W. Scherlis. 1998. "Internet paradox: A social technology that reduces social involvement and psychological well-being?" *American Psychologist.* 53:1017-1031.

Larsen, Jonas, Urry, John and Axhausen, Kay 2008. "Coordinating Face-To-Face Meetings in Mobile Network Societies " *Information, Communication & Society.* 11:640-658.

Larsen, Jonas, Kay W. Axhausen, and John Urry. 2006. "Geographies of Social Networks: Meetings, Travel and Communications " *Mobilities.* 1:261-283.

Larsen, Jonas, John Urry, and Kay W. Axhausen. 2006. *Mobilities, networks, geographies*. London: Ashgate Publishing.

—. 2007. "Networks and Tourism: Mobile Social Life." *Annals of Tourism Research.* 34:244-262.

Lasch, Christopher. 1979. *The culture of narcissism: American life in an age of diminishing expectations*. New York: W. W. Norton and Company

Latour, Bruno. 2005. *Reassembling the Social: An Introduction to Actor-Network-Theory.* Oxford: Oxford University Publishers.

Law, John and John Urry. 2004. "Enacting the Social." *Economy and Society* 33:390-410.

Licoppe, C. 2004. "Connected presence: the emergence of a new repertoire for managing social relationships in a changing communication technoscape." *Environment and Planning.* 22:135–156.

Ling, Rich and Birgitte Jttri. 2002. "Hyper-Coordination through mobile phones in Norway." Pp. 139-169 in *Perpetual contact: mobile communication, private talk, public performance*, edited by J. E. Katz and M. A. Aakhus. Cambridge: Cambridge University Press.

Lombard, Matthew and Theresa Ditton. 1997. "At the Heart of It All: The Concept of Presence." *Journal of Computer-Mediated Communication* 3:0-0.

Luhmann, Niklas. 1998. *Love as Passion: The Codification of Intimacy.* Stanford: Stanford University Press.

—. 1990. "Familiarity, Confidence, Trust: Problems and Alternatives." in *Trust: Making and Breaking Cooperative Relations*, edited by D. Gambetta. New York: Basil Blackwell.

Lupton, Deborah. 1998. *The Emotional Self.* London: Sage.

Lynch, Paul A. 2004. "Home Sweet Home: The significance of the home setting in hospitality." Pp. 456 – 465 in *The Council of Australian Tourism and Higher Education Annual Research Conference.* Brisbane, Australia.

Lynch, Paul A and M Di Domenico. 2004. "Home (Dis)Comforts and the Host/Guest Encounter." in *Tourism: State of the Art II Conference,.* University of Strathclyde, Glasgow.

MacCannell, Dean. 1976. *The tourist: a new theory of the leisure class.* New York: Schoken Books Inc. .

Mackenzie, Adrian. 2005. "From cafe to parkbench: Wi-Fi® and technological overflows in the city." in *Technological Mobilities*, edited by M. Sheller. London: Routledge.

Maffesoli, Michel 1996. *The Time of the Tribes.* London: Sage Publications.

Mai, Nicola and Russel King. 2009. "Love, Sexuality, and Migration: Mapping the Issue(s)." *Mobilities* 4:295 — 307.

Maines, D. R. . 2001. *The Faultline of Consciousness: A View of Interactionism in Sociology.* Hawthorne, NY: Aldine de Gruyter.

Markham, Annette N. 1998. *Life online: researching real experience in virtual space.* Walnut Creek, CA: AltaMira Press.

Mason, Jennifer. 2004. "Managing Kinship over Long Distances: The Significance of 'The Visit'." *Social Policy & Society* 3:421–429.

Massey, Doreen. 1991. "A Global Sense of Place." in *Marxism Today (Online:* http://www.amielandmelburn.org.uk/collections/mt/index_frame.htm), accessed September 2011.

Matsuda, Misa. 2005. "Discourses of Keitai in Japan" in *Personal, Portable, Pedestrian: Mobile Phones in Japanese Life*, edited by M. Ito, D. Okabe, and M. Matsuda. Boston: MIT Press.

McKenna, Katelyn Y. A. 1998. "The computers that bind: Relationship formation on the Internet." in *Unpublished doctoral dissertation*: Ohio University.

McKenna, Katelyn Y. A. and John A. Bargh. 2000. "Plan 9 From Cyberspace: The Implications of the internet for Personality and Social Psychology." *February* 4: 57-75.

McKenna, Katelyn Y.A., Amie S. Green, and Marci E. J. Gleason. 2002. "Relationship Formation on the internet: What's the Big Attraction?" *Journal of Social Issues.* 58:9-31.

McLuhan, Marshall. 1989. *The Global Village*. New York: Oxford University Press.

McPherson, Miller, Lynn Smith-Lovin, and James M Cook. 2001. "Birds of a Feather: Homophily in Social Networks." *Annual Review of Sociology.* 27:415-444

—. 2001. "Birds of a Feather: Homophily in Social Networks." *Annual Review of Sociology.* 27:415-444

Milgram, P. and H. Colquhoun. 1999. "A taxonomy of real and virtual world display integration." Pp. 5-28 in *Mixed reality: Merging real and virtual worlds*, edited by Y. Ohta and H. Tamura. New York: Springer.

Miller, Lynn C, John H Berg, and Richard L Archer. 1983. "Openers: Individuals who elicit intimate self-disclosure." *Journal of Personality and Social Psychology.* 44:1234-1244.

Molz, Jennie Germann. 2005. "Getting a "Flexible Eye": Round-the-World Travel and Scales of Cosmopolitan Citizenship." *Citizenship Studies* 9:517-531.

—. 2008. "Home and Mobility in Narratives of Round-the-World Travel." *Space and Culture.* 11:325-342.

Molz, Jennie Germann and Sarah Gibson (eds). 2007. "Mobilizing Hospitality: The Ethics of Social Relations in a Mobile World." Aldershot: Ashgate Publishing.

Moreno, Jacob H. 1953. *Who Shall Survive?* New York City: Beacon House.

Morley, David. 2000. *Home Territories: Media, Mobility, and Identity*. New York: Routledge.

Nie, Norman H. 2001. "Sociability, interpersonal relations, and the internet: Reconciling conflicting findings." *The American Behavioral Scientist.* 45:420-435.

Nippert-Eng, Christena. 1996. "Calenders and Keys: The Classification of 'Home' and 'Work'" *Sociological Forum.* 11:563-582.

Noll, Michael. 1995. *Highway of dreams: a critical view along the information superhighway*. New Jersey: Lawrence Erlbaum Associates, Inc.

Palen, Leysia. 2002. "Mobile telephony in a connected life." *Communications of the ACM.* 45:78 - 82

Parks, Malcolm R. and Kory Floyd. 1996. "Making friends in cyberspace." *Journal of Communication.* 46:80-97.

Parks, Malcolm R. and Lynne D. Roberts. 1998. ""Making MOOsic": The Development of Personal Relationships On-line and a Comparison to their Off-line Counterparts." *Journal of Social & Personal Relationships.* 15:517 - 530.

Parsons, Talcott. 1937. *The Structure of Social Action*. Glencoe: The Free Press.

Pellegrino, Giuseppina. 2011. "The Politics of Proximity: Mobility and Immobility in Practice." Abingdon: Ashgate.

Pennartz, Paul J. J. 2006. "Home: The Experience of Atmosphere." in *At Home: An Anthropology of Domestic Space*, edited by I. Cieraad. Syracuse: Syracuse University Press.

Plummer, Ken. 2000. "Symbolic Interactionism in the Twentieth Century." in *The Blackwell Companion to Social Theory*, vol. 193-244, edited by B. S. Turner. Oxford: Blackwell.

Pruijt, Hans. 2002. "Social Capital and the Equalizing Potential of the internet." *Social Science Computer Review*. 20:109-115.

Putnam, Robert D. 1995. "Bowling Alone: America's Declining Social Capital." *Journal of Democracy*. 6:65-78.

Putnam, Tim. 1999. "'Postmodern' Home Life." Pp. 144-154 in *At Home: An Anthropology of Domestic Space*, edited by I. Cieraad. Syracuse: Syracuse University Press.

Rabikowska, Marta and Kathy Burrell. 2009. "The Material Worlds of Recent Polish Migrants: Transnationalism, Food, Shops, and Home." Pp. 211-232 in *Polish migration to the UK in the 'new' European Union: after 2004*, edited by K. Burrell. Surrey: Ashgate.

Resnick, P. 2001. "Beyond Bowling Together: SocioTechnical Capital." Pp. 647-672 in *Human-Computer Interaction in the New Millennium*, edited by J. M. Carroll. New York: Addison-Wesley.

Rheingold, Howard. 2000. *The virtual community: homesteading on the electronic frontier*. Cambridge, MA: MIT Press.

—. 2003. *Smart Mobs: The Next Social Revolution*. Cambridge, MA: Perseus Publishing.

Robertson, Roland. 1992. *Globalization: social theory and global culture*. London: Sage.

Rock, Paul. 1979. *The making of symbolic interactionism*. London: Macmillan.

Rofe, Matthew W. *2003*. "*'I Want to be Global'*: Theorising the Gentrifying Class as an Emergent Elite Global Community." *Urban Studies*. 40:2511-2526.

Rojas, Hernando and Eulalia Puig-i-Abril. 2009. "Mobilizers Mobilized: Information, Expression, Mobilization and Participation in the Digital Age." *Journal of Computer-Mediated Communication*. 14:902–927.

Rosen, Devan, Pascale Roy Lafontaine, and Blake Hendrickson. 2011. "CouchSurfing: Belonging and trust in a globally cooperative online social network." *New Media & Society*. 13:981-998.

Rosenbaum, Milton E. 1986. "The repulsion hypothesis: On the nondevelopment of relationships." *Journal of Personality and Social Psychology* 51:1156-1166.

Rybczynski, Witold. 1986. *Home: a short history of an idea*. New York: Viking.

Ryle, Gilbert. 1971. *Collected papers. Volume II collected essays, 1929-1968*. London: Hutchinson.

Schegloff, Emanuel A. 1968. "Sequencing in Conversational Openings." *American Anthropologist* 70:1075-1095.

Schneider, Fabian, Anja Feldmann, Balachander Krishnamurthy, and Walter Willinger. 2009. "Understanding Online Social Network Usage from a Network Perspective." in *IMC'09*. Chicago, Illinois, USA.

Schug, Joanna, Masaki Yuki, and William Maddux. 2010. "Relational Mobility Explains Between- and Within-Culture Differences in Self-Disclosure to Close Friends." *Psychological Science*. 21:1471-1478.

Scott, John. 2000. *Social Network Analysis: A Handbook*. London: Sage.

Sennett, Richard. 2003. *The Fall of the Public Man*. New York: Penguin.

Sheller, Mimi. 2004. "Automotive Emotions: Feeling the Car." *Theory, Culture & Society* 21:221-242.

Sheller, Mimi and John Urry. 2006. "The New Mobilities Paradigm." *Environment and Planning A*. 38:207-226.

Sherif, Muzafer. 1967. *Social Interaction: Process and Products*. Chicago: Aldine.

Shirky, Clay. 2008. *Here Comes Everybody: The Power of Organizing without Organizations*. London: Penguin Press.

Short, John, Ederyn Williams, and Bruce Christie. 1976. *The Social Psychology of Telecommunication*. London: John Wiley.

Shove, Elizabeth. 2007. *The design of everyday life*. Oxford: Berg.

Shryock, Andrew. 2009. "Hospitality Lessons: Learning the Shared Language of Derrida and the Balga Bedouin." *Paragraph*. 32:32-50.

Simmel, Georg and Everett C. Hughes. 1949. "The Sociology of Sociability." *The American Journal of Sociology*. 55:254-261.

Simmel, Georg and Kurt H. Wolff. 1950. *The Sociology of Georg Simmel*. Toronto: Free Press.

–, David Frisby, Mike Featherstone (eds). 1997. *Simmel On Culture*. London: Sage.

Spencer, Liz and Ray Pahl. 2006. *Rethinking friendship: Hidden Solidarities Today*. Princeton, NJ: Princeton University Press.

Staub, Ervin. 1978. *Positive Social Behavior and Morality*. New York: Academic Press

Stephure, Robert J., Susan D. Boon, Stacey L. MacKinnon, and Vicki L. Deveau. 2009. "Internet Initiated Relationships: Associations Between Age and Involvement in Online Dating." *Journal of Computer-Mediated Communication*. 14:658-681.

Sterpka, M.K. . 2007. "The aesthetics of networks: A conceptual approach toward visualizing the composition of the internet" *First Monday.org*, vol. 12. (Online http://firstmonday.org/htbin/cgiwrap/bin/ojs/index.php/fm/article/view/2011/1886) Accessed September 2011.

Sweeney, Majella and Paul A Lynch. 2007. "Explorations of the host's relationship with the commercial home." *Tourism and Hospitality Research: Special Issue: Selected Papers from the 15th Annual Council.* 7:100-108.

Tan, Jun-E. 2010. "The Leap of Faith from Online to Offline: An Exploratory Study of Couchsurfing.org " *Trust and Trustworthy Computing: Lecture Notes in Computer Science.* 6101:367-380.

Thien, Deborah. 2005. "Intimate Distances: Considering the Questions of 'Us'." Pp. 191-204 in *Emotional Geographies* edited by J. Davidson, L. Bondi, and M. Smith.

Thoits, Peggy A. 1989. "The Sociology of Emotions." *Annual Review of Sociology.* 15:317-342.

Thrift, Nigel and Shaun French. 2002. "The Automatic Production of Space." *Transactions of the Institute of British Geographers.* 27:309-335.

Tocqueville, Alexis de. 1969. "Democracy in America." Garden City: Anchor Books.

Trafford, Abigail. 2000. "The Healing Power of Friendship." in *The Washington Post.* Accessed online http://community.seattletimes.nwsource.com/archive/?date=20001112&slug=4052659 September 2011.

Trexler, Richard C. 1980. *Public Life in Renaissance Florence.* Ithaca, New York: Cornell University Press.

Tuan, Yi-Fu. 1974. *Topophilia: a study of environmental perception, attitudes, and values.* Englewood Cliffs, NJ: Prentice-Hall.

Turkle, Sherry. 2011. *Alone Together: Why We Expect More from Technology and Less from Each Other.* New York: Basic Books.

Turner, Jonathan H. 1987. "Toward a Sociological Theory of Motivation." *American Sociological Review.* 52:15-27.

Tyler, Tom R. 2002. "Is the internet Changing Social Life? It Seems the More Things Change, the More They Stay the Same." *Journal of Social Issues* 58.

Urry, John. 2000. *Sociology beyond societies: mobilities for the twenty-first century.* London: Routledge.

—. 2002. *The Tourist Gaze (second edition).* London: Sage.

—. 2002. "Mobility and Proximity." *Sociology.* 36:225-74.

—. 2005. "The Place of Emotions within Place." Pp. 77-83 in *Emotional Geographies*, edited by L. B. Joyce Davidson, and Mick Smith. Aldershot: Ashgate.

—. 2007. *Mobilities.* Cambridge: Polity Press.

Uslaner, Eric M. 2000. "Social Capital and the Net." *Communications of the ACM.* 43:60-64.

—. 2000. "Trust, Civic Engagement, and the internet." in *Joint Sessions of the European Consortium for Political Research, Workshop on*

Electronic Democracy: Mobilisation, Organisation, and Participation via New ICTs. University of Grenoble.

Valenzuela, Sebastian, Namsu Park, and Kerk F. Kee. 2009. "Is There Social Capital in a Social Network Site?: Facebook Use and College Students' Life Satisfaction, Trust, and Participation." *Journal of Computer-Mediated Communication.* 14:875–901.

Van Dijk, Jan. 1999. *The Network Society, Social Aspects of New Media*. London: Sage.

–. 2005. *The Network Society: Social Aspects of New Media*: Sage Publications Ltd.

Vergeer, Maurice and Ben Pelzer. 2009. "Consequences of media and internet use for offline and online network capital and well-being. A causal model approach." *Journal of Computer-Mediated Communication.* 15:189–210.

Vittengl, Jeffrey R. and Craig S. Holt. 2000. "Getting Acquainted: The Relationship of Self-Disclosure and Social Attraction to Positive Affect." *Journal of Social and Personal Relationships.* 17:53-66.

Walsh, Katie. 2008. "Geographies of the heart in transnational spaces : love and the lives of British migrants in Dubai." *Mobilities.* 4:427-445.

Walther, Joseph. 1996. "Computer-mediated Communication: Impersonal, Interpersonal, and Hyperpersonal Interaction." *Communication Research.* 23:3-43.

Walther, Joseph, David Deandrea, and Stephanie Tom Tong. 2010. "Computer-Mediated Communication Versus Vocal Communication and the Attenuation of Pre-Interaction Impressions." *Media Psychology* 13:364-386.

Walther, Joseph B. 1995. "Relational Aspects of Computer-Mediated Communication: Experimental Observations over Time." *Organization Science* 6:186-203.

Wang, Hua and Barry Wellman. 2010. "Social Connectivity in America: Changes in Adult Friendship Network Size From 2002 to 2007." *American Behavioral Scientist* 53:1148–1169.

Watters, Ethan. 2003. *Urban Tribes: Are Friends The New Family?* New York: Bloomsbury.

Wellman, Barry. 2001. "Physical Place and Cyberplace: The Rise of Personalized Networking." *International Journal of Urban and Regional Research* 25:227-252.

Wellman, B. 2002. "Little Boxes, Glocalization, and Networked Individualism " *Digital Cities II: Computational and Sociological Approaches: Lecture Notes in Computer Science.* 2362:337-342.

Wellman, Barry. 2004. "The three ages of internet studies: ten, five and zero years ago." *New Media & Society.* 6:123-129.

Wellman, Barry and S.D. Berkowitz. 1988. *Social Structures: a network approach*. Cambridge: Cambridge University Press.

Wellman, Barry and Milena Gulia. 1999. "The network basis of social support: A network is more than the sum of its ties." *Networks in the global village: Life in contemporary communities*: 83-118.

Wellman, Barry and Wortley, Scott. 1990. "Different Strokes from Different Folks: Community Ties and Social Support." *American Journal of Sociology* 96:558-88.

White, Harrison. 1992. *Identity and Control: A Structural Theory of Social Action*. Princeton, NJ: Princeton University Press.

—. 1992. *Identity and Control: A Structural Theory of Social Action*. Princeton, NJ: Princeton University Press.

Wilkins, H. 1991. "Computer Talk: Long Distance Conversations by Computer." *Written Communication.* 8:56–78.

Wittel, Andreas. 2001. "Towards a Networked Sociality." *Theory Culture and Society.* 18:51-76.

Young, Kimberly S and Robert C Rogers. 1998. "The Relationship Between Depression and Internet Addiction." *CyberPsychology & Behavior.* 1:25-28.

Yum, Young-ok and Kazuya Hara. 2006. "Computer-Mediated Relationship Development: A Cross-Cultural Comparison." *Journal of Computer-Mediated Communication.* 11:133–152.

Websites Used During Ethnography

www.autostop.pl

www.carpooling.com

www.carpooling.co.uk

www.carpooling.pl

www.couchsurfing.com

www.chatroulette.com

www.craigslist.com

www.hospitalityclub.org

www.mitfahrgelegenheit.de

www.mitfahrzentrale.de

www.foursquare.com

www.facebook.com

www.facebook.com/places

www.gumtree.co.uk

www.gumptree.pl

Warsaw Studies in Culture and Society

Edited by Jacek Wasilewski

Vol. 1 Magdalena Góra / Zdzisław Mach / Katarzyna Zielińska: Collective Identity and Democracy in the Enlarging Europe. 2012.

Vol. 2 Paula Bialski: Becoming Intimately Mobile. 2012.

www.peterlang.de